THE STAR

who made movie history from the moment she dared to appear opposite the great John Barrymore in *A Bill of Divorcement*, through her unforgettable triumphs in *Morning Glory, Little Women, Alice Adams, The Philadelphia Story, The African Queen, The Lion in Winter*, and *Long Day's Journey into Night*.

THE WOMAN

whose youthful first marriage broke all the rules, whose romantic attachments to Leland Heyward and Howard Hughes ignored the conventions, and whose deep relationship with Spencer Tracy created a new kind of love story for our times.

THE REBEL

who beat Hollywood's most powerful figures at their own power games, whom success couldn't spoil or fiascoes deter, and who refused to be anyone but her inimitable self in public or in private.

There has never been a star like Katharine Hepburn—and never a biography as good as this one.

"Loaded with anecdote, insight, happiness, pain, and sadness, and writing so acute it hurts . . . impossible to put down!"

—PROVIDENCE JOURNAL

Kate

The Life of
Katharine Hepburn

by
Charles Higham

A SIGNET BOOK

NEW AMERICAN LIBRARY

For Richard Palafox

"Listen to the song of life."

—Inscription on the fireplace
of the Hepburn family home
at 201 Bloomfield Avenue,
Hartford, Connecticut

Acknowledgments

Katharine Hepburn was the subject of my first interview, done at the age of eight with my godfather, Gilbert Frankau, the author of *Christopher Strong,* on which her second picture was based. "Why is she so terrifying?" I asked him. "Because she's a tornado," he replied.

Writing this book has been an intense pleasure. Returning to the subject three decades later, I have talked not only to Kate herself but, through her warm cooperation, to some of the most fascinating people I have ever met in my life—her friends and colleagues. I will never forget Laura Harding, with her air of sturdy good sense and forthrightness, sitting in an elegantly cluttered Beekman Place apartment while a maid buzzed around the room with a Hoover; George Cukor, with his piercing glances, lower jaw shooting out as he emphasized a point in a phrase, voice high and sharp, a man of vivid intelligence, at once forceful and profoundly cautious; Pandro Berman, darkly saturnine and compact, tough and shrewd and kind, with a stabbing executive's voice; rugged assistant director Eddie Killey, looking at her photographs with the wonder of a child; Joel McCrea, huge and lovable, a rancher to the fingertips.

I liked Dorothy Arzner, Gertrude Steinish, sweet-natured, living in a coolly elegant house in the middle of a desert; Victor Heerman and Sarah Y. Mason, both in their eighties, in a house filled with cobwebs and moldering antiques; the exquisitely fragile Lillie Messenger.

Then there was the deeply serious, reflective George Stevens, his marvelous rocky face deeply lined with wisdom and suffering, speaking slowly, deliberately, in a near whisper through the ruthless chatter of the Beverly Hills Hotel Polo

ACKNOWLEDGMENTS

Lounge; Fred MacMurray, handsome and gentle, in a room alive with brassware and chintz, his wife June Haver dancing into the room, singing a number from one of her Fox musicals; Andrea Leeds, still the sad charmer of *Stage Door,* in her Palm Springs jewelry shop; Howard Hawks, like an eagle carved out of teak; the fastidious, careful, clever Armina Marshall.

There was Elia Kazan, sharp and profound; dapper Dan Tobin; the volatile Italian-American genius Frank Capra; Clarence Brown, a sweet teddy bear of a man, who at eighty-four walked almost a mile to greet me at the gate of his desert country club; shewdly witty Henry Ephron; John Houseman, deliberate and disillusioned, with the gloomiest eyes I have ever seen; the electric, fiercely intense Stanley Kramer; sleepily witty James Stewart; Ely Landau, massive and jovial, his shrewd eyes missing no detail; Tony Richardson, tall and spindly, with a high forehead and surprised, mistrustful glances; Michael Bennett, taut and vibrant as a harp string. They made writing the book a fascination I have not experienced before, bringing me to a small truth: great people confer a touch of greatness on those they work with. I can sum this up with a remark of Laura Harding, who knows Kate better than most. I had mentioned that she and Kate had sailed from Miami to Mexico on the S.S. *Morro Castle* a few months before the ship burned at sea with a loss of hundreds of lives. "Maybe," Laura says, "Kate left a spark behind."

Of all the meetings which the writing of this book brought about, the most extraordinary was my confrontation with Jed Harris, legendary "boy wonder" of the Broadway theatre of the 1930s, whose productions of *The Front Page* and *The Royal Family of Broadway* are still talked about with humble admiration among older theatre people. He had not produced anything significant since his celebrated presentation of *The Heiress,* with Basil Rathbone and Wendy Hiller, in 1947, and he seemed to have disappeared off the face of the earth—many people thought he must be dead. Letters from old addresses came back unanswered; a lead to a town in Florida fizzled out. The Theatre Guild had no idea of his whereabouts; even such stalwarts as John Houseman and Elia

ACKNOWLEDGMENTS

Kazan could not offer a clue. I was about to give up when that veteran figure of the theatre, Jean Dalrymple, mentioned that she knew someone who still kept in touch with Harris: the old-time theatrical agent Charles Abrahamson, who used to be Preston Sturges' right-hand man. Sure enough, Abrahamson knew where Harris was—living in Atlantic City —and he set up a meeting on condition that I paid five hundred dollars. Even though I had never paid for an interview before, the opportunity was too good to miss, as Harris had produced Hepburn's greatest disaster, *The Lake*, and she herself had urged me to see him. People were awestruck when I mentioned that I was going to meet the Great Man, the subject of several novels, including *The Saxon Charm*, and one asked me if I were armed. "With information?" I asked. "No, with a gun," he replied.

When I received a call in my hotel room that Harris was in the lobby, I felt a moment of sharp apprehension, which certainly turned out to be justified. As I reached the lobby, I immediately picked Harris out of several hundred conventioneers. Tall and dressed in funereal black, he bristled with a melodramatic menace. His hooded eyes were at once secretive and coldly observant. He began with a tirade against the hotel we were in, lamenting its loss of former glory. The interview started off with a violent monologue at Hepburn's expense, and frequently, during the course of it, he failed to answer anything. Several times, exasperated, he rose to his feet and started toward the door, sitting down only when he remembered my fee. Fortunately, I had taken the precaution of placing the money with his agent until a satisfactory interview was completed. An unseemly struggle was avoided only by the arrival of Charles Abrahamson, who made him sign the clearance and escorted him, violently protesting, to the elevator. I was never happier to see anyone go. Yet the interview, when I transcribed it, was the most remarkable I have ever conducted in my life.

Aside from those specially mentioned in the foregoing, I am indebted to over a hundred people for their memories of Katharine Hepburn. These include Sir Ralph Richardson, Cary Grant, Sidney Lumet, Victor Saville, Lawrence Weingarten, Joel and Frances McCrea, Barbara O'Neil, Margaret

ACKNOWLEDGMENTS

Barker, George Coulouris, the late Benn W. Levy, Phyllis Lawton Seaton, the late Merian C. Cooper, Daniel Selznick, Brooke Hayward Hopper, the late Alan Campbell and Dorothy Parker, Dolores Costello Barrymore, Adolph Zukor, Mel Berns, David Manners, Sid Hickox, William Wellman, Mary Pickford, Walter Plunkett, Joan Bennett, John Beal, Francis Lederer, Jane Loring, John Collier, Brian Aherne, the late John Ford, the late Donald Crisp, Eve Arden, Howard Hawks, Fritz Feld, Virginia Christine Feld, Lew Ayres, Donald Ogden Stewart, Annie Laurie Williams, Mrs. Philip Barry, Robert Sinclair, Worthington Miner, Joseph Cotten, Joseph Ruttenberg, Ruth Hussey, Joseph L. Mankiewicz, the late Hedda Hopper, Ring Lardner, Jr., Mrs. Elliott Nugent, Audrey Christie, Hurd Hatfield, Aline MacMahon, John Howard, Marguerite Roberts, Vincente Minnelli, Jay Robinson, John Huston, Joe Hyams, Ted Scaife, Aldo Ray, Cyril Ritchard, John Marven, David Lean, the late Harald Bowden, Colin Baskerville, Lindsay Browne, the late Josephine O'Neill, Robert Wise, Ralph Thomas and Betty Box, Lester Cowan, James Wong Howe, Joseph Anthony, Charles Lang, Jr., Joan Blondell, Alfred Drake, Boris Kaufman, Sam Leavitt, Martin Poll, Peter O'Toole, Richard Chamberlain, René Auberjonois, the late Roger Edens, Frederick Brisson, George Rose, Colin Higgins, and Roy Moseley.

Sherry Huber did an inspired job of editing the book, and suggested many important revisions. Ann Bloch typed it. And Kate Hepburn stood back nobly, not asking to see the book in manuscript or proof, clearing everyone, and not even calling me to see how I was progressing. There never was, and there never will be, another like her.

CHARLES HIGHAM

Prologue

Sometime in the 1940s, Louis B. Mayer, the powerful boss of MGM, kissed Katharine Hepburn's forehead.

"What did you do that for?" she snapped in her best New England schoolmarm, how-dared-you-touch-me manner.

"I just wanted to kiss the Blarney Stone," Mayer replied.

For the record: I have never kissed Katharine Hepburn.

But meeting her was kissing the Blarney Stone just the same.

We had two afternoon-long encounters, one at the end of 1973 and the other at the start of 1974, in which she talked about the whole of her life. At the first meeting, I dropped by her comfortable, leather-furnished cottage in West Hollywood to speak to her for the New York *Times*. On a chilly, foggy afternoon, she opened the door herself, showed me her Christmas wreath, and sat me down by the fire. She proudly pointed out the wreath's intricately woven leaves. She so often plays embittered, broken-down, aged women on the screen, it was a relief to find her as alive with enthusiasm as a young girl, cheeks ruddy with sunburn, movements quick and precise, her figure almost as attractively skinny as it was when she played *The Philadelphia Story* more than thirty years ago.

It was a wonderful meeting, in which she talked for many hours about her youth and upbringing, her life in Hollywood, and her admiration for her beloved Spencer Tracy. At sixty-four, she was an Alice-Sit-by-the-Fire with the fine lines of a Connecticut gentlewoman, cheekbones delicately chiseled, nose sharply patrician, and a mind of piercing sharpness which could dampen any pretentiousness. Only the smoky blue-grey eyes and trembling mouth suggested the pain she still feels years after Tracy's death. For all her oaklike strength, she is among the walking wounded.

She liked the article, and sent me a beautiful note about it, saying it was one of the few things written about her she had been able to finish. With extraordinary modesty, she wrote, "I must say you make me sound most fascinating." How could any writer, however doltish, make her sound anything else?

Several weeks on, after I had written her that I wanted to do a book about her, she called me over to tell me she was writing her own book and to lay off mine. Many hours of magnificent conversation later, as I was preparing to leave, she said, "You're going to do it anyway, aren't you?"

I told her, "Yes."

"Well then, I'll help you. I hope you don't write any *really* good stories or it will hurt my book. But if anybody's reluctant to see you, get them to call me. I'll talk to them."

"Do you want to see the book?"

"NO, NO, NO, NO, NO! I hate reading anything about me. I had the temerity to read your article about me in the *Times*. We were lucky enough to have had a most interesting afternoon. But a book? Oh, God! No!"

"You don't enjoy reading about yourself?"

"Can't stand it. Won't even *talk* about the *thing* Gar Kanin did.* It bores me to think of the past, and almost everyone who knew me is dead. You're going to have a hell of a job writing this. There's nobody left."

"I have a list of two hundred people. Want me to start reading it out?"

"I don't believe you. You're lying! Mention two names."

"Victor Heerman and Sarah Y. Mason."

"Oh, my *God!* The adapters of *Little Women!* Are they still alive?"

"They are, and send their best regards. They live in a fantastic old house in Hollywood, with cobwebs on the chandeliers."

"They saved *Little Women!*"

"And Lillie Messenger, who directed your first screen test,

* *Tracy and Hepburn,* by Garson Kanin (New York: The Viking Press, 1971).

and Sid Hickox, who photographed you in *Bill of Divorcement*, and Joe Ruttenberg, who photographed you so nobody saw your neck . . . and . . ."

"Don't you *dare* go on. And who else?"

"John Beal, your co-star in *The Little Minister*. He was terrified of you then and he's terrified now."

"You're not supposed to tell me that!"

"And all your directors and assistant directors, your fellow actors, your makeup men, your camermen, your costume designers, your friends!"

"STOP, STOP, STOP, STOP, *STOP!* That's enough! I'll do what I can to help you" (she did, enormously), "and mind that step as you go out!"

In her mid-sixties, Katharine Hepburn is still, wonderfully and emphatically, Katharine Hepburn. She now enjoys the same friends she cherished when she started out on her career, and lives in homes she has occupied for many years: a beautiful tall, narrow-staired, white-painted house on East Forty-ninth Street in Turtle Bay, New York; a lovely summer place called Fenwick, near Old Saybrook at the mouth of the Connecticut River; and the old Spencer Tracy cottage in Hollywood. She is as outrageously bossy, overpowering, funny, good-natured, challenging, cantankerous, and enchanting as she always was. At times, she is Saint Katharine, secretly generous, adoring of her peers, living a clean-cut, simple life of pure devotion to her work and her intimates. At other times, she is Alice's Red Queen in *Through the Looking-Glass,* a darting, maddening gadfly of a woman, stinging everyone's hides.

I fell in love with her at first glance. Meeting most stars is rather like meeting royalty: a maid ushers you into an enormous, regal living room apparently decorated by the Cunard White Star Line; there is an obligatory wait, the length of which may be judged by the commercial importance of the star, while he or she is presumably hiding in a nearby room, looking at a watch and deciding how many millions were earned that year. Then the star enters—coming downstairs or through a French window, as though onto a stage, followed by a business manager or press agent who sits on your left while the star sits on your right. It is extremely rare to be offered even a thimbleful of tap water. The instant the star says anything remotely controversial, the press agent changes the subject to football or the price of artichokes. A golden rule: never mention anybody other than the star, especially including yourself, or the eyes will glaze over.

With Kate it's different—to say the least. She comes to the door herself. She offers a festive afternoon tea, with a silver service and a splendid array of cookies, cakes, and pies. If it happens to be Christmas, she'll show you her Christmas wreath. If the weather is good, she'll take you on a walking tour of the Hollywood Reservoir. She'll dispense with any other company except her bony British secretary, Phyllis Wilbourn. Wonder of wonders, she doesn't even *have* a press agent.

She talks in her superb voice, a cross between Donald Duck and a Stradivarius. She is full of exclamations, such as "fascinating," "thrilling," "enormous," and "exciting." Well-scrubbed, well-honed, cheeks shiny, blue-grey eyes alive with humor and sadness, she looks as leathery and comfortable as her own living room. Her tender glances rest on brassware rubbed to a fine polish, landscapes of Cuba—pale and cool and evocative—painted by herself, good books crowding the walls, tables of old wood. She is still, at heart, the New England lady of the house, formidable, kindly, stern, worlds removed from Dorothy Parker's definition of a movie star: a woman with a long white glove and a diamond bracelet, and in the palm of the hand a bagel with a bite out of it.

She's the Statue of Liberty, Eleanor Roosevelt, and Lady Luck. The American ideal personified: the image of discipline, drive, the Puritan ethic fulfilled. She has been Liberated since birth. There is nobody like her.

She's KATE.

This book—that she may never read—is my tribute to her.

One

She was born to a maverick clan. The Hepburns—Kate's mother was a Boston Houghton—had the reputation of being one of New England's most extreme rebel families. They were of Scottish descent: the Earl of Bothwell, lover of Mary Queen of Scots, had been a Hepburn. The clannishness survived: the family clung together as aggressive freethinkers fighting the world of New England convention.

Dr. Thomas Norval Hepburn, Kate's father, was a Southerner from Virginia. A graduate of Johns Hopkins Hospital and a distinguished surgeon on the staff of the Hartford Hospital, he specialized in the field of urology and pioneered the study of sexual hygiene. Lean, athletic, a fine golfer, he was strikingly handsome, with carved features, hollows under his cheekbones, and dark red hair. Aside from his other accomplishments, he was a highly skilled investor, who had become rich from inspired buying and selling of stocks, shares, and real estate.

Mrs. Hepburn, Katharine Houghton Hepburn—known familiarly as Kit—was cousin to the ambassador to Britain, Alanson Bigelow Houghton. Slender, angular, beautiful, she was famous for wearing a Chinese tea gown which set off her thoroughbred's figure. She was a headstrong and gifted intellectual who set herself against her Boston contemporaries. Like her husband, she was ostracized by many society people.

She was committed to the suffragette movement, was an early advocate of birth control, and picketed the White House to ensure better working conditions for women. She dragged Kate along, at the age of four, to appear with her in soapbox public speeches against women's enslavement by domesticity. Paradoxically, she herself was the mother of six children: in bearing them, she had expressed her love for her husband, who profoundly wanted children, but she was aware of the fact that, for many poorer women, bearing children was simply an onerous duty, seriously affecting their health, welfare, and psychological development. What she carried off with great flair was for other women an intolerable drudgery. Dr. Hepburn enthusiastically shared her views as an early supporter of birth control, seemingly unperplexed by the contradiction of his own multiple fatherhood.

Named after her mother, Kate was born in Hartford, Connecticut, on November 8, 1909. Kate's elder brother, Tom, and two younger brothers and two sisters, Dick, Bob, Marion, and Peggy, were all raised to live a life of free speech; as soon as they could talk, they were urged to express themselves on every conceivable subject, arguing a point of view until everyone was exhausted. No one could leave the room until an argument was finished. Along with freedom of thought, the Hepburn parents encouraged freedom of movement.

Intensely happy with each other and deeply involved physically and mentally with their children to a degree extremely rare in upper-crust New England society, they stimulated Kate and her siblings to run, swim, bicycle, and play tennis better than anybody else. Both boys and girls would climb trees, invade deserted houses, tackle raging surfs, make cross-country excursions, run up hills, ride horses, and train hunting dogs. Dr. and Mrs. Hepburn taught their children that everything in life must be earned by severe effort; nothing must be freely given or received.

The Hepburn house, at 201 Bloomfield Avenue, was large and commodious, with a huge, shady garden. It constantly resounded to violently gabbled arguments, screams, shouts, tumbles down stairs. No one, ever, was told to shut up, though the entire family in concert was apt to say that to some unsuspecting fuddy-duddy Hartford conservative who happened to visit. In that odd case, he would be needled, cajoled, and mocked by everyone, until he fled in terror.

Kate's earliest memories are of sprinting down a gravel drive, bringing down the neighborhood boys in football tackles, shaving her hair each summer so her opponents couldn't grab it, wearing slacks and loafers long before it was acceptable for girls to wear them, reading newspapers, expressing her views on politics, taking deep gulps of freezing winter air when her father flung the windows open, doing physical exercises and ballet dancing on the lawn, and discussing childbirth, sexual intercourse, free love, and the problems of marriage with her parents.

There was no subject forbidden in the Hepburn household. Everyone spoke up loud and clear with his or her opinion, but the parents' word was more often final than Kate later cared to admit. Theirs was a commune in terms of shared views and domestic and garden tasks—but it was a commune with leaders.

She was spanked as a matter of course, plunged into cold showers, forbidden candies. She campaigned with her mother, holding placards high and calling herself "Jimmy." When a woman neighbor told her she looked frail, she lowered her head and charged into a tree, then turned around, head bleeding, and said, "I'm tougher than the tree."

Kate, referring to the icy baths, said, years later, "Those baths were responsible for my later perversity. They gave me the impression that the bitterer the medicine, the better it was for you. That may be one reason why I came to think that the more insulting the press was, the more it stimulated me."

From her earliest days, Kate was aware that her parents were socially criticized. This made her tackle the world head on, and no doubt stimulated that need to conquer the world on her own terms which made her a star. She was allowed to wear what she wanted: she chose to use her elder brother Tom's castoffs. She traveled around, appearing with her mother in suffrage speeches. She was extremely gauche at social events. When she went to her first dance, escorted by Tom, she wore a dress for a change: it fitted so badly she looked impossibly awkward. Kate heard another boy ask Tom, "Who's that goofy-looking wallflower standing over there?" Kate, angular and freckled, brazened the situation out, clodhopping her way around the dance floor, treading on Tom's feet. She told a friend years later, "I was never a

member of the feminine club. I never knew what other girls
were talking about."

She fell in love with silent movies, shoveling snow or trim-
ming lawns so that she could buy tickets and gaze ecstatically
at the solemn, horse-faced Western hero William S. Hart, the
shining, kiss-curled Mary Pickford, or exquisite young Lea-
trice Joy. She recalls she was haunted by the huge, glistening
images, the flowered titles, the fantastically exaggerated stories of love, death, and adventure, and dreamed of becoming
a movie star.

Kate's parents didn't take her ambitions very seriously. But
they allowed her and her brothers and sisters to convert the
dining room of their summer home, Fenwick, at Old Saybrook, Connecticut, into a repertory theatre, with the aid of
bits of furniture dragged from all over the house. There the
children appeared in a version of *Bluebeard*, with Kate in the
leading role in a beard stained blue. She murdered her wives
with great relish. Soon after this production, a Bishop
Howden of New Mexico gave a sermon at the local Connecticut church in which he discussed the severe plight of the
Navajo Indians. Kate and her brothers and sisters gave a
benefit performance of *Beauty and the Beast* for the local
parents and children, charging fifty cents a ticket. When the
parents of some children in the cast complained about the
ticket charge, Kate fired those children. She was a great
success as the Beast in her blue velvet Little Lord Fauntleroy
suit with silver stripes and her marvelous cloth donkey's
head. The sixty dollars earned from the performance went to
buying the Navajos a phonograph.

Up to the age of ten, Kate was an uncomplicated, open-
faced, freckled, harum-scarum tomboy. But then something
happened which altered her character overnight, and made
her, for many years, a violent antagonist of the world.

She was spending Easter, 1920, with her brother Tom at a
friend's house in Boston. On the Saturday night, the friend
had a party, with Tom leading the jokes and the fun. The
following morning, Kate went to waken him and found him
missing from his bed. She searched the house until at last she
came to the attic. She noticed an odd shadow on the floor.

Then she looked up, too numb with terror to cry out. Tom, with a noose around his neck, was hanging from a beam.

She collected herself, cut him down, and tried to revive him, but he was quite gone. She ran to the home of a local doctor and rang the doorbell. A maid answered, and Kate sobbed, "My brother's dead. Please help me." The maid replied coldly, "If he's dead, the doctor can't help him," and she slammed the door in Kate's face. Kate managed to find a policeman, and another doctor, who said that Tom had been dead since three o'clock in the morning. He was only sixteen.

The exact reason for Tom's death was never known. Suicide seemed unlikely for a handsome, healthy, highly intelligent boy. Instead, Kate felt that it must have been an accident: a week before, she had gone with Tom to see *A Connecticut Yankee in King Arthur's Court*, in which a man was hanged from a tree. Maybe, she figured, Tom was imitating the actor.

Kate's agony was so extreme that she became a highly nervous, moody girl, suspicious of people, arrogant and disrespectful, bitter, and hateful of religion. After seeing Tom dead, she no longer believed in a benign destiny or in a life after death. The physical evidence of lifelessness in his once energetic and healthy body crushed any hope she might have had that something survives the cessation of the functions. Her desire to become a movie actress, her image fixed forever on glittering celluloid frames, may well have been a realization of mortality.

At thirteen, Kate appeared in *Marley's Ghost* (from Dickens' *A Christmas Carol*) and *Bluebeard* in a special benefit for Navajo Indian children at Fenwick. At the West Middle School, she became known for her enthusiastic poetry recitals, especially of "The Wreck of the Hesperus." At sixteen, she entered Bryn Mawr, her mother's alma mater, a fresh-faced, freckled dynamo who hated studies but fought hard to improve her grades so she could appear in college theatricals.

Kate made an extraordinary impression at Bryn Mawr. The first night there, she entered the dormitory dining hall as though she were making an entrance in a play. Rawboned, she strode in bolt upright, haughtily, in a blue-and-white

Iceland sweater, trying to conceal her terror with an enormous air of bravado. The roomful of girls fell silent, staring
at her in astonishment. Finally a voice said, "Ah, self-
conscious beauty!" Everyone laughed, and Kate fled. She did
not eat in the dining room again for months, spending her mea-
ger allowance in the cheaper restaurants of nearby towns.
She was always getting herself involved in some kind of
prank to work off her nervous energy and to conceal her
terror at everything: jumping in the college fountain and
rolling around in the grass until she became dry, standing
nude on the roof with snow falling around her until she
looked like a living snowwoman, dashing late into class and
falling flat on her face, leaping up and executing a dance
before she slumped into a seat, propping her feet on the
shoulders of the girl in front of her. She also admits she
invaded the houses of total strangers when they were away,
both at Bryn Mawr and at Hartford. In one case, she entered
through a skylight and dropped three stories into the first-
floor hallway; miraculously she was not injured. She wasn't
popular, refusing to join in college activities, missing many
classes, and proving useless as a team player in games.

Performing in an angular, mannered style in college theatricals, she appeared in A. A. Milne's *The Truth about Blayds*
and in *Cradle Song*. In the spring of her senior year, she
made a bigger splash, as Pandora in John Lyly's *The Woman
in the Moone* in the Bryn Mawr May Day Revels of 1928. She
was spare and edgy in a long white robe, barefoot, and with
a wreath on her flowing red hair, and she played the part in
a style which fitted the playwright's description: "The Plan-
ets each give her their own humor for a time, so that she is
sometimes sullen, sometimes vain, and sometimes martial."
Kate earned a powerful burst of applause from both parents
and students: she decided at that moment to make definite
plans for a theatrical career.

Meanwhile, though, there was still the pleasure of her
family, and above all the summers at the paradise of Fenwick. Fellow students often came home to Fenwick, and the
icebox was always stuffed with bottles of pop. Kate dug clams,
gathered seaweed and pink mallow, sailed a boat named

Tiger, worked with a fisherman cutting fish fillets in a little hut.

Kate emerged as a fine athlete in her late teens, winning a bronze medal for figure skating at the Madison Square Garden Skating Club, shooting golf in the low eighties, and even reaching the semi-final of the Connecticut Young Women's Golf Championship. She was a good tennis player and a vigorous swimmer. She retained the family custom of saying and doing exactly what she felt like at any given moment—a habit which may have made for good psychological health but tended to infuriate almost everyone she came in contact with.

By eighteen, Kate's character was fully formed. Beautiful, with reddish hair, smoky blue-grey eyes, her father's carved features, and her mother's angular, aristocratic body, back held very straight, she had far more sex appeal than she realized. Her voice was high-pitched in those days, piercing and repetitive. She still walked with a lanky stride. When she went on a date, she would talk incessantly for hours, then announce sharply to her beau, "We're going home—right now!" A good-night kiss would be a sharp peck on the cheek. A pass would be rejected briskly. Her opinionated behavior cooled many a young man's desires, and she continued to be an awkward Alice Adams at the Senior Prom.

At eighteen, she set out to turn herself into a career woman. A friend, John S. Clarke, gave her an introduction to a young producer called Edwin H. Knopf, who had a stock company in Baltimore.

Kate remembers telling her father of her decision to go to Baltimore as she was driving with him from Bryn Mawr to Hartford. She said, very quickly, "I'm going to be an actress, Daddy!" He looked at her in silent horror, then shouted with rage, "You just want to show off—and get paid for it!" "But, Daddy," Kate replied, "you let Mother make speeches for the suffragettes!" Dr. Hepburn snapped, "That was for a political purpose. This is just stupid vanity!" Kate yelled and burst into tears. Finally, after much argument, as they neared home he climbed down and said, "All right. Here's fifty dollars. If you don't make it to first base, that's the end." Kate rushed off to Baltimore.

There are two versions of what happened next. According

to Kate, she arrived at a rehearsal, sat in the orchestra for
five hours, and was spotted by Knopf, who told her to report
for rehearsal. According to Knopf, she stormed into his Baltimore office, a red-haired, spindly, freckle-faced vision, all eyes
and talent, passionately insisting on being given a role. Affected by her eagerness, Knopf gave her a part as lady-in-
waiting to Mary Boland in his production of *The Czarina.*

At first, Mary Boland was dismayed by the trousered red-
head in the wings with her shiny face, a scarf twisted awkwardly around her neck. She felt Kate's eyes burningly turned
on her during rehearsal, and demanded that Knopf have her
taken away. But when Mary Boland saw Kate in a ball dress,
she was surprised. She said later, "The ugly duckling became
a swan—it was incredible! I never saw anything like that
eager girl, so proud to walk across a stage she seemed to be
borne up by light."

Next week, Kate played an alternating role as a flapper in
a play called *The Cradle Snatchers.* Again, she looked marvelous the moment she stopped wearing her usual clothes and
dressed up elegantly. But Edwin Knopf hated her shrill voice,
and the stage manager, Kenneth McKenna, bundled her off
to Frances Robinson-Duff, a voice coach in New York, when
the season closed. Mrs. Robinson-Duff specialized in the Del-
sarte method of actor training, made up of extravagant gestures of the kind seen in silent films. Kate learned to dance
with the Russian Michael Mordkin. When Knopf moved to
New York, she took on the role of a secretary in his production of *The Big Pond.*

About a week before the scheduled opening in Great Neck,
Knopf fired the leading lady and replaced her with Kate.
Kate was totally unprepared for the part, and terrified of it.
She was so overcome with nerves on opening night, she drove
off to a nearby railroad station and ate blueberries. When she
finally reached the theatre, with everyone in a state of terror
that she wouldn't turn up, her lace panties scratched her, and
she dropped them, shook them off her feet, and handed them
to an astonished stage manager. She stumbled through the
part, mixing up lines, tripping over her feet, and talking so
rapidly she was incomprehensible. She was fired at once. Incredibly, she managed to get more work: in a flop called

These Days, which lasted for eight nights, and then as an understudy to Hope Williams in *Holiday.*

She told me, "I was *always* getting fired! I was what might be called a 'flash actor.' I could read a part without knowing what I was doing better than anyone in the whole world. I could laugh and cry, and I could always get a part quickly—but I couldn't keep it! They got on to me after a while. I would lose my voice, fall down on lines, get red in the face, talk too fast, and I couldn't act! The sight of people out there just petrified me!"

Two weeks after *Holiday* opened, she impetuously accepted a proposal of marriage from Ludlow Ogden Smith—whom she called "Luddy"—one of four beaux she had been dating for the past few months, and left the stage.

She had been discouraged from marriage by her mother from the outset, but she probably felt that since her stage career was rapidly going nowhere, it might be as well to give herself some insurance for the future by marrying. The bachelor she settled on was a figure in the Philadelphia Social Register, tall, handsome, elegant, educated in France, and extremely sophisticated. His Philadelphia Main Line background and exquisite tailoring and manners evidently impressed her deeply. Also, he reminded her of her father in his authoritative bearing. There was the added advantage that he was a long-term friend of the family and a frequent visitor both to Hartford and Fenwick, where a room was set aside for him always. The engagement was very brief. Kate apparently was conscious that if she hesitated too long she would certainly change her mind. She married him secretly in Hartford.

The marriage was a disaster. Kate had such a horror of domesticity that the whole experience was a nightmare. She managed to persuade Luddy to call himself Ogden Ludlow, since she hated the idea of being called Kate Smith. She also had him shift his base from Philadelphia to New York and moved with him into a tiny apartment on East Thirty-ninth Street. They were drastically unhappy there.

She evidently realized that she had married on a whim and that marriage was totally incompatible with her need for absolute freedom of thought and action. She could not commit herself unselfishly to another human being, putting his desires and needs before her own, subordinating her will—in fact, doing everything which her mother had spoken against from soapboxes during Kate's childhood. Her mother had accepted the paradox of her own situation because of her love for Dr. Hepburn. Kate knew from the outset that her move into marriage had been as reckless as her move into the theatre, and as inspired by her passion for novelty, with one important difference: only the theatre was her vocation.

Three weeks after the marriage took place, the couple separated. Faced with the fact that he had a failed marriage, Luddy sensibly decided to continue with Kate on a Platonic basis. She, in her turn, much preferred him when he was not physically and domestically her husband, and in fact he became her lifelong friend. All the qualities that had attracted her to him—great intelligence, emotional security, and financial stability—became all the more appealing when she no longer had to resent his marital command over her life. She remained legally married to him for several years—clearly a defense against having to face marriage again, and an effective deterrent to men who might be attracted to her.

The problem with Kate in that period was that she was not really dedicated to her vocation as an actress. She was a stagestruck girl playing at acting. Mrs. Hepburn used to come to her rehearsals, but Dr. Hepburn, who still did not approve of the theatre, only came to her first nights, and gave his frank, and usually unfavorable opinion.

After understudying *Holiday*, Kate appeared as a rather foolish young girl who falls in love with the Prince of Darkness in a play called *Death Takes a Holiday*. "I was kicked out of it," Kate says. "I called home and said, 'I've been fired again! You'd better come and see the play before I actually leave.' Dad came and said, 'It's a silly play, because no girl of eighteen would want to go off with Death unless she was a psychopathic case. Obviously you're playing a psychopath. I thought you did it extremely well!' And I thought, 'Well, Daddy, now I know why I was fired!' "

At heart, she still remained as deeply involved with her family as she was with the theatre. She was fascinated, then and later, with the development of her brothers and sisters. Marion and Richard were both amateur writers, even at this early age, pouring out vivid, erratic stories and essays. Bob showed a scientific bent, and later followed in his father's footsteps as a doctor. Peggy also became fascinated by science, and worked later in a laboratory. All the siblings were handsome, freckled, dark-skinned, their hair streaked with red, athletic, clean-limbed, and slender. Kate's happiest hours were spent with them, and in her old room at Hartford, with the maple bed, the chintz drapes, the old, badly stuffed teddy bear, and, downstairs, the big uncarpeted hall constantly scuffed with golf shoes, tennis shoes, and riding boots, the French windows opening on to the sweep of green lawns, the nearby golf course, the woods for walking in. She adored the whirlwind life of early breakfasts, hikes, endless afternoon teas, lights out at 10 P.M.

Kate's next role was a brief appearance as a maid in *A Month in the Country,* for the Theatre Guild. The director, Rouben Mamoulian, has never forgotten the impression Kate made on him: "I had prepared the acting version of it myself. Alla Nazimova was the star. There was a very big part in the play for a young girl, and I began interviewing some unknowns. I saw about fifty girls. One day I was at the Theatre Guild offices when this youngster walked in—freckled face, red hair tightly combed back. She was shaking. I tried to put her at ease. I asked her to sit down, and I said to her, 'Have you ever done anything?' She said, 'No.' I told her, 'This is going to be difficult because it's a very big part. It would be very tough for someone without experience. However, here is a scene—you go in the next room and read it, and then come back.' She returned and she read it to me. She was obviously inexperienced, and I told her she wasn't ready for it. 'However,' I told her, 'if I have a chance for you, an opening for a smaller part, I would like to call you.' Then I walked out into the next office—there was Cheryl Crawford, who was the casting manager. I said, 'Cheryl, I want you to take this girl's name down because the kid has something. Whenever I have an opening, remind me.' She took the name down, and four weeks or so later the maid in the play who had two lines had to drop out, so we got this kid in. There was something about her—it's very difficult to describe in words. You can't describe music. There was—is—a kind of luminosity I noticed about her at the beginning; there are some faces that project the light; hers does. She was obviously set for stardom—even as a maid!"

After *A Month in the Country*, Kate studied again with the drama coach Frances Robinson-Duff. Mrs. Robinson-Duff was a massively fat, powerfully impressive woman who had lived much of her life in Paris, where her mother had coached the singer Mary Garden. Now she lived in a little brownstone house on East Fifty-second Street, decorated with French antique furniture, and equipped with a tiny, creaking, hand-operated elevator so small it could barely accommodate its enormous-hipped lady owner. Everyone else used the stairs. Kate would climb several times a week to the top floor, where Mrs. Robinson-Duff would lead her carefully through key scenes of famous plays, never ironing out her angular, metallic diction, but teaching her tiny details of emphasis and timing.

Among the other pupils was Laura Harding, heiress to the American Express fortune, an adorably good-natured, athletic blonde with a gentle New England voice, who later became one of Kate's closest friends. Laura Harding remembers her first impression of Kate: "I met her very briefly in 1928. I thought, 'She's not my type. We'd never like each other.' Isn't that funny? She had long hair pulled back in a knot, a man's sweater pinned at the back with a big safety pin —what we called a Brooks sweater—and a tweed skirt. She always rushed impetuously into class."

Frances Robinson-Duff said later, "The first time I met Kate, it was raining. She had run up the stairs. She burst in the door, unannounced, and flung herself down on a chest. Rain came from her red hair and down her nose. She sat in a dripping puddle and stared. 'I want to be an actress,' she said. 'I want to learn everything.' Why did I work with her? Sometimes we have an inward vision, a flash. I looked at her, huddled there, bedraggled and wet—at the terrific intensity of her face—and something inside whispered, 'Duse—she looks like Duse.' "*

Frances Robinson-Duff suggested that Kate should do a

---

*Eleanora Duse (1859–1924), the great Italian actress.

season of summer stock at the Berkshire Playhouse, Stockbridge, Massachusetts, with Laura Harding. Kate, eager to
learn everything she could about the company at Stockbridge,
asked Frances to arrange a meeting at the Robinson-Duff
house with Laura, whom she questioned eagerly for hours.
Laura, on this new acquaintance, found Kate charming, and
Kate was delighted with Laura's sweetness of character and
her warm, witty manner of expressing herself. The two women
met again at Stockbridge and developed a deep affection that
was to last a lifetime. They shared rooms rented for them by
the management in a large old clapboard house belonging to
and English minister named Bradley. The minister was a
model of propriety, but he was married to a "wild" southern
woman and had three teen-age daughters. Laura says, "The
three daughters sat up all night and drank whisky, leaving
the dirty glasses for the maid, and had different 'fiancés' every
week! At one point, Kate and I figured there were eighteen
people living in the house—the clergyman and his family,
theatre folk—and all sharing *one bathroom*. For some reason,
I was given the best bedroom, charming, and in no time Kate,
who had a tiny room, had moved in.

"The room was next to the bathroom, and she was determined to be first into the bathroom every day. She took endless baths—it was summer—and she was so *clean!* We got to
know each other very well, and we'd laugh an awful lot! Such
fun!

"Another person in the house was Osgood Perkins, Tony
Perkins' father. And there was an actor called Richard Hale,
who was always challenging Kate to debates. George Coulouris was another paying guest. He was in the stock company
with us, and he later became an Orson Welles actor and
appeared in *Citizen Kane*. He and Kate had a wild effect on
each other—sparks *flew!* He finally said to her, after a terrific
quarrel, 'You don't make any sense at all. You're just a flibber-
tigibbet and a fly-by-night!' And Kate replied, 'You can say
what you want, but I'll be a star before you're even heard of!'
They'd have this funny endless battle, then they would chase
through the house, up and down the stairs. We laughed and
laughed all summer."

George Coulouris says, "Bradley's was a wonderful place.

I remember when I arrived there, this tall, skinny, red-haired girl ran in saying, 'I've come all the way from Hartford with a golf tee between my teeth!' in what was then rather a high, squeaky voice. She drove a marvelous LaSalle convertible. She wore jeans all the time, she ate her meals with her knees almost up to her face, and had to pass her knife and fork over her knees. There were two stodgy English actors at Bradley's, and they thought she was *awful!*

"She was a complete individualist in every way. I watched her, fascinated by the things she said. One day, we were discussing Francis Thompson's 'The Hound of Heaven,' and she asked, very fast, 'Why does he use words of three syllables when he could use two?' I thought, 'What a nerve!'

"My wife, Louise, and I had the next bedroom to hers. Sometimes she would come in very late, about one o'clock, run a hot bath immediately, and shout French poetry, very loud.

"Her husband, Smith, came up every weekend from Hartford, and she promptly sent him off to the village for a quart of ice cream. He washed her hair in the tub, and that, and fetching the ice cream, was about all he did that weekend, so far as she was concerned! He never even stayed at Bradley's!

"Some people thought she was terrible, because she was sort of amateurish, but she was marvelous-looking on the stage; she came on looking stunning. We used to get together after the show. I used to scare her by hunching my shoulders and shining a flashlight in her face; she would always squeal."

Kate and Laura appeared in Sir James M. Barrie's *The Admirable Crichton* at Stockbridge, as two English girls stranded on a desert island. Kate brooded constantly over the fact that Geoffrey Kerr and June Walker, in the leading roles, never spoke to her or Laura. She had a Robin Hood hat decorated with spears of jungle grass, and she would turn her head onstage so that a long piece of grass stuck in the crown brushed Geoffrey Kerr's face. But he completely ignored her. She also used to giggle uncontrollably, in scenes that didn't call for giggling, when the actor Robert Coote, who had a facial tic, seemed to be winking at her.

As well as being in *The Admirable Crichton*, Kate was the

lead in a play called *A Romantic Young Lady*, for which she designed her own costumes, made up of bits and pieces borrowed from Laura, and sometimes worn back to front, to make the collars look high, because she had a horror of her own long, thin neck. She was a great hit with the local audiences, but the moment she achieved the leading part, she lost all interest and decided to move on to better things. She left the season halfway through, tired of pitting her wits against everyone else.

Later, Kate managed to land a role as the daughter of Jane Cowl in a Broadway play by Benn W. Levy, *Art and Mrs. Bottle*. The melting, soft-spoken Jane Cowl, with her marvelous bovine eyes and exquisite genteel catch in the voice, adored Kate, and Kate adored her. But Benn W. Levy was annoyed from the beginning by Kate's red topknot, loose sweater done up with a safety pin, pants, and headlong, stagestruck manner, and said, "She looks a fright, her manner is objectionable, and she has no talent."

The English actress Joyce Carey, who appeared with her in the play, has never forgotten her then: "They tested lots of girls in the part of the daughter. Kate was entirely different from any girl I'd ever seen. For one thing, she was obviously from a slightly higher drawer than anyone else I'd met in the theatre—she looked like a boy, she wore almost no makeup, her hair was scraped back. She wore—this I remember very well—a little sort of twist of felt around her neck to disguise it. Her voice was much higher then than it is now. For a couple of days at rehearsal, I thought, 'Strange girl!' She had a tremendous personality even then, a very brusque manner. She seemed rather rude, but she wasn't at all; it was simply her way of speaking. I got to like her very, very much. She was a little anxious, but she took a very grand attitude, which I rather admired. She looked wonderful. She was— and is—one of the great eccentrics."

Benn W. Levy fired her from the play, then rehired her after fourteen other actresses failed at auditions. The moment the season was over, she drove off helter-skelter to Ivoryton, Connecticut, to appear with Henry Hull in a season of summer stock. She was a great hit, and even managed, in

the late summer of 1931, to land the important part of Daisy
Sage in Philip Barry's Broadway play *The Animal Kingdom*.

Kate and Luddy went with Laura to The Lodge, a Pennsyl-
vania mountain home belonging to Laura's family, to study
the part of Daisy Sage. All three walked and fished and swam
through the late summer. At the end of August, Laura went
to London and wrote back letters describing what a wonderful time she had had.

Kate was enthralled at the idea of playing in *The Animal
Kingdom*. She plunged into rehearsal with the icily effete
Leslie Howard, who hated her outrageous posturings and
bossy manner. He was also maddened by the fact that she was
taller than he. Gilbert Miller fired her after a week. Livid, she
found out Philip Barry's telephone number, and insisted on
speaking to him when he was in the bath. She shouted, "You
can't let them do this to me! I'm perfect for the part, and you
know it!" He yelled back over the phone, "Nobody who has
your disposition could ever play light comedy! I'm glad they
fired you!"

Kate felt a sharp sense of desperation after *The Animal
Kingdom* fell through. But she was rescued quickly by the
producer Harry Moses, who offered her the role of Antiope,
the queen of the Amazons, in Julian Thompson's *The Warrior's Husband*. She was ideally cast in the part of Antiope,
which called for an aggressively energetic and athletic leading lady who was capable of making an entry carrying a
stuffed deer with an arrow in its back and leaping spectacu-
larly down a flight of stairs.

The play went into rehearsal at the Morosco Theatre in the
late winter of 1931–32. Kate bicycled or—when the streets
were too slushy—hiked to work each morning. She was always the first to arrive, bustling, trousered, her eyes gleam-
ing with the enthusiasm of a fifteen-year-old. She rehearsed
in her loose, safety-pinned sweater and pants, very much
part of a team, constantly bombarding the director, a sleepy
mediocrity named Burk Simon, with a fusillade of suggestions. Often, he simply shrugged, let her take over, put his
feet up on the orchestra seats in front of him, and nodded off.
His snores floated up through the auditorium as Kate rat-tat-
tatted her instructions on the stage.

Phyllis Seaton, who was stage manager of the production, remembers, *"The Warrior's Husband* was a perfect vehicle for Kate—it called for exactly the qualities that she had in abundance. She was young, lithe, vigorous, feared nobody, including herself, and it was as though she had been *plucked out of the sky*. I don't think I've worked with anyone before or since who had as much vitality as Kate. She felt no fatigue, ever. She was always, *always* 'on' at the end of a day's exhausting rehearsals! She rushed home and back again, tirelessly, always on time, *tremendously* able to cope.

"She had no patience at all for anyone who bemoaned his or her fate; self-pity in any shape or form *infuriated* her. Since she was able to conquer *her* fate, she felt there was no reason at all why everyone in the whole world couldn't do just that. This sometimes made her seem harsh. And yet it was never a conscious or deliberate harshness. It was simply that she wanted everyone to 'get up and do it.' She was impatient with anyone slow or dull. It was only later that she learned compassion—through suffering.

"Sometimes her sense of humor then was odd—disconcerting. She would think something was a joke which turned out not to be. Let me give you an example. We had a big company, and a lot of girls had to dress in the basement. They were feeling very insecure—*all* of us were, except maybe Kate! And the notices had been mixed. We didn't know whether we were going to close or not. I don't know what possessed Kate to do what she did one evening. She ran through the basement dressing rooms in the very first week, with everything terribly shaky, and yelled out, 'Well, we'll all get a vacation after Saturday!' Lord *knows* what was in her mind! I went down to call 'Fifteen minutes before curtain time!' And there were weeping ladies—they all thought Katie meant the show was going to close. I went to Katie and said, 'What on earth did you mean, saying we were closing Saturday night?' 'I said no such thing!' she replied. 'We're doing well!'" And then she added, 'I simply meant we'd have a Sunday vacation after Saturday night. Well, won't we? I'm going to the country.' I said, 'What were you doing? Pulling their legs?' She replied, 'Maybe.' So I told her, 'Go right down there and tell them you made a mistake.' And she did!"

Phyllis Seaton remembers that *The Warrior's Husband* was a troublesome, very difficult production. "First of all, it was very controversial. The women were masculine and the men very effeminate. The whole thing was a 'sex change'— years before its time. Katie was the 'man'—the one in charge of this little nation—and her husband, played by Romney Brent, was the 'woman'—simply a girlish plaything of hers. Then came Theseus, a 'real' man, played by Colin Keith-Johnston, a heroic figure, who conquered her and changed her into a *true* woman.

"I'll never forget opening night. The audience was *amazed* by Kate. Her beauty shone through her face. Her skin was transparent, alight with color and health. Her red hair *blazed* around her face. She had terrific grace—she was always complaining to me she had no grace as she crossed a stage, but she was more graceful than anyone else I ever saw. She couldn't make one *movement* that wasn't graceful. She came down a ramp of great stairs, running onto a platform, and then jumping onto the main stage. She *jumped* at the audience. The audience responded to her immediately. This was a star! You could smell it, you could feel it! It was all around you—the perfume of success!"

Kate and the play received excellent reviews, and would have been a huge hit if Romney Brent, whose funny, effeminate playing was so crucial to its appeal, had not suddenly left the cast after only two weeks. Phyllis Season says, "We had to put an understudy on. That was difficult for Kate—she had to give up time to rehearse with the understudy, and that made her very irritable. I had to say to her, 'Don't make such a fuss about this. You were once an understudy.' And she said, 'Yes, but I didn't get this kind of attention.' I replied, 'Maybe you didn't need it!' It was ghastly for her to do over and over and over what she knew so well. But she still got talked about. She was the talk of New York!"

Two

When *The Warrior's Husband* began to wane, and audiences dwindled, Harry Moses decided to take the production to London, using a British cast in support. Kate had been excited by Laura's vivid and affectionate descriptions of the social life of Mayfair and asked if Laura would come along for the length of the West End run. "I'd love to," Laura said at once. But finally the play's backers decided not to transfer the production. Audiences in the last days of the Broadway run were so small the show would have to be written off as a flop.

Once again, Kate seemed to be high and dry. She made a screen test of *The Warrior's Husband* for the tough, cigar-chewing Irish-American director John Ford, when Fox Studios in Hollywood showed an interest in the rights, but she lost the role to Elissa Landi. Not really wanting to go to Hollywood—which theatre people traditionally despised, and which to a New England girl of her background seemed like the end of the world—she virtually threw away the performance.

Other offers began to come in. Mrs. Kermit Roosevelt, who had seen her in *The Warrior's Husband*, had cabled Merian C. Cooper, head of RKO-Radio Pictures, that Kate was "exciting and must make a star," and David O. Selznick, the head of RKO production, had seen the show and liked her. His brother, Myron, who was an agent, sent an associate, Leland Hayward, to pursue Kate and try to make her agree to a new screen test.

"An agent is after me," Kate announced to Laura.

"What's an agent?"

Kate explained. "His name is Leland Hayward."

19

"Leland! I know him!"

Laura had dated Hayward when she had been a debutante. He had been one of the brilliant, enameled young men in the stag line—very "Scott Fitzgerald," like a John Held, Jr., cartoon come to life, with his black sealskin hair neatly parted and slicked down, his sideburns immaculately clipped, his slender figure elegantly attired. He had often spun Laura across the polished floor of the Plaza at the tea dances of the mid-1920s, where "the nice young people" went. Fair-skinned, handsome, and smooth, he fascinated Kate, and managed to push her to the point at which she stated a price. She took a deep breath and said, "Fifteen hundred dollars a week!"

At the moment she said that, her salary was seventy-five dollars.* Hayward wired his partner Myron Selznick the absurd request. In a fit of extravagance, Myron's brother David wired back, "O.K., if her test's good." He wanted her badly for a very important part: the unhappy British society girl, Sydney Fairfield, whose father, Hillary, has been shattered by shell shock, in a version of Clemence Dane's play *A Bill of Divorcement*.

Kate was astonished when she heard that the studio could possibly be prepared to pay $1,500 for her services. She felt that, in view of the generosity of the offer, she might as well go to provincial, despised Hollywood, see what it was like, and, if it was unbearable, return home the moment the picture was over. Also, she thought it might be a marvelous experience to become, however briefly, a movie star like the great silent-screen idol of her youth, Leatrice Joy. Along with these mingled feelings of reluctant submission, excitement, and adventurousness was another—a feeling of extreme fear. She knew that Katharine Cornell had made an enormous hit with *A Bill of Divorcement* on the Broadway stage, that the role of Sydney Fairfield had in fact helped create Cornell's reputation. Dared she follow in Katharine Cornell's footsteps?

Kate's screen test was shot at a special studio hired by RKO on West Fifty-ninth Street and Tenth Avenue, under the

---

*Some sources go as high as $78.50 and $100.

direction of the RKO talent scout Lillie Messenger. Kate asked her great friend, Alan Campbell,* who had appeared with her in *The Warrior's Husband,* to sit in a tall wing chair opposite her while she acted a scene from *Holiday.* She played with desperate earnestness, miserably conscious of the camera, and overemphasizing all the wrong words. When Lillie Messenger ran the test that night, she was dismayed by Kate's awkwardness. But she was also impressed with Kate's effulgence. She felt just sufficiently confident to send the test to Hollywood by train.

Meanwhile, David O. Selznick was in a hurry to get started. Aside from the fact that he did not yet have a leading lady, his biggest problem was that John Barrymore, who was cast as the shell-shocked Hillary Fairfield, would only be available for two weeks on loan from MGM, which had released him in the first place because of last-minute delays in preparing the epic film *Rasputin and the Empress.* Selznick had to make a snap decision between Anita Louise, whose test had indicated a touching quality of nervous fragility, and Kate, who was virtually an unknown quantity.

The moment the test arrived on the train, David Selznick had it rushed to RKO by special limousine. He and his director, George Cukor, walked over to the private executive screening room and ran the test. As the scene began, both men felt a sense of shock. They were looking at a fierce, clumsy girl who was so totally original she unsettled them completely. Cukor says, "There was this odd creature; she wasn't strictly speaking 'pretty.' She was unlike anybody I'd ever heard. I watched her in the sequence from *Holiday,* and I wasn't knocked sideways, I didn't say, the way they do in pictures, 'Aaahh, great!' It doesn't happen that way. Instead, you use little *indications,* things that might be promising, and sometimes you're wrong. But I think I have a nose for what's good.

"She was 'in the mode' of Philip Barry. That was in the time when there was a slightly affected, almost 'singing' way of speaking lines, in rhythm. Barry had his own 'note' as a dramatist, and she 'oversang' that note. Years later, after she

*The husband of Dorothy Parker.

did *The Philadelphia Story*, Spencer Tracy said, 'All you people sang Barry's play so nicely.'

"The test was slapdash, and she kept 'oversinging,' and I thought, I suppose right away, 'She's too odd. It won't work.' But at one moment in a very emotional scene she picked up a glass. The camera focused on her back. There was an *enormous* feeling, a *weight* about the manner in which she picked up the glass. I thought she was very talented in that action. David Selznick agreed. We hired her."

On July 1, 1932, Kate and Laura Harding—who went along as Kate's companion—set out on their momentous journey to Hollywood. Kate, loaded down with luggage, her red hair screwed into a casual knot, wearing an ill-fitting dark grey silk costume by the New York designer Elizabeth Hawes, and a pancake hat stuck awkwardly on her head, joined the train in Harmon, New York, and strode down the corridor to her compartment. Laura had boarded the train at Grand Central. The two girls embraced happily, then settled back in their seats to enjoy the journey. As the sun set, they took supper in the dining car, and enjoyed the rich gleam of expensive silver in the fading light.

"It's going to be a marvelous adventure," Kate said, looking out at the landscape being swallowed up in the deepening dusk. Talking about their families, they realized they hadn't known each other very well, that even at Stockbridge their friendship had been very much on the surface. Now, on the train, bound for California, a bond, far stronger than they had known at Stockbridge, was permanently forged. They knew instinctively they would be friends for life.

At first the journey was pleasant enough. But after the first hours, the heat of summer began to become oppressive. There was no air conditioning on the train in those days. Chicago provided a welcome break: the girls visited art galleries and museums during a brief stopover, and dropped by the Blackstone Hotel for afternoon tea and the hotel's famous chocolate cake.

When the journey recommenced, it was severely uncomfortable, with hot cinders blowing through windows open in the heat. But the trip provided a romantic panorama of a still largely unspoiled America, and Kate and Laura, bathing their foreheads with water-soaked Pullman towels, talked about the pioneers, the painful early journeys by wagon train, and the dangerous promise of the New Land.

The train made a fifteen-minute pause in Albuquerque, New Mexico. The girls looked down, fascinated at the Indian traders below the windows, and alighted at the dusty depot to buy magazines and stretch their legs. A fox-faced little man came up to them, wearing an odd, high-crowned cap several sizes too large for him, and stuffed with tissue paper. "My name is Adolph Zukor, head of Paramount Pictures," he announced. "You're Miss Hepburn, aren't you? I almost engaged you for a role." "I turned you down, didn't I?" Kate said. Fascinated to meet the man who had been responsible for so many of her favorite silent movies, she talked to him cheerfully for a while, pleased to find he was on the same train.

As the train chugged out of Albuquerque and Kate walked out onto the observation platform, a cinder flew into her left eye. Then another stung her retina, slightly scratching the surface. She grabbed a Pullman towel and began wiping the eye. Laura begged her not to. "It will only go in deeper," she insisted. By the time the train arrived at Pasadena, California, where stars traditionally concluded the trip west, Kate was in acute pain, barely able to see; the other eye had swollen sympathetically, and she looked terrible as she stepped down to the platform, leaning on Laura's arm. She saw the look of dismay on the faces of the two agents who had come to greet them: Leland Hayward and Myron Selznick. She heard Selznick mutter to his partner, "My God, Leland, is this what we're sticking David fifteen hundred a week for?" Against the brutal insult, Kate's defense was to put on her bossiest and most contemptuous manner, while Laura tagged along, helping to sort out the luggage.

The oddly assorted little group—Kate with her straggling red topknot, crumpled grey costume, and watery red eyes, Laura trim and blonde, Leland and Myron in dark business suits—made their way to a yellow Rolls-Royce that was waiting to take them to Hollywood. All four sat in the back of the car. The atmosphere was filled with unrelieved tension. Finally, as they neared Los Angeles, Myron tried to break the ice with, "Miss Hepburn, did you bring your clubs?" A pause. "I understand you're very good at golf." Kate gazed out of the window at the dried-up grass and the purple mountains. "I don't think I'd care to play golf in California," she said, still smarting at his previous insult, and still in acute pain from her eye. "I hope you like the Château Elysée, where I've booked you," Leland said. Kate didn't reply.

At last, the journey was over, and the yellow Rolls-Royce stopped outside an executive building of RKO Studios in the worst part of Hollywood. It was a depressing neighborhood, with lean-to shacks, prisonlike structures, and mysterious towers, all shimmering under a savagely hot sun. Their hosts took Kate and Laura up to David O. Selznick's office, done in Hollywood desert beige, and there was an awkward, very formal introduction. Pandro Berman, Selznick's clever, saturnine young assistant, conducted the girls downstairs to the office of George Cukor, who looked at Kate with subdued horror. In an attempt to make her feel at ease, he showed her the costume designer Josette de Lima's drawings for the film. Kate squinted at them through her inflamed eyes and decided they were terrible: far too flouncy for an English girl of Sydney Fairfield's background and class. She said, "They're no good!' '

Cukor was furious with her for daring to comment at all. "It's not your place to criticize," he told her. "And look at what you're wearing!"

She wasn't rattled. "I thought these clothes were pretty fancy. I paid a great deal for them."

"Well, they're terrible. You look ghastly."

"I want my clothes to be designed by Chanel," Kate said. Assuming that a Hollywood person would not be well informed, she asked, "You know Chanel?"

Cukor was furious at the slight. "The first thing I'm going to do," he told her, "is to get you into makeup, so they can do something about your hair."

Despite their unpleasant first confrontation, Kate liked Cukor at once. He was forthright, tough, direct, and he would stand no nonsense: he was a kindred spirit. Thirty-three years

old, plump, with dark hair and flashing, intense eyes, he
threw off nervous energy like a shower of electric sparks.
His voice, high, insistent, repeated certain adjectives and
adverbs like a litany ("She's enormously, enormously, enormously, *enormously* talented!"). He had an odd, disconcerting
tendency to offer ideas, opinions—streams of opinions!—
then suddenly withdraw into a shell, becoming guarded,
tense, irritable. Sensitive, he could be cut to the quick by a
tiny mistake in taste, judgment, or expertise. He was a per-
fectionist, intolerant of weakness. His eyes were like gun
nozzles, his jaw so urgently protuberant that a champion
boxer's punch would probably rebound off it. Kate stood on
her crane's legs, in her unbecoming New York costume, looking at him with admiration as he stamped about the room,
picturesquely giving her a piece of his mind.

At the height of this tirade, Kate's co-star, John Barrymore,
walked in. She was fascinated at once. But now, she noticed,
the great star was past his prime. Though his tall swordsman's
figure still retained its handsome outlines, he was beginning
to develop a paunch. His eyes were lightly poached in nests
of wrinkles. His voice slurred on certain syllables. His skin
was grey and slack. He had an air of flustered hauteur, as
though he were a butler caught robbing a safe.

He walked unsteadily over to Kate, peered into her flaring
eyes, and beckoned her to step outside Cukor's office into the
hall. She followed him. She was shocked when he said, "I also
hit the bottle occasionally, my dear. But I have a perfect
disguise. You see this little phial of eyedrops? When I use it,
it clears up the inflammation right away. People think I've
been cold sober."

"But Mr. Barrymore, I have a cinder in my eye!" Kate
protested.

"That's what they all say, my dear," Barrymore replied as
he ambled off.

Cukor poked his head through the door. "I've got to get
you down to makeup," he said. He walked Kate and Laura
to the back lot, took them across a small concrete pathway,
and showed them Kate's dingily furnished "star" dressing
room. Then they climbed one flight up a steep wooden stair-
case and walked into the makeup department. There, Cukor

introduced them to the makeup man, Mel Berns, a dark little man with a toothbrush mustache, who looked exactly like Walt Disney, and a young hairdresser, Jean Woodhall. Cukor left, and Kate walked over to a basin, took a toothbrush from her pocket, picked up a bar of soap, and began scrubbing her teeth until her mouth was full of bubbles.

Then she sat in Jean Woodhall's barber chair and began talking in her educated, clipped New England voice about the value of Roosevelt's economic policies and the excellence of George Bernard Shaw's plays. Neither Mel Berns nor Jean Woodhall had met an intellectual actress before: most of the stars they had handled talked about men, parties, and beauty care.

As Jean started pulling her hair knot apart, Kate said, "There's nothing you can do about it. It's baby hair." Jean said, "It's not. It's beautiful," and immediately prepared a medium long bob for her. In the midst of the rinsing and combing, George Cukor poked his head around the door and inquired, "What can we do about her freckles?" "Nothing," Mel Berns said. "They look great. Why play with nature?" George popped out again, but not before Mel cautioned him, "She has natural looks, high cheekbones, and whatever you do, don't put a voice coach on her. Her diction is absolutely unique. Audiences will love it."

When Jean finished her work, Kate asked for a mirror and said to Jean, "Let me see my hair. If I like it, I'll tell you; if I don't, I'll tell you that, too." She liked it. Cukor came in to see the finished job, and was amazed at the transformation. Even with her inflamed eyes, Kate looked vastly more attractive. "Well!" he said, happily. "There's Katharine Hepburn at last."

While she was in makeup, Cukor called the studio doctor, Sam Hirschfeld, and obtained the name of a woman eye specialist downtown who could fit Kate in between appointments. An assistant of Leland Hayward's drove Kate and Laura to the doctor's office. Kate had to sit absolutely still in a chair while the doctor picked away at the surface of her eye. Finally the doctor stepped back and said, "The cinders are removed, but you'll have to wear an eye patch for several days, until the surface heals."

Kate and Laura and Leland's assistant emerged from the doctor's office to a shockingly cold Los Angeles night. The assistant dropped them at an intersection and rudely told them to find their own way to the hotel. They were freezing in their summer clothes, depressed, and close to tears. There were no taxis about, and they had to wait an hour before a cab arrived in answer to their phone call.

At last, the girls reached their hotel, the dowdy Château Elysée. They were exhausted and collapsed on the bed, wanting only a hot supper and sleep. Laura called room service and the man at the front desk said, "We have no room service!"

After a first day of makeup and costume fittings, Kate returned exhausted to the Château Elysée. She was cheered only by the fact that Laura's close friend, Carlton Burke, who owned property locally and had a lot of money, promised to help them house-hunt. The very next day, Carlton Burke found a place for them, a small four-room cottage with a tiled roof, surrounded by trees, in Franklin Canyon. It had a live-in maid, Joanna, whom Kate and Laura virtually adopted for years.

Once they were settled in the house and Kate's eye was healing, they felt much more cheerful. They very grandly had Carlton Burke arrange for them to rent a huge Isotta-Fraschini automobile with a chauffeur. But they discovered to their distress that the car was a former prop, used for numerous films, and that everyone in town laughed at them as they drove by in their tailored costumes and white gloves, gazing haughtily from the windows. They were embarrassed, but, characteristically, refused to be moved by scorn. They kept the car.

Kate's attitude toward Hollywood was complex. As a Fabian conducting her own private war against capitalistic exploitation of the masses, she naturally despised the character of this factory town. Yet, paradoxically, she wanted to show by driving in the Isotta-Fraschini that she was independent of Hollywood financially; she made it clear to everyone

that her money had been from family, not from a cheap,
chiseling business background. She was disgusted by the taw-
dry ostentation of Hollywood, yet her parading in the car was
certainly ostentatious. She refused to hobnob with Hollywood "society," partly out of a contempt for the *nouveau
riche* which her Fabian background had instilled in her, and
partly out of a feeling that she would soon be returning
home, that her stay in Hollywood could not be lengthy.
There can be no question that Kate at the time was an intellectual snob. This unsettled most people she met. But gradually people began to see her qualities. Certainly, she was not
a social snob. She liked the ordinary people around the studio
—Mel Berns, Jean Woodhall, the electricians and "grips," the
carpenters and engineers. Uneasy with Hollywood executives, she felt at ease with the film studio crews. She knew
them on first-name terms, knew their wives, sent over food
and medication when their children were sick. This, of
course, was in keeping with her Socialist background: a contempt for get-rich quick businessmen, a love of simple working people.

She also adored those men she felt to be truly artistic and
talented: Selznick, Cukor, Pan Berman, and other directors
and producers. She watched the big RKO star, blond and
sophisticated Ann Harding, making a picture. She was fascinated by the processes of movie-making, acquainting herself, even then, with details of lighting, the composition of
shots, the use of music and dialogue in a scene. Within a
month, she could virtually have directed a picture herself.

The people around RKO were fascinated by her: this
leggy, rather gauche New England bluestocking probing
into everything with the eagerness of a student of Egyp-
tology. They had never seen anything like her. She was
worlds removed from the sleek, satin-clad platinum blondes
or sultry brunettes who populated the houses of Bel Air and
Beverly Hills, looking like angels and swearing like Marines.
Unlike almost everyone else except Garbo, she refused point-
blank to see the press.

Just before the shooting of *A Bill of Divorcement* started,
Kate told the RKO press agent Perry Lieber that she would
do nothing about giving interviews or posing for picture

layouts, or shots with male stars intended to give an aura of spurious "romantic interests."

After playing her first scene with Barrymore, she was heard to mutter, "He's all beaten up. He's overacting." Between takes that first day, Barrymore invited her into his dressing room. Once there, without warning he flung all his clothes off. Kate was astounded and shrank against a wall.

"My dear," Barrymore said, "any young girl would be thrilled to make love to the great John Barrymore."

"Not me," Kate said in terror. "My father doesn't want me to make babies!"

Later, Barrymore pinched her fanny. "If you do that again," she said, "I'm going to stop acting."

"I wasn't aware you'd started, my dear," Barrymore snapped.

There were, from the outset, problems on the set. The picture had begun without a completed script, and the writer, Howard Estabrook, had to sit behind the camera typing new pages and handing them to Kate and the players to be learned. For Kate, who was used to the theatre, this was particularly trying. Another writer, Harry Wagstaff Gribble, had to come in and write additional scenes. David Selznick kept trying to push Cukor to a faster schedule, while MGM's bosses screamed for Barrymore's quick release.

The strain undoubtedly told on Kate. She hated the fact that pictures were shot out of sequence, making it impossible to build a role naturally from beginning to end. She barely endured the constant demands of the cameraman, Sid Hickox, a very fast worker borrowed from Warner Brothers because of his speed. He kept using additional filters to soften her rather angular features, begged her to refrain from moving so rapidly that she would go out of frame, ordered her to quit nervously shaking her head, and compelled her to calm down and to subdue her gestures for the camera.

Sometimes she was so nervous she made impulsive, meaningless gestures. Her juvenile co-star, the classically handsome and hypersensitive David Manners, was standing with her by a fireplace in a romantic scene when she noticed some dust on his shoes. While Cukor explained the point of a scene to him, Kate suddenly sank to her knees and started cleaning his shoes with the hem of her expensive organdy dress. Cukor said, "What are you doing? That dress cost a fortune!" Kate came awkwardly to her feet and played the scene without a murmur.

Cukor was often forced to correct Kate in front of everyone. But she never weakened, listened carefully to what he had to say—and learned, reluctantly, that screen acting involved the subduing of the personality. Cukor says, "For all Kate's rough edges, she was a complete pro from the outset. This odd creature had her own grace, her own style. I was excited by her.

"It wasn't so much a question of letting her act as though she was on a stage. It was a question of bringing out that quality in her which was 'made for the screen.' Her face moved correctly for the screen, it had a light, a radiance. She had a natural aptitude. I taught her that acting for the stage was acting with the body and the voice, but that acting for the screen was acting with the eyes. Also, that acting for the screen had to be totally 'on the level,' sincere, and real. You couldn't get away with anything false, as you could on the stage. There wasn't the protection of the distance of the stage —the camera was right next to you, and you could not lie. The camera *unmasks* you.

"Kate was real. At times she'd get too mannered, highfalutin, actressy. I'd bring her down. I'd say, 'Be yourself, draw on your own emotions, keep your voice down. The audience is at your shoulder.' " Cukor showed Kate that a director is himself also an audience; he must know how to applaud, how to condemn. Cukor liked to create a climate on the set in which the director takes chances.

"Kate was quite good at rehearsals," Cukor says, "but she didn't really come alive until the camera closed in on her. I had a rough idea she was doing well, but she sprang to life when I saw the rushes. Her odd awkwardness, her odd shifts of emphasis, these were proof of her being alive on the screen. She wasn't too smooth, she was *fresh*."

Assistant director Eddie Killey observes, "She had the beauty of a clean, wholesome *lady*. You felt you could have put your arms around her and hugged her."

During the making of *A Bill of Divorcement*, Kate's day

was disciplined to the last minute. At 6:30 A.M. she rose, showered—sometimes she would have several showers a day —breakfasted on eggs, fruit, and coffee with Laura Harding, put on slacks and a sweater or old shirt, and then she and Laura were driven in the Isotta-Fraschini to the studio in Hollywood. At 7:30 she checked in with Mel Berns, scrubbed her teeth with soap, and sat down with Jean Woodhall for a shampoo. Jean washed her hair with eggs, rinsed it with lemon juice and water, and dried it. While Kate was under the dryer, Berns would begin sponging her face with pan-cake foundation. She went to her dressing room and put on her clothes for the day's shooting. She usually had lunch not in the commissary or in the restaurant nearby but in her dressing room, where her chauffeur brought her small, thinly cut sandwiches, green salad, milk, and a piece of homemade pie.

She lay down and studied the afternoon scenes. At 1 P.M. the afternoon shooting began. At 3 P.M. she always insisted on a break, during which she would drink limeade made with plain water. At 4 P.M. she had a custom, absolutely unvary-ing, of passing out candy to each member of the cast and crew.

At 6 P.M., at the end of the day, she went home in her makeup, which could be easily washed off with soap and water. She took a shower and went to bed; a maid served her dinner in bed. She read her mail, studied next day's lines, and telephoned her family in Hartford. She heard all their news but didn't bore them by giving them any of her own.

"Father and Mother never came to Hollywood," Kate told me. "They were not remotely interested in picture-making, and why should they be? Their own life was far too interest-ing, and far removed from the drudgery of Hollywood. The only thing fascinating in our conversation was what *they* told *me*."

Kate was intensely concerned with what happened to her brothers and sisters. Robert succeeded in entering the Sig-net, the literary society at Harvard, and became a member of the Hasty Pudding Club. He graduated with high honors and went into medical school. Dick also went to Harvard, after a year at Trinity College in Hartford. He continued

with his earlier activity of writing plays, basing the structures
on Greek drama and dealing in aggressive, left-wing, anti-
capitalist themes. Of all the family, he most strongly resembled Kate both in his clothes—an unsightly combination of a
loose white sweater, baggy pants, sockless feet, and sneakers
—and in his red-headed, high-cheekboned, horsey look.

Marion was married young, to an industrialist, Ellsworth
Grant, and settled down in Hartford. Margaret married an
engineer, Thomas Perry, and bought a 250-acre farm at Can-
ton, New Jersey, where Perry had his own workshop, full of
ingenious mechanical gadgets of his own invention.

Kate liked to read poetry, particularly Emily Dickinson,
with whom she had a spiritual affinity, and fairy stories, because of their timeless, pure, and abstract quality. Most of the
time, though, she read scripts sent to her by the studio.

Aside from reading, playing tennis and walking, her private life consisted of little more than sleeping. On the rare
occasions when she dated a handsome young Hollywood
bachelor, she was always left safe at the front door. Laura
would go to parties and return to find Kate asleep with a book
and an empty milk glass beside her bed. Since Kate rose at
dawn, before Laura was up, Laura could only tell Kate about
the parties on weekends—and she usually found Kate quite
uninterested.

From the beginning, Kate showed a passionate concern
with the personal affairs of the crews. She liked "her" crew
to be with her on every picture, from assistant director Eddie
Killey down. It gave her a feeling of confidence, of joy in a
"family," and it was devastating to her when a member of the
family died. Her favorite cameramen, Henry Gerrard and
Robert de Grasse; her editor, Jane Loring; her costume designers, Howard Greer and Walter Plunkett; and the always
staunch and reliable, sharply intelligent Pan Berman were
her great supports, giving her the strength she needed, the
warm feeling of being part of a team.

Kate rushed ahead into her career, filled with enormous
enthusiasm, excessive dismay, and then enthusiasm again.
Nervous as a well-trained racehorse, she flung herself into
her work, driven by wildly conflicting moods. She was interested in every aspect of a picture, and absorbed the diverse

crafts of producer, director, writer, photographer, and set designer in every fiber of her being. Often she was intelligent, often drastically wrong in her choice of vehicles. She refused to do anything that didn't suit her and Laura Harding's idea of a good subject. She refused point-blank to make a term contract. She insisted on signing for a specific film that would guarantee her a minimum of four weeks' work. She signed a new contract for every new movie. This meant that she could never be forced to do anything; if she was offered something she didn't want to play, she would laugh and take a suspension. With her background—her home, her family, her money—she didn't have to do anything she didn't want to do, and she was blunt in making that fact clear to everyone.

To show how much she despised the florid vulgarity of Hollywood, Kate showed herself off as something of a professional eccentric. She sat down on a sidewalk outside RKO Studios to read her fan mail while traffic roared past her. She had the studio electricians wire various star and director chairs so that anyone who sat in them would get a shock. She loved dogs, but in addition to these pets she also went around with a pet monkey clinging to her shoulder.

Kate and Laura formed a kind of two-woman Fabian revolution against the phoniness of Hollywood. Both women recall that they invaded vulgar, oversized houses when the owners were abroad. They piled into the trunk of the *nouveau riche* director William Wellman's oversized car and didn't emerge until he reached home, jumping out and making funny faces. One night—with Leland Hayward—they crept up to the house of the producer Walter Wanger. They peeped through the dining-room window and saw him, Mrs. Wanger, Charles Boyer, Madeleine Carroll, and several others sitting in complete silence. They went into the kitchen, bribed the maids and butler, and put on their uniforms. Then they served the meal. Looking straight ahead, nobody noticed them until Mrs. Wanger glanced up and said, "Mary, has anyone told you you look like that new girl in town, Katharine Hepburn?"

On the rare occasions when they went out to dine, Kate would lean back in her chair until it almost fell over, and prop her feet on the table. When asked why she did this, Kate would say, "I can't digest anything unless the seat of my pants is higher than my head." Sometimes she, George Cukor, and Laura Harding would spend weekends wandering about beaches and going into shooting galleries. "What do you suppose she does?" a sailor asked Cukor in one shooting gallery. "She's a schoolteacher," Cukor replied, referring to her schoolmarmish demeanor.

During one weekend luncheon at Cukor's house, Kate dived into the pool naked and swam about. Just as she surfaced, Cukor said, "Garbo has arrived." Kate hastily grabbed a towel and was making her way, dripping wet, to the guests' changing room when she ran smack into Garbo coming up the path. Holding a towel in front of her, she curtsied and said, very solemnly, "Oh, Miss Garbo, how nice to meet you!" She was embarrassed, and ran into the shrubbery. Later, she and Garbo became good friends.

Often, at weekends, Kate shut herself up and refused to see anyone. Mary Pickford sent an invitation to dinner at Pickfair—in those days that was like being asked to Buckingham Palace—and Kate sent a note of refusal: "I never go out to dine." Then the impossible happened. At ten o'clock one Sunday morning, Ford Johnson, a polo-playing friend of Laura's, arrived at the front door with Mary Pickford herself in a pink wrap, and Mary said to Kate, who fascinated her, "Won't you come up?" Kate felt compelled to accept.

That night, Kate and Laura drove with Laura's date, Ford Johnson, to Pickfair, where Doug and Mary entertained Gary Cooper and the Countess di Frasso, among other guests. The conversation had an absurd provincial snobbishness. After dinner, Douglas Fairbanks showed his new movie, *Mr. Robinson Crusoe*. Ford Johnson, to Kate and Laura's acute embarrassment, fell asleep in the middle and snored loudly. "Shall I waken him?" Laura asked. "Oh, no, he's going to qualify as a member of the New York film critics," Fairbanks quipped. Next day, Kate told George Cukor that she and Laura had been to Pickfair, and Cukor, looking them up and down, replied, "As maids—through the back door?"

Three

Kate's greatest pleasure in those months was at weekends: swimming, playing tennis at the Beverly Hills Hotel tennis court, and wandering over the still unspoiled and smogless hills of Hollywood. Pine trees and eucalyptus, plunging green slopes, dirt tracks, views of the distant glitter of the ocean—Kate loved to walk through the mists of summer mornings, gazing as far as the horizon. She may not have liked or wanted to pursue Hollywood social life, but she loved the terrain, the cool evenings after the hot days, the magical nights when the stars seemed as large and glittering as fireflies. She knew how to enjoy watching, and grew fond of the bird life of the hills: the blue herons, the jays, the ravens, and, in the undergrowth, red foxes, nimble squirrels, chipmunks. Away from the stifling artificial asmosphere of the studio, she could respond to clouds, children's kites flying, the sun, the moon, the sea. It was hard to go back on Monday mornings to the struggle of picture-making, but the moment she started to work, her enthusiasm took over.

The shooting of *A Bill of Divorcement* was finished on schedule in a month; John Barrymore reported for work in *Rasputin and the Empress* at MGM. *A Bill of Divorcement* was previewed out of town, with most of the RKO executives, including Cukor and David O. Selznick, in attendance.

George Cukor says, "I'll never forget the preview. The audience had never seen a girl like that—she seemed to *bark* at them. She didn't play for sympathy at all. At first, the audience wasn't quite sure whether it liked her or not. Well, there was an early scene that captured them a little. She was seeing her mother off to church—*church!* It sounds like Jane

Austen! She smiled, touchingly, and showed these perfect white teeth.

"Then came the big moment. She walked across the large set as Barrymore came out of a room. He was asking for 'a breathing space.' She picked up a pillow, and lay down on the hearth alone. The audience could 'see' her now for the first time. They could see she moved beautifully, and it was at that point she became a great personality, the beginnings of a star, a major Movie Queen. But the audience had to have time to get *used* to her. She never was the sort of person the people could cotton to immediately."

Visibly ill-at-ease in many early scenes, talking in a shrill or harsh voice and seemingly unaware of the other players, Kate was marvelous in the picture's second half, when she had to show a deep affection and tenderness for her shell-shocked father. Despite—or because of—her clumsy movements across the set, she held the eye, and she was exquisite in repose, seeming modern today against Barrymore's skillful but dated theatrical attack. She conveyed a gruff affection, a combination of sweetness of character and extreme aggressiveness which made the performance agreeably unpredictable and contradictory. From the first shot, it was obvious that an original had been born.

Kate decided that the instant the film finished shooting, she would have her chauffeur drive her to the more "civilized" San Francisco. She left on a weekend and had reached Santa Barbara when a message came from the studio indicating that the preview had been on the whole a success, but that she must return at once to reshoot two serious scenes which had made the audience laugh.

Annoyed, Kate drove back to Hollywood and completed the scenes. Leland told her the studio was picking up her option. Kate and Laura spent a rainy day going over the new contract, making notes of the many things Kate wanted, including leave to travel after each picture, and right of approval of all properties designed as star vehicles for her.

The next afternoon, Kate and Laura went out to David Selznick's beach house at Malibu. Laura remembers, "Myron was there, very drunk, and Mr. and Mrs. Lewis Selznick,

David's parents, were fast asleep on sofas. When Kate asked for tea, everyone was in a state of shock—they only drank hard liquor and coffee—and had to send out for it. David came rushing in, surrounded by lawyers, and discussed the contract, agreeing finally to everything. But when the contract was given to Kate to sign the following week, nothing had been changed, and she had to have it completely rewritten by Leland Hayward."

Irritated by what she felt to be David Selznick's dishonesty, Kate decided to abandon California for a while. Reluctantly, she canceled plans to go to San Francisco. Laura returned to her family in New England, and Kate took a ship from New York to Europe with her husband. They went steerage. When someone asked her why, she said, "I always get seasick. I don't see why I should get seasick on a first-class ticket."

She and Luddy traveled to the Tyrol, walked and climbed and looked at the mountains, and forgot all about Hollywood. They received a telegram from David Selznick in Vienna: *A Bill of Divorcement* had opened very successfully in New York, at a charity premiere for Mrs. William Randolph Hearst's Milk Fund, and had enjoyed rave reviews. Kate was to make another picture immediately—*Three Came Unarmed,* from the novel by the British author E. Arnot Robertson, to be directed by Gregory La Cava. She cabled her agreement and took the *Paris* home.

Reporters came aboard when the *Paris* docked in New York, preceded by the New York publicity corps of RKO. While in Europe, Kate had been amused to read the absurd stories that RKO people had made up about her: that she was a direct descendant of Mary Queen of Scots and the sixteen-million-dollar heiress of A. Barton Hepburn, chairman of the board of the Chase Manhattan Bank. When a gang of pressmen invaded her cabin—first class this time—and asked her if she were really married to Luddy, she smiled sweetly and said, "I don't remember." They wrote notes furiously. "And any children?" a woman reporter asked. "Two white and three colored," Kate replied.

With very mixed feelings, Kate returned to Hollywood in

the late fall of 1932. She didn't look forward to the idiotic
gossip, the obsession with foreign aristocrats, the brutal concentration on shoptalk. On the other hand, her success in *A
Bill of Divorcement* and the experience of working with
David O. Selznick and George Cukor had given her a con-
suming interest in making pictures.

She was eager to get back to work, and read E. Arnot
Robertson's novel *Three Came Unarmed* on the train. It was
an intriguing book, a study of the three children—Herel,
Nonie, and Allen—of an alcoholic missionary in Borneo, who
spend their days hunting, fishing, and trapping in the jungle.
They accept an invitation to go and live in Wales, where at
the village of West Mersea they are little more than curiosi-
ties, shocked by the greed and social climbing of civilized
life, irritated by the constant lying and deceit.

Kate was fascinated by the story, and felt she would be
intensely happy in the role of Nonie, the jungle girl who sees
through the pretensions of a British provincial town. She also
relished the idea of playing the early scenes in animal skins,
carrying a spear.

Laura was tied up with family and had to follow Kate on
another train. Kate, leaving Luddy behind, made the journey
alone; Perry Lieber at the studio had arranged for her to be
met in Pasadena by Joel McCrea, her co-star in *Three Came
Unarmed*, because he hoped to foster rumors of an imaginary
romance. McCrea says he will never forget seeing the leggy
young woman striding down the platform toward him carrying an oversized bag stuffed with an assortment of clothes,
books, and papers, and walking right past him, not knowing
who he was. He grabbed her by the arm, told her he was from
RKO, and bundled her into the RKO Cadillac limousine. She
sat stiffly next to him as the chauffeur drove them to Hollywood. The conversation was desultory.

"And what do *you* do?" Kate asked grandly.

"I'm Joel McCrea. I'm an actor," he replied.

"And how did you get that tan?" she asked.

"At the beach."

"You must take me there," she insisted. (He did, soon after,
and within an afternoon she was surfing like an expert.)

Joel McCrea says, "When we arrived at the studio, she suddenly got out and sat down on a grass patch in the middle of all the buildings, excited at being back, drinking it all in. Then she stood up and ran headlong into David Selznick's office."

The same afternoon, Kate began to make costume tests for *Three Came Unarmed*, running around—just as she had hoped—in skins and carrying a spear. But it soon became apparent to the studio that the picture would not "work," and it was shelved. This was particularly annoying to Kate, after she had cut short her Tyrolean vacation. She sat around, waiting for the studio to come up with something new.

The "something new" was a script by the celebrated Broadway dramatist Zoë Akins based on Gilbert Frankau's best-selling British novel, *Christopher Strong*. It was the story of an aviatrix who falls in love with a married man, becomes pregnant, and kills herself by pulling off her oxygen mask while breaking the altitude record at thirty thousand feet. After David Selznick left the studio to make independent pictures, Merian C. Cooper handed the project over to Pandro Berman, who had meanwhile become RKO's head of production. David Selznick had already chosen Dorothy Arzner, one of the few female directors in Hollywood, to handle the story.

At first, Kate was fascinated by the idea of making a picture with a woman director. But she was rapidly disillusioned. Both very strong-willed, the two women had a somewhat awkward relationship from the outset.

Kate was Arzner's second choice for the role of Lady Cynthia Darrington, the aviatrix (the first choice, Ann Harding, had been unavailable). Being "second choice" was rather irritating and depressing to Kate. Then, as on *A Bill of Divorcement*, there was the major problem of a script. Arzner was working daily with Zoë Akins at Akins' house in Pasadena—a showplace filled with liveried flunkies and priceless British antiques—but Akins' husband, a British aristocrat, was in an oxygen tent, stricken, and the author was painfully distracted. A page took days to complete, and Kate never saw anything approaching a finished script. She filled the weeks of waiting by reading Gilbert Frankau's original novel and biographies of famous aviatrices, including Frankau's model for Lady Cynthia, the British flier Amy Johnson.

At last about half the script was finished. Kate motored to
Dorothy Arzner's elegant imitation Greek house on Los Feliz
Terrace evening after evening for dinner, discussions of the
role, and careful readings. Howard Greer, an amusing, dog-
loving raconteur Kate adored, was the clothing designer, and
created a very "English" wardrobe for Kate, to which Walter
Plunkett added one costume. Once the script was finished,
Kate and her fellow players, led by Colin Clive—cast as her
lover in the story—held a series of on-set discussions. Everyone sat in a semicircle as Zoë read them the entire screenplay, line by line, rather clumsily taking the different roles.

Shooting started in the rain-drenched winter of 1932–33.
Kate didn't enjoy it at all. For Arzner, making the picture
was a challenge. As a woman in a man's business, she dared
not have any failures; she would have been "let out of the
club." This made her directing of the film purposeful and
grim; she took little or no time getting to know Kate on a
personal level; they didn't really hit it off.

Kate missed the intense friendship of Cukor, his concern
for her personal welfare. Shooting *A Bill of Divorcement* had
included a lot of joking, clowning around among the crew,
often when Cukor was unaware of it. When shooting *Christopher Strong*, Arzner insisted on a cathedral hush, with everyone talking in low-pitched voices—no hammers, no saws, no
laughter—as she instructed Kate and the rest of the cast in
a subdued, level, sometimes almost inaudible voice. The
point of the near inaudibility was to force everyone to attend
to every word. Nobody ever dared to call Miss Arzner "Dorothy"—let alone "Dotty." And she addressed Kate as "Miss
Hepburn" throughout.

Many scenes—of Kate getting into her plane and taxiing
along an airfield, cut in to actual pilots taking off—were shot
in sheets of rain at the old Van Nuys airfield. Morning after
morning, Kate and Laura drove up with tureens of soup for
the cast and crew, but despite all precautions Kate came
down with influenza, complicated further by gynecological
problems. Dorothy Arzner drove her very hard, and the two
women frequently quarreled.

Miss Arzner says, "I remember one night I was working on
a shot of a truck and a motorcycle colliding. The actual colli-

sion would have been too difficult, so we had to have the
drivers barely miss each other, then cut to give an impression
of an impact. Hepburn was watching, and each time the
drivers came closer and closer to hitting, she'd cry out,
'That's it!' She was concerned for the safety of the players—
she always stood up for the small people on a picture, the
underdogs. After the fourth time, she yelled out, 'You can't
get any closer than that!' She was *directing*, you see. And
when I ordered another take, she said to me sharply, 'I'd
heard you were a cruel woman. Now I know it!' "

Miss Arzner adds, "Kate wasn't someone you could mold
easily, that you could control. She was extremely strong-
willed. Her *tone* was all wrong; I had to soften her constantly.
But sometimes she was wonderful: there was a scene in a boat
with her married lover, and she said, 'Do you love me, Chris?'
and he replied, 'Call it love if you like.' I wanted the scene
played without any emotion at all. I canceled a whole morning's work because I just couldn't make the scene 'play,' and
finally I decided it had to be two people looking just dead
ahead, two people who couldn't express any emotion—just a
monotonous emptiness. At first she played the scene headlong, but when I told her to look blank, she did, and her voice
went wonderfully flat and toneless. She and Colin Clive
played it superbly—people said it was the best love story on
the screen."

Aside from weather, there were a number of problems in
the film. Walter Plunkett designed a costume for Kate to
wear in a fancy-dress-ball scene in the form of a moth which
was made entirely of bits of metal. It was unbearably heavy,
and when she removed it, each portion of it had to be peeled
off with infinite care, or it would have skinned her alive.
When she rested in the costume, she couldn't sit down, but
had to lie, in pain, on a slantboard. Another problem was with
the cameraman, Bert Glennon. After two days, shooting had
to be called off because Dorothy Arzner fired him when he
refused to shoot the setups she had ordered, and replaced
him with Sid Hickox.

Still suffering from various internal problems, Kate collapsed after three weeks' work and was rushed to the Good
Samaritan Hospital, closing down shooting for several days.

She recovered, but played the last scenes listlessly, and her co-star Colin Clive was radically concerned for her health. Her performance shows signs of strain, and Dorothy Arzner's direction looks stiff and conventional today. However, the reviews were excellent. Regina Crewe wrote in the *Journal American*, "That troubled, masque-like face, the high, strident, raucous, rasping voice, the straight, broad-shouldered boyish figure—perhaps they may all grate on you, but they compel attention, and they fascinate an audience. She is a distinct, definite, positive personality—the first since Garbo."

The personality was certainly distinct, definite, and almost alarmingly positive. Rash and headstrong at first, Kate had by 1933 toughened into a vividly opinionated, fast-talking, and aggressive young woman who generally liked to listen to other people's arguments only just so long as it would take to find a logical reason why she should shoot them down. Even at that early stage, she did not want to pause long enough between opinions to get a seriously considered opinion of herself. She was looking out for herself so much she had no opportunity to look into herself. Her attack on the world was her greatest defense against the pain of existence. Her working life was a challenge she met head on; a contemplative life was a challenge she worked desperately hard to avoid.

Christopher Strong was not a success at the box office; the audience was put off by the strained, artificial script written under such duress by the unfortunate Zoë Akins, and by the evident lack of emotional rapport between actress and role. Perhaps fortunately, Dorothy Arzner abandoned her immediate plan, to do another Zoë Akins screenplay, *Morning Glory,* for Kate. Instead, Pandro Berman took over the subject as a personal production.

Morning Glory was a perfect story for Kate. It was an account of the career of a struggling young actress, Eva Lovelace, who is ignored by New York producers until a friend and mentor, the veteran actor Robert Hedges, takes her to a party for the Broadway star Rita Vernon. Eva becomes drunk on champagne and without warning gives everyone present a bizarre but forceful demonstration of acting

—Juliet in the balcony scene. She becomes an understudy to Rita Vernon, and takes over from her triumphantly when Vernon walks out of the show.

Like Dorothy Arzner before him, Pan Berman used to drive over to Pasadena daily to work with Zoë Akins, whose husband was sinking fast. Kate still did not know that Pan had her in mind for the part, though she heard rumors to that effect. While Pan and Zoë toiled away, Kate had a marvelous time playing tennis and golf, and taking long walks with Laura into the Hollywood hills, discovering strange places. Her social life was as restricted as ever: only the very occasional lunch at George Cukor's, or dinners at Pickfair, interrupted a Spartan regime of regular hours, swims in her pool, lights out at ten or earlier.

During those weeks of preparation, Kate became seriously involved with her agent, Leland Hayward. For an awkward, impressionable girl crashing headlong into Hollywood movies, Leland Hayward was irresistibly attractive. He had all of the polish, the smoothness, the elegant appeal she so signally lacked. His clothes were flawlessly tailored, his hair impeccably brushed, his shoes brilliantly shined. He was like Gatsby: "He smiled understandingly—much more than understandingly. It was one of those smiles with a quality of eternal reassurance in it, that you may come across four or five times in life." In New York he drove a splendid Rolls-Royce, in Hollywood a Hispano-Suiza. He piloted his own plane to and from New York. He constantly made long-distance phone calls when few people made them. He knew everyone and everything that mattered. He spoke with a rapid, thrusting directness and could argue anybody into anything. He loved many women, but was incapable of being faithful. He even owned a gold mine.

Kate thought he was dashing, even finding his ruthless business dealings on behalf of his clients—who included his mistress Margaret Sullavan, Fred Astaire and Ginger Rogers, Ben Hecht, and Miriam Hopkins—appealing. She always worshiped strength, especially when it had a cutting edge. Leland held her spellbound. She did not feel for him the deep, overpowering love she later felt for Spencer Tracy. In the parlance of the time, he was a "capital beau," full of

gossip, wisdom, toughness, engaging treachery, a *man*. In
the spotlight of her young girl's eagerness, he was a star. He
betrayed her often with other women. Her aggressive, innocent mind blotted out the knowledge. She loved him at the
time he was hers: that was all.

He did not act as her investment counselor. After the first
picture, Kate sent all her money back East for her father to
invest. Thrifty and cautious, Dr. Hepburn bought shares in
property so wisely that he made her a rich woman. She relied
utterly on his advice.

Work stopped on the script of *Morning Glory* when Zoë
Akins' husband died. Pan Berman says, "One day I went over
to Pasadena. Zoë greeted me weeping: he was dead, the poor
fellow. She continued to work—I don't know how; she was
very broken up, but she had show business back of her all the
way, and she wasn't about to give up. I remember the day we
finished work, she took me into her bedroom and showed me
the death masks she had made of her husband—it was as
though he were still in the room with her. She was quite a
character—old Zoë Akins. Little, old, fat—talented."

As soon as the script was finished, Berman called Laura
Harding and asked her, in a skillful strategy maneuver, to
come to his office. Inevitably, Kate tagged along, and Berman
counted on this. While Kate waited outside, edgy with curiosity, pacing up and down in enormously flapping trousers,
Laura sat and read the script from beginning to end. She was
very pleased with it, and looked at Berman, telling him all he
needed to know. His secretary called Kate in. Laura told her,
"It's wonderful." Kate sat down, read it right through, and
exclaimed, "Laura's right. When do we start?"

Berman replied, "As soon as I have a director." Within a
few days, he had signed one: Lowell Sherman. Fresh from a
great triumph as the leading man of George Cukor's *What
Price Hollywood?*, Sherman was skilled both as leading man
and director, prevented from being a star only by the fact
that he was an alcoholic. He was not physically attractive: he
was plump and round, with a heavy, swarthy face, and a
biting, disillusioned touch in his voice. People didn't warm
up to him immediately, and many people disliked him.
Though he did not, for Kate, have the intense fascination of

Cukor, she respected him, and admired the speed and efficiency of his approach, as well as his profound knowledge of the theatre.

Sherman made the picture with miraculous speed and economy. It was almost certainly the first Hollywood movie rehearsed and directed in continuity, not just in individual scenes. Sherman told Pan Berman, "If you'll give me a week with this cast sitting around a table, I'll make you the fastest picture you ever heard about."

Kate and the other players sat around with Sherman for a week and did exactly what he said they would do. He excited Kate, and she excited him. He shot the entire film in eighteen days. It was a record in Hollywood.

A mutual tension existed at first between Kate and her co-star Douglas Fairbanks, Jr.

Douglas Fairbanks, Jr., says, "I remember disliking Kate because here she was, virtually a complete unknown, and she was getting far more publicity than I was! But when I got to know her, I fell in love with her. Head over heels. I asked her for a date. She refused. I kept on trying for weeks—until after the picture was finished. Finally, she allowed me to take her out to dinner. Halfway through dinner, she developed a sick headache. I drove her home, then didn't leave right away. I wanted to sit and savor the experience of having dated Katharine Hepburn, thinking about her, feeling her close, seeing her, hearing her. I expected the lights in the house to go out after a while, that she would go to bed. Suddenly, the front door flew open and Kate came running out. Another car I hadn't noticed before was hidden farther up the driveway under some trees. She hopped in, and I saw a man at the wheel.* I never saw his face. They drove right past me without even noticing me. She was laughing happily, her hair blowing over her face! That was why she had cut her date short! I never did find out what it all meant!"

Making *Morning Glory* was a pleasant experience for Kate. As soon as the picture came out, both previews and premiere were enormously successful, and the reviews were ecstatic. Kate's performance as Eva Lovelace—heartbreak-

* Almost certainly Leland Hayward.

ingly tender, sensitive, eager, filled with the spirit of youth
—established her once and for all as a very great star. Sherman's direction of her showed a deep understanding of her
skills and her limitations.

The influential Richard Watts, Jr., wrote in the New York
Herald Tribune: "The striking and inescapably fascinating
Miss Hepburn proves pretty conclusively in her new film
that her fame in the cinema is not a mere flash across the
screen . . . it is . . . Miss Hepburn who makes *Morning Glory*
something to be seen." *Time* magazine wrote: "From this
immemorial fairy tale, the delicate, muscled face of Heroine
Hepburn shines out like a face on a coin. Of the brash little
provincial she makes a strangely distinguished character, a
little mad from hunger and dreams, absurdly audacious and
trusting." Eva Lovelace was the first part Kate had played
which was based on her own experience, desperate youthful
yearnings, and crazy trust in her own talent; it brought out
the best in her, and had the raw, jagged edge of truth. It was
her greatest triumph to date.

During the break following *Morning Glory*, Kate had a
terrifying experience. After a couple of moves, she was living
in an odd, triangular house set against a hillside in the upper
reaches of Coldwater Canyon. Kate and Laura had noticed
something strange about the house from the beginning. In
the early summer of 1933, Joanna, the maid, who had stayed
with them from the time they had lived in Franklin Canyon,
kept insisting that a small guest apartment under the house
was haunted. Although it was never occupied and was kept
locked, whenever Joanna went in there the furniture had
been moved about.

One night, Kate called Laura, who was with her family
back East, from her bedroom saying that "someone was in
the house." Kate's close friend and stand-in, "Murph" (Eve
March), had seen the latch on Kate's bedroom door moving
for no apparent reason. When the two women opened the
door, there was nobody there. Kate and Murph were terrified, and Laura by long distance suggested they call the
police. But Kate was horrified at the idea of the publicity, and
she refused. Next day, Kate and Murph were at the pool

turning off the hydraulic pump when they noticed the figure of a man turn and walk into the lower apartment. When they went to check, the door was locked, and no one could be seen inside. Kate called Laura again, insisting she come out at once.

Laura arrived from New England with her dogs, but the dogs failed to flush out the ghostly intruder. The hauntings worsened and the sense of a foreign presence became increasingly overpowering. Kate's brother Richard appeared for a visit; Kate and Laura housed him in the guest apartment, saying nothing about the haunting. After he had been there a week, he told Kate, "There's something the matter with this house. I haven't slept one single night since I've been here. I've had the feeling someone is standing at the foot of the bed looking down at me." Later, Boris Karloff took over the house. ("We felt," Laura says, "rather sorry for the ghost.")

Another odd experience occurred at the same time. Kate and Laura often went for long walks in the hills on Sundays. One Sunday afternoon, above Mulholland Drive, they ran into some men who were standing near an open fire in defiance of the regulations, shooting rabbits. Kate shouted at them, "You're not supposed to be here!" She and Laura came toward them, waving angrily, and the men deliberately shot within a few feet of them, so close that Kate was afraid the bullets might hit the dogs. Then, without warning, the men turned on them and began firing at them. The girls ran, tumbling through the scrub, and finally fetched a policeman. The men escaped, and by nightfall Kate's house was full of police.

Despite pleas from friends—including George Cukor and Leland Hayward—she and Laura refused to give up the haunted house. And soon the urgent business of making a new film, *Little Women*, was at hand. David O. Selznick had been fascinated by Louisa May Alcott's novel for years: he loved the story of the March sisters in Concord, Massachusetts, during the Civil War, with their father at war and their mother, Marmee, trying to preserve some semblance of family unity in his absence. The characters were still fresh and alive: Jo, the headstrong tomboy who longs to be a

writer, was a wonderful part for Kate, and Selznick returned
to RKO by special arrangement just so that he could make
the film with her.

Selznick had two scripts written, neither of which worked
very well, before Kate was told about the venture. When
Selznick asked George Cukor to direct, Cukor shocked him
by saying he had never read the novel. Cukor had always
assumed the book was grossly sentimental, like *Elsie Dins-
more;* but when he looked at it he was amazed to find it was
austere, severe, full of evocative details of New England life.
He knew it would be perfect for Kate, because of her own
New England emphasis on duty, severity, self-sacrifice, and
avoidance of self-pity. He says, "Kate was born for the part
of Jo. She's tender and odd and funny, sweet and yet tough,
intensely loyal, with an enormous sense of family and all of
Jo's burning ambition, and at heart a pure, clean simplicity
and firmness." He and Selznick worked out the other casting
with care, differing only on Selznick's choice of Spring Byington as Marmee—Cukor felt that Byington was too Middle
Western, too saccharine, too "enveloping" for the role,
which called for a kindly sternness. A new actress, Jean
Parker, was lovely and fragile as the tragic Beth, Joan Bennett had a perfect self-reliance as Amy, Frances Dee was a
flawless Meg, Paul Lukas was perfect as the stuffy but considerate Professor Bhaer.

David Selznick decided to hire Victor Heerman, who had
written the script for *Rupert of Hentzau* for his father, Lewis
Selznick, to prepare the screenplay for *Little Women* with
Mrs. Heerman, the accomplished Sarah Y. Mason. Sara Y.
Mason had been in love with the book for years; she felt that
every young girl in America at the time had read it. She
herself had become obsessed with it. She even signed her
letters, "With love, Beth."

The Heermans took the previously written scripts home,
read them, and returned to Selznick's associate, Kenneth
MacGowan, saying that both versions were "lousy." Victor
Heerman remembers, "During the conversation, George
Cukor arrived at the MacGowan office. MacGowan said to
him, 'The Heermans don't like the scripts.' 'What don't they
like about them?' Cukor asked. 'They're all bits and pieces,'

I told him. 'No beginning, no end, nothing. The novel tells it all beautifully, from beginning to end. But these scripts are just disconnected incidents.' George said, 'You're perfectly right. What's your idea?'

"I told him I wanted to be faithful to the book, and he asked Sarah and me to come back with a straight outline. We prepared the treatment with Kenneth MacGowan coming over constantly to our house and asking us, 'What are you doing? No, that's not right.' He nagged and nagged, and we kept saying, 'Be quiet, and let us alone.' We worked night and day for four weeks, and we forgot about the outline—we went ahead and did the script. Day and night—every minute. I blocked out scenes, then I rehearsed them, playing every role. Sarah would be at the typewriter, while I was all the women in the story—Meg, Jo, Beth, Amy, Marmee."

At the end of the four weeks of work, the Heermans were exhausted. They took the script over to the RKO stenographic pool, and when they discovered the typists' excitement—found that the girls read to each other, acting out the roles of Meg, Jo, Beth, Amy, and Marmee—they knew they had a winner. Cukor summoned the Heermans to his house. Heerman told him he was worn out, and that Sarah was in bed, but Cukor insisted they come over. "When we arrived," Heerman recalls, "George said, 'It's delightful, it's magnificent. Have a brandy.' I felt, 'Something's wrong. He's tense —he's going to say something.' I was right. He said, 'I don't want Jo's novel to be a success in the picture. I want it to be a failure.' I said, 'Holy Christ, we've worked so hard, and now you want to make this change! I'm tired, worn out, sick, I won't do it.' George said, 'I know you better than you think I do. You do wonderful things up to a certain point, and then, because somebody wants to do something, you walk out.'

"George bargained, 'You sleep on it, and tomorrow talk it over with Sarah.' I did, we talked it over, and we decided he was right. We changed the concept." Today, Kate says, "The Heermans saved *Little Women*. That's all there is to it."

Kate hugged Laura with excitement when she heard she had the role of Jo. She immediately read the novel twice, and made notes on the characters. She rushed into makeup tests with Mel Berns, who gave her the absolute minimum of rouge and face powder, and costume fittings with Walter Plunkett, who had meticulously followed the realism of the book by making the girls' clothes of cheap, worn materials, not at all glamorous or fancy. By the time Kate was through memorizing the entire script—including the other roles— Kate knew more about Louisa May Alcott, the character of families in Massachusetts in the 1860s, Christmas customs, and the modes and manners of the Civil War than Selznick's entire research staff rolled together.

Hobe Erwin designed exquisite sets of the small Massachusetts town, with exteriors to be shot on Civil War-period sets at the RKO ranch. Cukor directed meticulously, Victor Heerman and Sarah Y. Mason sitting behind the camera, making notes and providing new pages where needed, their typewriters set up on small, rickety tables. Often, Cukor would pace up and down impatiently, then snatch new pages from their machines.

One day, Heerman had a call from his son, who was in summer camp: the boy wanted to come home. Heerman drove all the way to Big Bear and found that his son had changed his mind. Driving back, irritated, to the set, Heerman found an atmosphere of total panic. "Where were you?" George Cukor screamed. "And where is Sarah? We can't proceed with work. This scene in which Jo comes in the house and walks into the conservatory—it won't play!" Heerman rewrote it in an instant, peeled off the page, and handed it to Cukor.

Another problem Kate and the others were faced with was the pregnancy of Joan Bennett, who played Amy. Each day she seemed to grow alarmingly larger, in scenes which called for Amy to be slim, yielding, and demure.

One morning, all the girls were on the set at 9 A.M. except Joan Bennett. George Cukor was furious, and sent assistant Eddie Killey to fetch her. Killey walked into her dressing room and snapped at her, "There are all these people out there waiting for you. Now, why can't you be ready at 9 A.M.? Goddamn it, from now on I'm going to give you an earlier call, so you can be ready. I'll see that you get here even if I have to go to your house and bring you here!" She retorted, "You S.O.B. Are you through now? I'm pregnant!" There was an unholy quarrel, and Joan Bennett was half an hour late on the set.

A couple of days later, Joan was at the bottom of the stairs with Kate, and the other two girls were at the top. Jean Parker ran down the stairs so fast she knocked Kate and Joan Bennett over in a heap. Cukor and Ed Killey rushed to Joan Bennett, terrified she would have a miscarriage and the picture would have to be closed down. Fortunately, she had no ill effects.

Next day, the unit was working at Warners at a rented house exterior when word came that the sound technicians were on strike. Shooting was called off for the day. For three weeks, all filming was closed down and by then Joan Bennett's pregnancy was so far advanced that her dresses had to be completely remade.

Frances Dee, who played Meg, recalls, "I'll never forget Katharine. She used to sit between scenes in a window seat in her severe, austere dresses with a straight back, reading a slim volume. She could have been Jo herself. She had such a grave, sweet expression on her face, with her hands folded in her lap, and looking so austere and yet so beautiful. She was always the first on the set every day, lines perfect, glowing with health, and never the slightest sign of temperament. Sometimes while she was reading or just contemplating alone, we girls, Joan Bennett, Jean Parker, and myself, would creep up and peek at her, absolutely awestruck by her concentration. I'm sure she knew we were watching, but she never looked up or around."

Cukor and Kate sometimes quarreled during the picture. Cukor remembers, "In one scene, Kate had to go headlong up a flight of steps with a tub of ice cream in her hands. I told her she must be extremely careful because Walter Plunkett had made only one copy of the dress, made of very rare old material, and whatever happened she mustn't upset the ice cream. She got halfway up the steps, and she accidentally spilled the ice cream all over her skirt, completely ruining the dress. Then she had to go and change into something much less appropriate. I was furious with her, and I slapped her hard across the face and called her, in front of the entire cast and crew, a rank and hopeless amateur. She stuck her chin high and said, 'Well, that's your opinion.' But she didn't cry or apologize. That was Kate.

"On the whole, she handled everything wonderfully. When the sound men went on strike, the scabs who were working against union regulations deliberately or accidentally ruined take after take by not having the microphones in the correct position. Kate was playing a scene after her sister Beth had died, and she had to cry over and over again for hours. At last she had a perfect take, and once again those incredible tear ducts opened on cue. She waited until the take was over and said, 'Do you have it perfectly?' When I said, 'Yes,' she said, 'All right. I can throw up now.' And she did. That was Kate again."

It was on *Little Women* that Kate introduced her custom of picnics for both cast and crew. Joanna, the maid, and Laura would prepare the food—finger rolls, bacon sandwiches, delicious stews—and Joan Bennett and her husband, Gene Markey, not to be outdone, bought the most expensive food they could find in a Beverly Hills delicatessen. Unfortunately, the Markeys lost the competition, as everybody much preferred Joanna's and Laura's home cooking. In the afternoon, Kate insisted on having afternoon tea served, which caused Cukor to say, "You come round here and bring this goddamned country-club atmosphere."

But Kate's decision was right: the picnic lunches and teas helped give the whole picture a wonderfully relaxed feeling, an important ingredient of its success. Cukor's direction was perfectly in keeping with the spirit of the novel, and Kate's Jo was nothing short of magnificent. Once again, as in *Morning Glory*, she gave a sensitive, deeply moving portrait of ambition, of girlish dreams, and yet of a fundamental firmness, discipline, control. Her striking face, delectably lit by the cameraman Henry Gerrard, was alive with wonder, sadness, shifting moments of hope and despair. Cukor had always understood that screen acting lay in the expression of the eyes, and Kate's eyes were mirrors of a spirit noble, daring, and tender. Once again, the reviewers threw their hats in the air. Richard Watts wrote: "It is the unashamed straightforwardness of the writing, the unpatronizing shrewdness of George Cukor's direction, and above all, Miss Hepburn's beautiful playing, which make *Little Women* an exquisite screen drama."

Little Women also proved to be the first film of Kate's which was an enormous box-office hit. At long last, her stock stood high in money-conscious Hollywood.

Four

Intoxicated by the success of *Little Women*, Kate at twenty-four decided in an impetuous moment to make an immediate return to the stage. Like most theatre people of her generation, she didn't believe that even the greatest film success could possibly match the importance of a major hit on Broadway. And again like most actresses of her time, she felt that the ultimate accolade would be to do a play with the thirty-two-year-old producer Jed Harris. Thin and dark, with hooded eyes, he was the maverick boy wonder of the American theatre, its greatest 1930s genius before the advent of Orson Welles.

After the great success of *A Bill of Divorcement*, Kate had received several urgent messages from the fearsomely intense Harris, who was determined to have her appear in a production of Mordaunt Shairp's *The Green Bay Tree*, a play about homosexuals, in which she would be co-starred with the up-and-coming young British actor Laurence Olivier. Kate had enormously admired Harris' productions of *Broadway*, *Coquette*, *The Royal Family*, and *The Front Page*.

Harris says, "I first met her when she was still in New York, before she went to Hollywood. She came in to see me at the Morosco Theatre, where I had my offices on the top floor. I talked to her for a few minutes about her ambitions. She had an odd combination of sweetness with a certain Scottish determination that I saw on her face, and I knew Gilbert Miller was looking for a girl for *The Animal Kingdom*, so I recommended her.

"I had no interest in having her play for me, because it was obvious that with her everything began with *her*, and with me everything began with the play. The only flattering thing

54

I have ever heard said about me was that if Jed thought his mother was wrong for a part, and her life depended on it, he would still fire her. I never thought in terms of getting plays for people.

"After she had her great hit in *A Bill of Divorcement*, she wrote and begged me to find a part for her in the theatre. She wanted to come back to Broadway. My original suggestion was *The Green Bay Tree*, which had been done in London in a rather obvious, brash way, with Hugh Williams, Mordaunt Shairp's stepson, in the leading role of a homosexual. I decided to take the obscure young Laurence Olivier for the part in New York.

"I thought it would be modest and brilliant for Hepburn to come in and take a small part, subsidiary to the men, in which she would have two or three really marvelous moments. I would have built scenes for her which would have made her tremendous. Hepburn would have been perfect for it. Larry's then wife, Jill Esmond, played the part. Katharine Hepburn didn't have the good sense to take a subsidiary role like this after her huge success in Hollywood.

"She didn't have brains or anything like that, she was just a terribly stagestruck girl, with certain odd components which I thought would be successful in the theatre, just by being herself. So I found *The Lake* for her."

The Lake, by Dorothy Massingham and Murray MacDonald, had originally been produced in London. Harris hated it, but thought it might succeed in New York. The story was thin: Kate would play Stella Surrege, an English girl with an overbearing mother and an unhappy, beaten father. Stella marries, elopes, and she and her husband crash their car into a lake. Surviving the accident, Stella discovers loyalty to her family. Harris says, "I thought *The Lake* was common, stupid, sentimental, but I sent it to Kate for her to read. She loved it. I suddenly found myself saying, 'All right, I'll do this play.' From that moment of decision, I hated myself. It's the only time in my whole life in the theatre I ever ventured into 'show business,' which is all that *The Lake* with Katharine Hepburn amounted to."

At first, Kate was unable to obtain a release from RKO to do the production. She wanted to spend four weeks training

with Jed Harris privately, but reluctantly agreed to make
another picture, *Spitfire*, a ridiculous concoction in which
she played a wild mountain girl. She made an agreement that
she would film the picture in four weeks for $50,000, but if
the production ran one day over, she would be paid $10,000
a day for any extra days. The picture, directed by John Cromwell, who did not admire Kate, did in fact run one day over.
She forced Pan Berman to pay.

Kate left for New York in the late fall of 1933, feeling
irritable after the experience with Cromwell, but looking
forward to working with Jed Harris and to what she expected
to be a triumphant Broadway return. Harris says, "We went
into rehearsal. Becoming a star had changed her from a simple, spontaneous girl into someone who acted scenes with
self-pity, weeping tears constantly. I found her totally inept.
There was a moment in a particular scene when I was horrified by her. I found she had no imagination in playing it, she
couldn't move out of a certain mold. She was inexperienced,
she didn't know what to do, she was very naïve, complexity
of feeling was something beyond her wildest imagination.
Finally I said something sharp to her. She burst into tears and
threw her arms around me, and I was shocked to hear her
say, 'I could have loved you so.' I had never thought of loving
her or being loved by her. I was intensely embarrassed, yet
my heart was full of pity for her. I had no way of expressing
it. I couldn't do anything. She clearly felt she could have been
in love with me. I made a terrible mistake. Instead of calling
off the rehearsal, taking her to her dressing room, talking to
her, I decided not to direct her any more, and left the work
to my stage manager, Tony Miner. To all intents and pur-
poses, the play was fully directed, but I didn't want anything
further to do with the play after that. Miner was one of these
people who are worshipers of movie stars, and he said, 'Oh,
I think she's just great.' Well, she wasn't great, she was really
bad.

"When she came to rehearsal, she hadn't the slightest
doubt she could play it. She was a big star from Hollywood
and she could do anything she wanted. I could see she was
hopeless. I fought with her—I begged her to stop posing,
striking attitudes, leaning against doorways, putting a limp

hand to her forehead, to stop being a big movie star and *feel* the lines, *feel* the character. I was trying the impossible, to make an artificial showcase for an artificial star, and she couldn't handle it. *Tremendous* artificiality! It's as though she had seen her own performance and liked her own rather charming babbling at everything, and she had decided that was acting.

"I blame myself. I shouldn't have done it, I should not have sent it to her. I should not have been moved from A to B by her enthusiasm for it. I should have been on guard, and I was not."

The distinguished theatrical director Worthington ("Tony") Miner insists that Jed Harris' accounts of these events is entirely false. "I began directing the play for him." he says. "I treated Kate sensitively, and she needed sensitive treatment. She was unsure, and we were getting along fine, when Harris fired me. He wanted to destroy every actress he came in touch with, and he brutalized her so completely that by the time we got to the production in Washington, she was totally demoralized. She cried helplessly, and I had to beg her to go."

Jed Harris says, "I wanted to close the play in Washington. I was told I couldn't close, I was committed to open at the Martin Beck Theatre. I had an ironbound contract to go in there. I said, 'Get in touch with Mrs. Beck and find out what it would cost me not to come in.' In those days, I put up all my own money for my own plans. I didn't have backers, or anything like that. So not to have gone in would have been a considerable loss to me. I was forced to go ahead, because Mrs. Beck insisted even a bad play would sell tickets with Katharine Hepburn as the lead. I was disgusted. When the show had been running six weeks, Hepburn wanted out. My manager made her pay $15,000 to release her. I heard she was very bitter—apparently she thought she could just close a show when she chose.

"Looking back on the whole episode, I feel I should have been more patient with her, more considerate. I should have paid more attention to her. I felt sorry for her—she had spent her whole so-called love life with a nonentity she married called Smith, and then she was involved with an agent, for

God's sake, called Leland Hayward. She was an imbecile, a
damn fool, an idiot, yet I regret I wasn't more patient—there
was a barrier of language and feeling I could not cross to
reach to her. The other night I saw her in *The Glass Menagerie* on television, and she was still babbling with a fixed smile
on her face, the way she did in *The Lake,* and I thought, 'God!
She hasn't changed at all.'

"I don't want to take everything away from her. She was
sweet, she was well-bred, her face was stunning, people
thought she had breeding. But I should never have worked
with her, or she with me."

Laura Harding was the only friend whom Kate managed
to sneak in to rehearsals. Laura says, "Jed Harris was like a
snake. Whatever he says, he hooked Kate into doing *The
Lake,* then he behaved very peculiarly. Kate asked me to
come and see her work. She had to wear riding clothes in the
first act, and I helped her pick them out. Then I dropped by
the theatre. I sat way in the back, but after a few minutes Jed
stopped the rehearsal, called Kate down, and murmured
something to her. Kate was furious and walked off the stage.
I thought, 'This is queer, they're talking about me. But why
would they be? I'm just sitting here.' Pretty soon, someone
came up and said, 'Mr. Harris wants you to leave the theatre.'
I went backstage to see Kate and asked her, 'What goes on?'
She said, 'I won't go back on the stage.' I told her, 'It's not
worth it.' Finally she did go back, and found he had canceled
all her orders for riding clothes. Just making something out
of nothing. Then, in a really awful move, he got a rather
charming girl called Isabel Pell to come into the cast and
gave her everything Kate was supposed to be wearing. In the
end, Kate had to wear my riding clothes. Jed was horrible to
her. Kate was struggling so hard to do the play, and he insisted she be a big star—she didn't want to be a theatre star,
she wanted her part played down below the others in the
cast. He was cruel to her and in all his relationships.

"When she opened in the play, Harris gave her some false,
ridiculous, overblown publicity. It was a hideous moment for
her, the whole ordeal."

Kate herself admits she was a disaster in the role, deserving the horrible reviews and Dorothy Parker's quip that in the play Kate "ran the gamut of emotions from A to B."

On February 3, after fifty-five performances, an official announcement appeared in the New York *Times* saying that *The Lake* would close on February 10 after a seven-week run, and would not go on tour.

Kate decided to make a trip abroad. Since Laura was busy with her family, she took along a plump former opera singer, Susanne Steele, who had been giving her private coaching during the weekends for the run of *The Lake*.

Kate booked passage on the *Paris*, leaving on March 18. The day she sailed, she heard the news that she had won the Oscar for *Morning Glory*. It was accepted for her in Hollywood by B. B. Kahane, president of RKO.

The news cheered her as she hid from the press in her cabin, after hurrying aboard by the third-class gangway and calling back that she wouldn't be interviewed by anybody. When reporters knocked on her cabin door, she told them to go away. Finally, they were so persistent that Susanne had to come out and make a little announcement that she and Kate would be "abroad for four or five weeks, visiting Paris and the Riviera."

The crossing turned out to be an anguish. Susanne was constantly drunk; she horrified the temperate Kate with her alcoholism. On arrival in France, Kate canceled all plans for the tour and returned immediately on the *Paris* after only four days in port. She covered up her distress gallantly, and even consented to a press conference on board ship in New York Harbor on April 4. "I often make these hasty trips," she said. "I can't explain why I do it. I just do it and that's all there is about it." Then she lied, "I came home because I was homesick. I had nothing to say when I left, and therefore I saw no occasion for saying anything." She added that she would shortly be making the film *Joan of Arc*, from a screenplay by Thornton Wilder, and that Garbo was her favorite actress.

From New York, Kate went to Miami, where she set out on board the S.S. *Morro Castle* on an odd little expedition to Mexico with Laura, to obtain a Mexican divorce from Luddy. She filed the petition from the Hotel Itza in Mérida in Yucatán, where she was registered as Laura's maid Katharine Smith. She had a meeting with a Mexican attorney named by Luddy at the seaport called Progresso, and then appeared at a court in Mérida on May 8 to give her deposition. The divorce decree revealed that the couple had joined in a petition that the usual thirty-day restriction upon remarriage be not imposed. The court ruled that, as the request had been made jointly, showing that each was willing for the other to seek a new partner, there was no need to apply the restriction. This released Luddy to marry his girl friend, Elizabeth, a few days later. Kate was intensely happy that Luddy had fallen in love and smiled on the marriage from the outset.

Kate and Laura, after canceling plans to return on the *Morro Castle* to Miami—the *Morro Castle* burned at sea shortly afterward—flew to Miami instead, and took the train to New York. At Turtle Bay and her family home of Fenwick, Kate began reading scripts sent her by RKO—a revised draft of the *Joan of Arc* script which proved to be unworkable, a life of George Sand, a version of *The Forsyte Saga* written by Jane Murfin. She also considered appearing for Arthur Hopkins in a stage production of *Pride and Prejudice,* and almost went into an Ivoryton summer theatre production of *Dark Victory,* later made into a film starring Bette Davis, only to have all plans canceled when her co-star, Stanley Ridges, withdrew because of family problems.

At last she found a subject she really wanted to do: Sir James Barrie's *The Little Minister,* which had been a great triumph for her idol, Maude Adams, on the Broadway stage and for Betty Compson in a silent-film version. Set in Scotland in 1840, it was the story of Lady Babbie, who is democratic at heart and loves to dress as a gypsy, mingling with the humble weavers of a Scottish valley. She is involved in the weavers' rebellion against her stern foster father, Lord Rintoul, and horrifies the villages by falling in love with the diminutive and prim young minister, Reverend Gavin Dishart, who begins by trying to flush her out of the glen. The local townspeople threaten the Reverend, but forgive him when Babbie's true lineage is disclosed.

Sentimental, absurdly overromanticized, and snobbish, the play was virtually impossible to adapt for the screen. The first draft screenplay, which Kate liked, was by Victor Heerman and Sarah Y. Mason, but while Kate and Laura came out by train and took a new house, William Sistrom, the studio manager, became impatient with the Heermans' delays—they could not beat the sentimentality out of the play—and put Jane Murfin on the job. Jane Murfin failed to write a good script, and the Heermans were called back for more work.

Driving into the studio with Laura Harding in her station wagon for costume tests one morning, Kate spotted the Heermans. "What's the trouble?" she yelled out. "They took us off the picture," the Heermans said. "Who took you off?" "Pan Berman." Kate talked to Berman. Shortly thereafter, the Heermans were hired back to finish the script. But they never really conquered the problems presented by the material.

John Beal, Kate's young co-star, had read the play and had an overwhelming determination to act the Little Minister. He pestered Pan Berman constantly for the role, and finally Franchot Tone, who had turned the part down, recommended Beal for it. Kate heard he had been given the part the day she met him for the first time in a restaurant opposite the RKO studios. Beal says, "She came to the table. We were introduced, and she told me, 'You're too tall! He's a *little* minister!' She was that forthright. When I started work, they had to shave down my heels. Then she towered over me!

"When we started to work, I was fascinated by the excitement she created, the energy, the health. And the niceness. Once she'd accepted me—with my heels shaved down—she was very kind and considerate. The very first day of work, she and Laura arrived with baked chicken for us all for lunch—unheard of. And then each day we had wonderful food, out of picnic hampers, spread on the tables.

"We began shooting at Sherwood Forest. She was up a tree, singing! I'm supposed to be furious—I'm a minister—here's a gypsy, misbehaving in the glen. I was awestruck with her; it was hard to be furious.

"I remember how I felt during our first love scene. We were standing near a little stone bridge, and in the script I realized I was falling for her. I thought, 'It's her scene, and I shouldn't move or anything to distract the audience attention from her. I was very respectful; too much, probably; I would bend over backwards to obscure myself.' She felt I was underplaying, and she drew me aside and said, 'Don't be afraid to do things on your own.' She said, 'Keep the screen alive.' It was a wonderful phrase. She made me feel I needn't be too careful about suppressing my personality. Her electric enthusiasm constantly recharged me."

The problem in shooting the film, both at Sherwood Forest and at a Scottish village in Laurel Canyon, was that the director, Richard Wallace, was much too soft. He let scenes drift away, forcing the players to take over the direction. Kate, who preferred a challenging mind and a strong directorial hand, became impatient. She had to make a complicated move down the side of a hill through branches and then stop dead because she saw the Little Minister approaching through the glen. It took all morning to get the shot—fifty-seven takes—because director Wallace was unsure exactly what expression he wanted her to register. This was particularly annoying for Kate, because she knew precisely what effect she wanted to create in the scene, and Wallace clearly did not.

The Little Minister never satisfied Kate, because she was never convinced that Wallace had a proper grasp of the material. And over the film, too, hung the sudden tragic death of her favorite cameraman, Henry Gerrard, during production. Stricken one night by appendicitis pains, he foolishly allowed himself to be operated on by an unlicensed chiropractor, and the clumsy, botched-up operation killed him.

The movie opened at Radio City Music Hall in late 1934, to the biggest audience in the theatre's history, but it failed in every other engagement. The news was a severe blow to Kate, and an even severer one to Pan Berman, who had been the prime mover in bringing her back to Hollywood. Berman says, "By this time, I realized Kate wasn't a movie star. She wasn't going to become a star, either, in the sense that Crawford or Shearer were—actresses able to drag an audience in by their own efforts. She was a hit only in hit pictures; she couldn't save a flop. And she almost invariably chose the wrong vehicles."

After the catastrophe of *The Little Minister*, Pan Berman began urgently casting around for another vehicle to recoup RKO's losses on the picture. While Kate returned home to Hartford, Victor Heerman and Sarah Y. Mason went to work adapting a story by Lester Cohen entitled *The Music Man*.* It was the story of a temperamental and brilliant conductor, Franz Roberti, who is married to a struggling composer, Constance Dane. Kate was delighted when she was offered the role of Constance Dane.

There was talk of engaging John Barrymore to play Franz Roberti, but MGM was unable to release him. Instead, the Heermans suggested Francis Lederer, the accomplished Czech actor, whom they had seen play a musician on the stage in *Autumn Crocus*. Kate was excited to learn that Pan Berman had hired as director Philip Moeller, the aging but reputable guiding light of the Theatre Guild, who had directed some of the Guild's most important productions.

She returned to Hollywood anxious to get to work, learned how to read a score to add conviction to her role, and interviewed composers and professional musicians. But from the first, she and Lederer failed to get along. Too professional to show her dislike of him openly on the set, she expressed her irritation privately to Moeller and the Heermans.

Victor Heerman says, "Kate came to me and said, 'I just can't work with Lederer.' I asked her, 'What's wrong?' 'Well,' she said, 'he's so slow, he doesn't grasp the lines, he's impossible.' 'Now,' I told her, 'we wrote the lines for a slow, halting man, who finds life hard.' If he had been Cukor, Pan Berman would have told her, 'I'll do the deciding on who's to play with you.' But Pan Berman was afraid of her."

Assistant director Ed Killey says, "There was *much* tension on the set. One morning, everything came to a halt. Lederer refused to come in a door because he was showing the bad side of his face. Well, I told Kate, 'I'm going to have this picture stopped. I'm going to have this man thrown off the picture.' She shrugged her shoulders and said, 'Why don't you go up and see what they say?' I took Lederer with me.

*The title was changed during production to *Break of Hearts*.

I said to Mr. J. P. MacDonald, the head of the studio, 'We've been rehearsing this thing with Lederer for two weeks now, this is our first morning of shooting, and I can't reconstruct the set just because he doesn't like us showing the wrong side of his face. And I don't think he has the right to tell the director where to put his cameras—he's just an actor.' MacDonald called Lederer in and said, 'Mr. Lederer, we feel we want to make a change.' I thought we'd have to close the picture down. When Lederer walked out, MacDonald said, 'Eddie, go back on the set, and within an hour we'll have someone there.' An hour later, down walks J. P. And who do you think he's got with him? Charles Boyer."

Kate liked Charles Boyer very well, and they worked comfortably together. But Philip Moeller proved seriously inexperienced as a movie director, and the Heermans' script, though extensively rewritten on the set by Anthony Veiller, was a bitter disappointment to Kate. The picture emerged as a confused, unsatisfactory work, and was not well received by critics or the public. After the disaster of *The Little Minister*, the flop of this new film came close to breaking her heart, as the title had prophesied.

Pan Berman, desolate following the collapse of *Break of Hearts*, decided to proceed with Kate's next vehicle: Booth Tarkington's touching story of small-town life, *Alice Adams*. Kate adored the book, and she accepted the idea at once. She knew that Alice, with her pathetic dreams of social success, would be perfect for her, and she hugged Pan gratefully when he told her he had chosen her for the part. Her only disappointment was that Laura would not be present to guide her in her work. Laura, upset by statements from Kate's colleagues that "you either get into this business or get out—stop living Kate's life for her," and anxious to return to her own life, remained East for many years.

Laura says, "People kept sympathizing with me and with her, saying that it must have been a terrible wrench for us to be separated after our intense friendship of three years. But it became clear to me that my presence in Hollywood was increasingly inessential to myself, to Kate, and to pictures. I had no interest in going into the industry, Kate was

firmly established as a huge star and was no longer depen-
dent on me, and I was tired of the rather meaningless, sterile
life of Southern California.

"You must remember that I came from a totally different
social milieu from either Hollywood people *or* Kate. Our
family was in railroads and the travel business, our friends
were East Coast old money people, and I never even approved of Kate's bohemian ways. I adored her and still do,
but in 1935 it had become obvious that I did not belong at the
center of her life. I traveled, went to Europe, found a new
string of beaux, and got back into my kind of society. Unhappy? No. I had come home."

Laura saw her dear friend only when Kate visited New
York, Laura's farm in New Jersey, and Kate's family at Hartford. The sensitive, perceptive film editor, Jane Loring, took
Laura's place as confidante, supporter, and adviser on all her
projects, and Leland Hayward, whom Kate was still dating
after three years, remained a wonderful friend.

Once Kate and Pan Berman had settled on *Alice Adams*,
they had to decide who was going to direct it. They narrowed
down the choice to two people: William Wyler, then approaching the height of his career after making *Dodsworth*,
from the novel by Sinclair Lewis, and an obscure thirty-year-
old beginner named George Stevens, whom Berman had just
allowed to direct his first feature-length comedy, a simple
Gene Stratton Porter story, *Laddie*. Eddie Killey urged Kate
to take Stevens.

"I think," Berman says, "Katharine was taken with George
in another way. I think she found him very attractive. One
night, we got together at my house to make the decision. I
was very torn, because I knew Wyler was just great, but I also
knew he was capable of being very difficult. I had to make
a special deal with him, and I didn't know how much I'd have
to pay him. I had George under contract, and I was paying
him a weekly salary.

"So we batted it around for an hour, and I said to Kate, 'I'll
tell you what let's do, let's toss a coin.' She said, 'Great.' So
I flipped the coin, and I said, 'If it's heads it's Wyler, if it's tails
it's Stevens.' It fell on the desk. It was heads—Wyler. I looked
at her, she looked at me. I said, 'Let's flip it again.' She said,

'Yes!' I flipped it again, it came up tails, and we took Stevens. Inside us, we both wanted him."

Once the die was cast, Kate shook hands warmly with Pan Berman, who called Stevens over to him on the set and asked him if he had read the novel. "We need another success for Kate," he said. Stevens dissembled: he hadn't read the book and was in the middle of shooting a film sequence that had him covered in mud and black dust and surrounded by a gang of stunt men. He said something that might have been "yes" or "no," and Berman asked him if he would go to Kate's house that evening to discuss the property. "You liked the book?" Berman said quickly. "Yes," Stevens lied.

Later, Stevens drove over to see Kate; she was ill, and sprawled exhaustedly in a chair. "We talked about a variety of subjects," Stevens recalls, "but we didn't say a word about the book itself, the script, or the film." It was a desultory conversation; Kate felt worse and worse during the discussion, and Stevens found himself getting quite uncomfortable. Next morning, Pan Berman called him in and said, "Kate says you had a very pleasant evening, but you didn't say a word about the picture. That puts me in a very difficult situation. I've got to get started." Stevens went off and read every word of *Alice Adams,* and within twenty-four hours agreed to do the picture.

The existing two-thirds of a screenplay hurriedly written by Jane Murfin was overlong and very bad, so Stevens engaged a young writer, Mortimer Offner, to revise it, going back to the book. Stevens copied the interior of a house he had seen in Los Angeles that struck him as almost deliberately designed as the kind of place a young person would have to escape from. He did not have a finished script when he started shooting, but instead acquired new pages from day to day.

At night, Kate insisted on showing him her new clothes for the picture. "She would always model them for me just when I was bushed and waiting to go home. She was completely tireless. She'd show me two dresses and ask which one I liked. If I chose the first one, she'd say, 'Well, don't you really think the second one is better?' I didn't know what she wanted. All

I was concerned with was that she dressed the way under-privileged people like Alice Adams would."

Kate was fascinated by Stevens, whose slow, controlled manner, seemingly sleepy but in fact intensely watchful, was completely the opposite of Cukor's energetic activeness. "We had instant harmony," they both say. But Stevens occasionally had major differences with her in interpretation of scenes. "I knew the Alice Adams people intimately," Stevens said. "Better than she did, intuitive and brilliant though she was. I knew how those people *thought*, what they were *after*. The father, for instance: he's never accomplished a damn thing, he's beholden to an old-man boss, Alice Adams is trying to reach beyond him, hurting herself, and wondering if she has the kind of intelligence, the kind of style which will make it possible for her to survive in a more privileged environment.

"Kate impressed me deeply with her effort to reach out to the role. She was the opposite of Alice Adams; she was a privileged woman, born to money. She was forceful, vividly expressive, strong, even strident, and now she had to be subdued, restrained, perhaps 'beaten by life' in a way that Kate never could have been. The audience would respond to Kate's bravery, honesty, and beauty, and her innate grace, but she had to play down all those qualities, let the audience discover them.

"Above all, I had to guide her in the love scenes. She had always thought that to play a love scene with a man involved standing up straight and talking to him strong, eye to eye. I made her have confidence in her beauty, so that if she sat in a chair, letting her head fall back, with a wide-brimmed hat over her eyes, she had a quiet assurance she was attracting her man; she didn't have to bulldoze him into submission.

"I had to teach her not to please herself—which is perhaps a great virtue in any activity. I had to teach her to follow only the concept of the original author. It was a discipline she learned uneasily. But it was so much more interesting to see her strength become vulnerable. To be vulnerable is the nature of any woman. But to be brave and strong and cavalier about things and then be wounded by life—that is deeply moving."

Fred MacMurray, who played Alice's suitor, says, "I remember a scene on a porch; Kate was in a porch swing and I was sitting in a chair. Her concept of the scene was entirely different from George's. He was quietly definite, and she was less quietly definite. Finally, he said, 'Let's shoot it.' We did it over and over, most of the morning, and we broke for lunch. We did it over. He said, 'It's not the way I want it.' After eighty takes, all day, at last she did it the way he wanted it."

Stevens says, "There was a long scene in which Alice is shown depressed by her hopeless existence. She says good night to everyone, goes upstairs in a long dress, and into her bedroom. Kate had in her mind that Alice Adams would open the door, fall on the bed, and cry. I wanted her to go to the window, see rain, lean her head against the glass, and let us look at the tears running down her face. Kate refused. I said, 'Why won't you cry on camera?' And she said, 'I wouldn't cry so anyone could see.' I said, 'You wouldn't, but Alice Adams would. Alice Adams wasn't an actress. If she was a hundred Alice Adameses and all actresses, every damn one of them would walk through the door, fall on the bed, and cry. You're not going to be actress a hundred and one. We want the audience to *hang on* to what you're doing.' Well, she agreed, a little. Eddie Killey gave me the signal she was ready to play the scene. She went to the window, looked at it, looked at me, looked at the window, and said, under her breath, 'Son of a bitch.' I could read her lips. I went over to her and said, 'Who's a son of a bitch?' She said, 'You are.' I said, 'Why?' She said, 'That's inhumane, to ask me to cry like that in front of millions of people.' I said to her, 'Who are you making happy? You or the audience?' I said, 'I'll tell you whom I'm making happy. I'm not making you happy one damn bit, I feel for all those Alice Adams girls who are watching this, who are going to know something about this kind of pain and find that somebody else can have pain as bad as they have.

"The girls are going to be sitting there at the Music Hall, and they want themselves to be up there, not a rich movie actress. Now, I'm going to put the camera outside the window, and I'm going to expect you to be enough of an actress to cry. Let's try it again.' I walked away, Eddie Killey gave me the signal again. She came in, she opened the door, she walked in without shutting it, realized she hadn't shut it, went back, shut it quietly, threw her coat on the bed, she looked as though her heart was broken, it was an empty world, and she really cried. It was painful—and *perfectly* what I wanted. By facing what for her was the excruciating embarrassment of showing an emotion, she came through and she was great."

Five

Stevens' considerate but determined guidance paid off. Kate's performance in *Alice Adams* was unusually soft and subdued, lovely in its details of timing and emphasis. She played the difficult scenes with intricate skill: Alice's emergence at the Palmer dance, glancing around flirtatiously, her eyes filled with provincial anxiety, for a man to fox-trot with; Alice on the porch—the scene that was so difficult for Stevens to shoot—in which she tries to divert her fiancé so that he won't feel compelled to enter her parents' shabby, depressing house; Alice's collisions with her dullard brother, played faultlessly by Frank Albertson; the scene at the window when she cries, filmed in a lingering take through the rain; Alice at a dinner party ruined by a slovenly black maid. Although it seems unlikely that so refined a creature would be born to such dull and unattractive parents as those played by Fred Stone and Ann Shoemaker, Kate overcame the audience's doubts by sheer force of technique and feeling.

Alice Adams was a perfect part for Kate: she had always been the awkward-girl-out at the ball, the wallflower, who had always been eager to please her parents, yet was devastated to find she had been deprived of any sense of social poise with her peers; she had always tried to please herself, yet felt she had failed to do so. Now she was nervous young Alice Adams in the provincial overlit ballroom of Hollywood.

George Stevens' direction, intimate, emphasizing luminous close-ups of Kate's delicately responsive face, effortlessly fluid in its evocations of the Adams house, remains the finest of his work of the 1930s. The house itself, cozily ugly, cluttered, with its flights of porcelain geese on the walls, its gloomy family portraits, narrow stairs leading to chintz bedrooms, endless connecting doors, becomes a living thing, reflecting the parents' dead hopes.

During this period, Kate's long romantic friendship with Leland Hayward dissolved: during a party at George Cukor's, she heard on the radio that he had married Margaret Sullavan. The news came as a severe shock; but characteristically she sent Miss Sullavan a telegram of congratulation, a telegram Miss Sullavan contemptuously tore up and threw away.

At that time, Kate met and became fascinated by Howard Hughes. She was enormously attracted to him: he was an individualist, an isolated loner, and a hypochondriac, who brought out the nurse in her. He was a renowned aviator, who gallantly dipped his wings when he flew over her house; and he even taught her to fly. Although they did not have a great deal in common in terms of their interests, he did like to play tennis and golf and to swim, and so did she. They could enjoy each other's company without becoming deeply committed to an intense personal relationship: as in all of Kate's relationships, there was never any question of marriage.

They made a physically well-matched pair. Tall, bony, angular, they were always dodging in and out of cars, trains, planes, in an attempt to avoid publicity, which, like Garbo's, inevitably resulted in an excess of it. The press followed them everywhere, and this annoyed them equally; quite often autograph hounds pursued them, and got brushed away like gnats for their pains. The leggy, fugitive figures in their ankle-length mid-thirties coats, playing tennis or golf, flying, swimming, laughing, joking, had as much chance of trying to hide as two daddy longlegs in a klieg light.

The great success of *Alice Adams* clearly went to Pan Berman's head, because he suddenly and nobly gave Kate *carte blanche* to do exactly what she liked, and in any manner she chose, in her next project. The result was *Sylvia Scarlett*, a serious mistake which Berman called "by far the worst picture I ever made, and the greatest catastrophe of Kate's thirties' career.

"I had nothing to do with it," Berman adds. "I despised everything about it. It was a private promotional deal of Hepburn and Cukor; they conned me into it and had a script written. I said to them, 'Jesus, this is awful, terrible, I don't understand a thing that's going on.' I tried to stop them, but they wouldn't be stopped; they were hell-bent, claiming that this was the greatest thing they had ever found."

It was true. Kate and Cukor had fatally fallen in love with a novel: the Scottish Compton Mackenzie's *Early Life and Adventures of Sylvia Scarlett,* a story about a young girl, Sylvia, who, with her larcenous father, escapes from France disguised as a boy. They meet a crook, Jimmy Monkley; Sylvia falls in love with a wealthy, good-looking artist, Michael Fane. Sylvia has to "become a woman" to avoid losing Fane to a predatory Russian adventuress, Lily.

George Cukor had wanted to make the picture for years. When Louis B. Mayer, to whom he was under contract, refused point-blank to take on the script, Cukor offered it to the RKO bosses and they approved it. Kate was enchanted by the story at once. She adored the idea of playing a boy, and making the picture became what was virtually a paid vacation. Cary Grant was cast as Jimmy Monkley, Brian Aherne as Michael Fane, and Edmund Gwenn as Sylvia's father.

It was a highly effective team, and the script by Gladys Unger and John Collier, with additional touches by Kate's friend Mortimer Offner, was audacious in its off-color references to sex changes. John Collier introduced a line of dialogue in which Brian Aherne, who is attracted to Kate in her boy's disguise, says, "There's something very queer going on here." A maid tells Hepburn, "You're very attractive," and they kiss.

Cary Grant says, "This part of the Cockney was a disaster for me in terms of a mass audience, and the whole joke was far too private; but I learned comedy timing from George; the whole part gave me a new lease of life as a comedian." Cukor adds, "Cary knew the kind of life we showed in the picture, when the Scarletts join a traveling fair. He had started his career walking on stilts in a British circus."

Brian Aherne has very happy memories of making the picture. He says, "We had a lovely time! We shot most of the

film down the coast beyond Malibu, and we swam and sun-
bathed and shouted with laughter. We were all young—very
young. Both George Cukor and Kate had cooks who used to
vie with each other to prepare the lunches. The meals were
equally delicious—served on benches on the cliffs above the
sea. One day, we were sitting down to eat when a biplane
roared up and settled on a landing strip. Out stepped Howard Hughes. He came over and sat with us, using that odd,
high-pitched voice deaf people have. Kate and George used
to say, *sotto voce,* 'Pass the bread, please' right in front of
him, and they'd roar with laugher as he strained to understand them. He didn't know *what* they were up to!

"Then he'd walk off and fly away, still without the remotest
notion what they were all laughing at. Kate was great fun all
the time. She asked me one day, 'What's it like, being
brought up in England?' I told her, 'Be seen and not heard.'
My father, I pointed out, never allowed us children to express
an opinion about anything. She said, 'Oh, that's *amazing!
Amazing!* We children would talk all at once, screaming as
loud as possible, vying for attention, and my father would say,
"If you have an opinion, express it as clearly as possible." If
we *didn't* have an opinion, he thought we were stupid!'

"Well, we all frolicked and carried on—I really think
George and Kate were hopelessly carried away by the whole
thing. Cary Grant had fun, too, except when one scene called
for him to dash into the Pacific Ocean surf to rescue a drowning girl. He refused. 'No, I won't go in there, I won't!' he
insisted, and Natalie Paley, a baroness who was playing the
girl, was out there bobbing up and down. It was *freezing,* and
she was really almost drowning, and occasionally you'd hear
'glug, glug, glug!' And George said, 'Oh, go in, Cary, she's
drowning!' and Cary said, 'I won't, it's too cold!' Well, Kate
was laughing so hard she was bent double, and she nearly fell
over. So George finally said, 'Oh, *Christ!*' And he sent in Kate
instead, and *she* rescued Natalie. You should have heard
what Natalie said after that!"

Kate enjoyed every minute of making the picture, and the
presence of her co-stars: Brian Aherne, golden and silken as
a prize-winning retriever; Cary Grant, cocky, bouncing, na-

sally humorous; Edmund Gwenn, Pickwickian and apple-cheeked, with a wine taster's relish of his lines.

Kate was so convinced *Sylvia Scarlett* would be a hit she even broke her usual rule and went to the preview in Huntington Park. Neither Kate nor George Cukor will ever forget that night. The picture was far too sophisticated for the general public. Three-quarters of the audience walked out, and the rest started to yell, hiss, and boo. Feeling rather ill, Kate went to the ladies' room and saw a woman lying on the floor. "Was it really so bad?" Kate asked her. The woman didn't reply, but simply raised her eyes and rolled them about. Kate went back and dragged Cukor out of the theatre. As they got into his car, she hit her head on the door. "Thank God I've knocked myself out," she said. Cukor drove her to his house. Pan Berman had already arrived, and had been let in by the maid. Berman was bristling with rage. "You got me into this crap," he yelled. "That plot! And not one person in the audience understood a word of those English accents! You recorded the words with complete indifference as to whether the audience could understand them!" Kate said, "George and I have been discussing this on the way up, and we want you to know how terrible we feel, after you let us go ahead with this against your own wishes. We'll make it up to you; we want to do another picture for you free of charge." Berman sprang to his feet. "Oh, God! No!" he cried. "I never want to see either of you again!" And he stormed out.

The humiliation of *The Lake*, George Stevens' painstaking reduction of Kate's mannerisms in *Alice Adams*, and the collapse of *Sylvia Scarlett* all had the effect of knocking the stuffing out of Kate, making her more sympathetic, softer, mellower, and less the nervous sophomoric iconoclast of the early years. Although she had no more patience with Hollywood social life than she had had in the early 1930s, she was more and more dedicated to her work, more and more considerate of others, and increasingly aware of the importance of the director in a motion picture. Her friendships deepened, because as she reached her late twenties she could commit herself to them with a more mature concern.

George Cukor remained a close friend. His wit, sophistica-

tion, stabbing powers of observation, all proved to be a continuing source of fascination. She retained Leland Hayward
as her agent and adviser even after his marriage to the difficult and neurotic Margaret Sullavan, a fact which says much
for her self-discipline and loyalty. She deeply admired the
withdrawn, contemplative George Stevens; and on trips to
the East, aside from visits with her family, there was always
Laura Harding (who worked for Leland for a period) to fascinate, absorb, delight, and advise her. And Pan Berman remained a staunch supporter despite his threat never to work
with her again.

In 1936, Berman saw Maxwell Anderson's historical play,
Mary of Scotland, in New York, and bought it for Kate,
co-starring her with Fredric March as the Earl of Bothwell.
RKO dragged out its old press releases, indicating that Kate
was a direct descendant of Mary; the studio research department gathered material on sixteenth-century Scottish clothes,
furniture, and jewelry; Walter Plunkett designed an elaborate
wardrobe, and the sets were as authentic as possible. Unfortunately, everyone forgot the importance of the script,
which was a complicated, wordy bore; and the director, John
Ford, was totally inappropriate for a "woman's" picture.

Bell-ringer of the Irish Mafia, ill-tempered, coarse, rough,
he looked like a ditch digger. He had no understanding of the
need for sensitivity in directing Kate, and handled her as
though she were John Wayne. Kate and Pan Berman used to
fall over laughing as they imitated Ford's Irish-American
accent and habit of spitting tobacco chaws into brass spit-
toons. But she respected Ford's great talent and had fun
taking the mickey out of him. They became friends later on.

She said to him one day, "You never change your shirt, do
you?"

He sat grumpily chewing on a pipe and said, "Yeah. Ever'
day."

She skipped behind him and, while he wasn't noticing,
made a red pencil mark on the back of the sleeve of his dirty
blue denim shirt. Next day, she and Pan crept up behind him
and the mark was still there. And it was there every day until
the end of shooting. Finally, Kate asked Ford, "You said you
changed your shirt every day?"

"Sure did."

"Well, why is that red mark still there on your sleeve?" Kate and Pan almost rolled on the floor as Ford twisted around, trying to see the mark behind his elbow. When he saw it, he went purple, almost bit through the stem of his pipe, and sank deeper into his chair. From under his cap he said, "God damn it, you caught me. Well, I'll tell ya, I'm superstitious. It was the shirt I wore when I made *The Informer* a couple years ago. I thought if I wore it again, *Mary of Scotland* might be a hit."

Mary of Scotland flopped, and so did its successor, *A Woman Rebels,* a story of a suffragette of the 1870s so tedious that everyone connected with it would prefer to forget it. Kate had been drawn to the subject because she wanted to honor her mother's suffragette activities, but the indifferent production was a great disappointment to her. But she took pleasure in agreeing to make *Quality Street,* from the play by Sir James Barrie, for George Stevens in 1937.

Stevens, by contrast, did not enjoy the making of the picture, and he and Kate had many differences during the shooting. Pan Berman groans at any mention of the pretty, chocolate-box movie and says, "Why did we do it? Here we were in the middle of the Depression, and we were doing a story about Phoebe Throssel, whose beau, Dr. Valentine Brown, courts her during the Napoleonic Wars, but never gets around to proposing. Jesus Christ! There are breadlines, and people are supposed to care about a rich girl in crinolines, carrying a parasol, and tossing up between several handsome young men? Maybe we thought it was 'escapist fare' or some goddamned thing. Well, the only thing that escaped was our money—down the drain."

Stevens came on the picture in a bad temper. With his deeply withdrawn, sleepy watchfulness, expressive of his part Indian origins, he could suggest a thunderous oppressiveness, and the first days of shooting were very uncomfortable. Assistant director Eddie Killey remembers, "He would walk to the edge of the sound stage, sometimes behind the flats, and brood, alone, brushing all of us away." The reason Stevens was in such a vile mood was that he had wanted to

direct Maxwell Anderson's *Winterset* that summer, and Kate
had pulled him off it for her picture instead.

He began shooting in an "English" stretch of country near
Malibu Lake. Kate tried to make everyone comfortable by
having afternoon tea served, English style, from silver pots,
and the period costumes were lovely. But Stevens didn't like
the movie, and decided she was conferring with her friends
too frequently. He finally had to forbid them to come on the
set during the shooting, because they were creating a reluctance in Kate to play scenes in the manner he wanted. One
afternoon, Kate discovered the whole group was missing.
"Where's Jane [Loring] and the others?" she asked Stevens.
Stevens said, "I don't want your stooges advising you. If they
must advise you, let them advise you off the stage." Kate said,
"That's an order?" Stevens told her, "Well, I wouldn't put it
that way. But we'll work without them." Stevens later con-
fessed, "The gang didn't come in after that. Kate was confused by them: their advice was so diverse she didn't know
what she was doing. She accepted my ruling: she had a very
good head on her shoulders, but she picked out lightweights
to think with, and that was a mistake. She doesn't need a
lightweight, she needs someone 'heavier' than she is, someone who will question her judgments."

There can be no question that the collision between Stevens and Kate's people caused severe tension on the set. And
Stevens feels he still let Kate influence him too deeply. "She
even tripped *me* up, and I was her strongest adviser. I had
rushed into *Alice Adams* full tilt, and by the time I got to
Quality Street, I felt I had become a student again, *her* student, and I didn't know enough to override her. I don't think
I did her any good. She became precious, and preciousness
was always her weakness; I should have helped her away
from that, and I wasn't strong enough. *Quality Street* was a
precious play, anyway, full of precious people, and that infected her; I myself didn't have sufficient familiarity with the
British background to save her. I was thinking about *Winterset*, all through the shooting—my bitter disappointment at
not making what could have been my best picture—and that
affected me too. That's it, in sum: I gave in to her, and the
film was bad, and it's all my fault."

With *Quality Street* a depressing failure, her mannered playing justly criticized, and her friendship with George Stevens severely strained, Kate was as relieved as everyone else at RKO when she announced she would make no more pictures for a time, and would return East to make a stage appearance for the Theatre Guild. This was the beginning of a recurrent association with the Guild, which was to prove most satisfying in the years to come, and the fathering of three great friendships: with the explosive Lawrence Langner, director and co-founder of the Guild; his fellow director, acutely intelligent Theresa Helburn; and Langner's wife, Armina Marshall, a warmhearted, shrewdly sophisticated woman who was to become, with Laura Harding, Kate's closest friend in the East.

Each of these people intrigued Kate enormously: Langner, with his swarthy Levantine face; Armina, sensitive and delicate, but with an impression of refined strength; Terry Helburn, short, stocky, mannish.

Theresa Helburn conceived the idea of starring Kate in a new adaptation of Charlotte Brontë's *Jane Eyre*, written by Helen Jerome, who had recently done a successful version of *Pride and Prejudice*, with Worthington ("Tony") Miner directing. The original plan of the Guild's board was to engage Laurence Olivier to play the role of Edward Rochester. Olivier was not available because of commitments in England, and Kate and Theresa Helburn were unable to find anyone else who could measure up to the part.

Several important stage actors were terrified of appearing with Kate, because they felt they would be overshadowed by her; others feared involvement with disaster after the collapse of *The Lake* and several of Kate's pictures; and a smaller number were unavailable. Finally, the Guild was forced to select a non-star, a character actor, Dennis Hoey, who was not equal to the demands of his role.

A further difficulty emerged at the outset. Kate and everyone else agreed that the third act of the play was quite hopeless. But Mrs. Jerome refused bluntly to change a single line. An early tryout in Boston proved a failure. Kate agreed the show was not yet good enough to open in New York, and instead settled on doing a tour. After a series of last-ditch efforts to make the author improve her work, Langner ordered the company to Chicago.

Kate and her fellow players flew there through a severe snowstorm that tossed the plane around violently. Howard Hughes followed the tour persistently by private plane, and attended some of her performances, with the result that Kate was again forced to dodge reporters, leaving cars several blocks before they reached her destination and darting around behind buildings, using freight or servants' elevators, putting "Do not disturb" notices on all of her doors. The notoriety packed houses in Chicago, Cleveland, and Pittsburgh, with the result that costs were fully covered through very limited subscription engagements. Impressed that a major star would come to their city, the Midwestern critics gave the play much warmer reviews than the Boston critics had done.

But when it became clear that Helen Jerome still would not answer Kate's pleas for changes, Kate decided finally not to take the show to Broadway. Aside from the weak third act, she was still not satisfied with Dennis Hoey as her leading man, and, with her characteristic sensitivity and selflessness, declined the idea of replacing him.

"It's all very sad," Tony Miner says today. "Kate's interpretation of Jane Eyre was fascinating. She played the role with a quiet wit, a delicate charm and sense of gaiety and exuberance. Joan Fontaine, in the film, showed the governess as mousy, beaten, shy, yet bold. Kate played the part with spirit, she *confronted* it, and she dealt with Rochester, her employer, with a certain sharp intelligence. It was the very best portrayal of the role I have seen, on stage or screen. But we had to deprive New York of the chance of seeing it."

Back in Hollywood in the winter of 1937, Kate began to take stock of her at that point miserable career. She was living at the time in a huge old mansion once owned by the silent-film director Fred Niblo. Alone, she brooded on the failure of most of her films to reach a mass audience. She felt guilty that Pan Berman continued to lose his shirt out of loyalty to her, and suffered a stabbing sense of despair that

her stage career had gone down the drain. Her associates—
her film editor and confidante Jane Loring, her dresser-secre-
tary Emily Perkins, her stand-in Eve March, Eddie Killey,
Mort Offner, and Howard Hughes—were all very supportive.
But she was uncertain what the future would be, characteristically concealing her fear behind a mask of bravado.

It was therefore with a great sense of relief that she received from Pan Berman a scintillating script, written by
Morrie Ryskind and Anthony Veiller, based on the play *Stage
Door*, by Edna Ferber and George S. Kaufman. Working
with Berman, the director Gregory La Cava, and the writers,
Kate spent the winter making subtle changes in the play
which served to improve her pivotal role of Terry Randall.

Terry Randall was as similar to her own personality as Eva
Lovelace in *Morning Glory* had been: strong, forthright, a
devotee of Shakespeare in the slangy, gum-chewing world of
a theatrical lodging house in New York. Like Kate, Terry is
an heiress, whose father has an ambiguous attitude toward
her career in the theatre; like her, Terry is enormously protective and considerate of underdogs, while seeming to be
harsh and proud; also similarly, she plays for an irascible
producer (based on Jed Harris) in a show resembling *The
Lake* and learns how to act scenes with true, piercing emotion instead of empty posturing.

Kate admired Gregory La Cava, whom she had met briefly
when the plans for *Three Came Unarmed* were afoot. He was
a remarkable polar bear of a man. With his steely grey hair,
dark, compelling eyes, face alive with animation, and powerful figure, he exuded energy and vitality. His mind was constantly inventive and sharp. Kate found every day on the set
fresh and stimulating because of him. Pan Berman says,
"Greg was one of the most talented men I've ever known,
and he worked effectively with Kate. He was an alcoholic
bum—he had almost been driven out of the industry because
of his drinking—but he had been brilliantly talented from
the beginning. He'd started out as a great cartoonist. He was
a hell of a fine director of screen *characters*. His technique
was odd: he never saw movies—didn't know one actor from
another. When I said, 'I'd like you to make a picture with
Katharine Hepburn,' he replied, 'Who's she? I never heard

of her.' But when he met her, he analyzed her at once, and came to her completely clear, without the faintest idea of what she had done. He saw her eagerness, awkwardness, enthusiasm, grace, and purity of spirit. Every word of dialogue he wrote for her was based on her own odd, exaggerated speech patterns. It was daring, completely original writing. He amazed me, and I gave him complete freedom. I went through a terrible ordeal on the picture, not knowing where we were going, what we were doing tomorrow, how the script would turn out. The picture aged me a hundred years every day we worked. Every single person on our boards here and in New York wanted me to fire Greg. It was pure hell! Greg got drunk all through the picture—he fell off the podium of the Biltmore Theatre in downtown Los Angeles while we were shooting a scene. Into the orchestra pit! But we dried him out, and he went on. And when he was sober, he never put a wrong foot forward." Kate, by this stage, had mellowed considerably in her attitude to drinking. She understood the acute sensitivity to daily experience which made creative people sometimes turn to the bottle, and she was extremely supportive of La Cava when studio executives threatened to remove him from the picture.

Andrea Leeds, who memorably played a tragic, defeated actress in the film, says, "Gregory La Cava had all of us girls in the movie come to the studio for two weeks before the shooting started and live as though we were in the lodging house itself. He had a script girl take down our conversations and he would adapt these into dialogue. He rewrote scenes from day to day to get the feeling of a bunch of girls together —as spontaneous as possible. He would talk to each of us like a lifelong friend. That gave us a feeling of intimacy. I remember he found out I was part Italian, and he was Italian, so he'd talk to me about spaghetti, pizza, and lasagna."

Kate was inspired by La Cava's improvisations, his ability to show the girls interrupting each other, in overlapping dialogue, which was used by Orson Welles later in *Citizen Kane,* and she stood on the sidelines watching all the scenes in which she did not appear. "At the end of a sequence, she would applaud loudly and cry out 'Beautiful!'" Andrea Leeds says. "It was a marvelous encouragement to all of us."

Another great blessing of *Stage Door* was that it introduced Kate to Constance Collier, who played a wonderful old actress in the picture, hard up but still proud. With her gypsyish black hair and dark eyes, heavy figure, and delicious, extravagant humor, Constance fascinated Kate, and her adoration is visible in their many scenes together in the picture itself. They were soon fast friends, and Constance came to occupy the role of those other inspired women in Kate's earlier life: Frances Robinson-Duff and Susanne Steele. She became mentor and mother, as well as drama coach and strong shoulder to lean on. A now softer, more tender and considerate Kate learned to draw from Constance Collier's vast experience of the British and American stage, giving her in return a sense of understanding of her worth that was not easily found in Hollywood.

Stage Door was an immediate success at the preview. The audience had never seen a picture like this before, in which characters interrupted each other, talked in non-theatrical, richly idiomatic speech, and in which a host of new players, edgy and funny, gave the very taste of New York theatrical life. Kate's Terry Randall was adored by critics and public alike: from the first entrance in dark costume and hat, a single austere figure in the confused babble of the Footlights Club, through the scenes in which her tenderness, consideration, and love of others break through her apparently gruff, aggressive, overbearing manner, Terry Randall *was* Kate. With great intelligence, La Cava showed Terry-Kate as being something of a shock to the other club members at first—they had never heard anybody quote Shakespeare before; it's as if Katharine Cornell had strayed into a chorus line—but gradually disclosing to these tough, slangy girls the purity and decency of her character, and the fact that she belonged among them. The scenes with the Jed Harris-like producer, deftly played by Adolphe Menjou, the rehearsals and first night of the *Lake*-like *Enchanted April*—these convey Kate's flaws commented on by Harris, and her emergence as the mature actress of *Alice Adams* and *Stage Door* itself. Stiff and mannered at rehearsal, she was shown emerging as sensitive, heartbreaking, completely open and free in

KATE   83

the playing of the show itself. It was a metaphor of her own
career that few critics noted at the time.

When Kate saw the finished picture—informal, full of life,
evoking the overcrowded, stifling, yet stimulating life of the
Footlights Club lodging house—she cried with happiness.
The film furthered the career of Ginger Rogers as Kate's
slangy, hard-bitten roommate and presented a whole group
of youngsters—Ann Miller, Eve Arden, and Lucille Ball,
among them—who were destined for major success. It was a
smash hit, Kate's first for many years, and it was a lifelong
disappointment that she never got a chance to work with La
Cava again.

After the depressing mid-1930s, Kate again felt optimistic,
and at last Pan Berman could face his board without the
painful embarrassment of trying to explain why he kept her
on the payroll. Pan had his writers cast about for another part
which would fit Kate perfectly, preferably a comedy this
time. A studio writer, Hagar Wilde, came up with a story
called *Bringing Up Baby*, about a zany Connecticut heiress,
Susan Vance, who falls in love with a shy paleontologist, and
a leopard called Baby, which causes them both some highly
amusing problems. Howard Hawks was hired to produce and
direct. He and Kate liked each other at once. Hawks, with his
narrow hatchet-blade face and hard, brown body, was resil-
ient, forceful, and overbearing in a quiet way: just what she
liked in a man. She also adored working again with Cary
Grant.

Hawks says, "I approached Cary to do the role of the paleontologist. 'I won't know how to do a thing like that,' Cary
told me. 'I wouldn't know how to tackle it. I'm not an intellectual type.' And I said, 'You've seen Harold Lloyd, haven't
you?' He nodded. That gave him a clue—the innocent
abroad. Katie was by contrast fascinated with her part. She
had not been trained in comedy at all, but she wanted to play
comedy.

"I felt she was like Carole Lombard: she might run around
like a tomboy, but she had beauty and the ability to wear
clothes and to look like a lady. The part in *Bringing Up Baby*
was her; she *was* a Connecticut heiress, she *was* full of opin-

ions, she *was* inventive and certain about everything. Lombard played herself—dizzy and quite touching—for me in *Twentieth Century* opposite John Barrymore, and now Katie was doing the same.

"We had a little trouble when starting the picture, because Katie rather thought she had to be 'funny.' She kept laughing, and she took the comic situations *too* comically. I tried to explain to her that the great clowns, Keaton, Chaplin, Lloyd, simply weren't out there making funny faces, they were serious, sad, solemn, and the humor sprang from what happened to them. They'd do funny things in a completely quiet, somber, deadpan way. Cary understood this at once. Katie didn't.

"So I thought, 'What shall I do?' Well, I had a marvelous comic under contract called Walter Catlett—I showed him the rushes, and I said, 'She's not handling it right, is she?' He said, 'No. She's being too obviously funny.' I asked him if he would work with her, and he refused. I said, 'What if she asks you to?' He replied, 'That's different.' I told her, 'There's a fellow here who can show you some things; would you like to be shown?' She responded immediately, 'I'd like to be shown.'

"Walter played a whole scene of hers out with Cary Grant, played it with every mannerism of hers, *very serious*, and she was entranced. She said, 'You have to create a part for him in the picture.' And I did. After that, she played perfectly—not trying to be funny, but being very, very natural and *herself*. All of her grimaces of disappointment and shock were greatly amusing to the audience. Katie kept everything deadly serious throughout. People laughed—*God* how they laughed!

"Once she got the hang of the role, she was wonderful to work with—she had the poise of a good fighter. When she turns, she's 'in balance,' she could knock you out if she wanted to. I'd play golf with her at weekends in the middle of shooting, and she had a lovely stroke. She was a fine tennis player, and she had a tennis player's timing in comedy. That marvelous coordination! As for her famous ability to 'direct,' I encouraged her to talk things over, as long as it wound up my way!

"I remember one very amusing incident. Katie was so full of life she was talking and talking and *talking*. The assistant director called me about something, and she went on talking right over him. He called 'Quiet on the set,' and she still went on. I told my assistant to tell everyone to sit down and just look at her. Finally she realized everyone was just looking at her, waiting for her to stop. She said, 'What are we waiting for?' I said, 'I was just wondering when the parrot was going to stop talking!' She said, 'I want to have a word with you.' Then she beckoned me to come behind the set. She said, 'Howard, these people are friends of mine, and if you say things like that to me, you're liable to get yourself into trouble.' I glanced up, and there was an electrician in the flies above us with a big lamp. I called up to him, 'Eddie, if you had a choice of dropping that lamp on Miss Hepburn or me, which would you choose?' And he called back, 'Step aside, Mr. Hawks!'"

Making the picture was completely informal. Fritz Feld, who played a comic psychiatrist in the picture, says, "Life in Hollywood in those days was wonderful. Often in the morning Howard Hawks would come in and say, 'It's a nice day today. Let's go to the races.' And we'd pack up and *go* to the races. Kate continued her custom of serving tea on the set. We all laughed and laughed, and were very happy. I remember Kate and I played a scene in which I begin by analyzing her and she ends up analyzing me. Just as Kate would in real life. We clicked together wonderfully, and lo and behold, at the end of shooting the scene, at five o'clock, two cases of champagne arrived. Howard Hawks gave us the cases. Those were the good old days!

"I remember a fantastic incident involving Nissa, the leopard which played Baby. In those days, the camera was in a huge booth on rollers, which had to be moved by ten or fifteen stagehands, with long cables trailing everywhere. I walked on the set one morning and opened the door of the booth! Someone inside yelled, 'Don't open the door! Stand still, don't move!' I obeyed, and suddenly the leopard—it was wild, never really tame—came padding and growling past me. I was *frozen!* And I suddenly realized that everybody on the stage—Kate, Cary Grant, Hawks, the entire crew—was inside the booth! I was the only one on the stage! And later on Hawks said to me, 'We have orders around here. Any time the beast escapes, get into the booth!' "

During the picture, Hawks was astonished by Kate's gift for improvisation. "In one scene, she broke the heel of a shoe. She was right on camera, and without fluffing a line, she said, as she limped, 'I was born on the side of a hill!' She and Cary were unbelievably quick.

"As for the leopard, when I said 'Cut!' Katie would whirl around, her skirts spinning wide, relieved at the break in the scene. And the leopard would paw rather violently at her skirt: the skirt frightened it. I had to tell Katie not to spin so fast. Leopards know if you are afraid of them. But Cary wasn't afraid of Nissa, and emphatically Kate was not, either! If anything, Nissa was afraid of her!"

Nissa's trainer, Mme. Olga Celeste, said later, "In Miss Hepburn's first scene with Nissa, the actress was required to pat the leopard's head, push her off a divan, and shove her in another room. Miss Hepburn, to my surprise, showed no reluctance at working with the leopard. She was amused when I insisted that she douse herself with perfume, which always makes Nissa playful and even-tempered, and put resin on the soles of her shoes. When I explained that I always resined my own shoes before working, lest my feet slip and frighten Nissa into doing something drastic, she did likewise. I think if Miss Hepburn should ever leave the screen she would make a very good animal trainer."

I spoke to Cary Grant about Kate at Universal in 1965, and he said, "Working with her was incredible. You never saw such timing! She had a mind like a computer—every detail worked out! Yet computers don't have instincts, and her instincts were infallible. She taught me just about everything I know about comedy—how to time my lines, the solemn way to say something comic, and if there was anything she didn't know, which I doubt, then Howard Hawks could fill in the rest."

The character of the Connecticut heiress Susan Vance was as perfectly tailored for Kate as Terry Randall in *Stage Door* had been. It brought out the comic side of her personality, which no other part had entirely done: her sense of the ridiculous gave a strong reality to Susan, with her rat-tat-tat delivery of suggestions, orders, cajoleries, madcap schemes, her determination melting into affection; and Cary Grant, Harold Lloydish in scholarly horn-rims, an overgrown schoolboy adrift in an ocean of Hepburn mannerisms, was very funny, too. Hawks taught both actors the delicious fun to be obtained by seeming to be the only serious, sane people in a world gone mad, and Kate and Cary responded with all of their formidable talent. The result was a masterpiece of thirties comedy: man, woman, leopard, they were, from the very moment of their confrontation, part of American screen legend.

Bringing Up Baby, hard and glittering, received excellent notices. But it proved too sophisticated for the mass audience, and it barely met its costs outside the big cities. Harry Brandt, president of the Independent Theatre Owners of America, was provoked by the film's near failure to announce publicly that Kate was "box-office poison," along with Marlene Dietrich, Garbo, Kay Francis, Joan Crawford, and other stars. Kate's comment was, "They say I'm a has-been. If I weren't laughing so much, I might cry."

She decided to get out of RKO for good, and not even Pan Berman felt like arguing with her. When the studio contemptuously offered her a role in a B picture called *Mother Carey's Chickens*, she bought up her contract for $200,000. She never worked for RKO again.

Fighting depression, Kate accepted an offer from Columbia to appear in Philip Barry's *Holiday* for George Cukor, opposite Cary Grant and Lew Ayres. Cukor strove to reduce the "singing" quality of Barry's lines and directed Kate with all the watchmaker's care he had devoted to her in *A Bill of Divorcement*. It was a very happy picture, made without incident, and Kate even liked the gruff, mad bulldog Columbia boss Harry Cohn.

When *Holiday* was finished, George Cukor threw a traditional end-of-shooting party. Kate says, "I stole the old *Holiday* test from RKO and ran it for the guests. I laughed when I saw myself. I *led* the laughter, and everyone just fell over

—Cary, George, *everyone*, laughed themselves *sick*. I was so terrible! It was heartbreaking to see how eager, how hard I was trying to impress—too eager. I turned to George and said, 'Oh God, why did you hire me?' "

Kate's performance in *Holiday* was among her most famous of the period. She played Linda, an unhappy sibling of a Park Avenue family, who clings to her nursery, yearns for her dead mother, and feels a kinship with a would-be dropout (Cary Grant), the fiancé of her conventional sister; she wins him at the end. It is easy to see what had attracted her to the role, first when she played as understudy in the stage version, later when she acted a scene in her first screen test, and finally on the screen. Linda is a rebel against convention: she believes that her prospective husband should throw up his job and exist freely, taking a long holiday from life, and living on her money if necessary. She constantly fights her father's manic concern with dollars; she aims to live simply, quietly, without ostentation; and she refuses to seduce the man she wants, preferring to wait until he sees her true qualities. Kate played the role with a golfer's attack, suggesting a combination of the lacquered society girl and the liberated woman, indicating how the freethinking of her future lover changes her attitude from a conventional concern with income and position to a realization that life holds more than the American ideals of work, gain, and competition. Cukor glamorized her, making her face shine with the glow appropriate to a major star; her hair was faultlessly groomed, her powerful stride de-emphasized. Only her voice—too harsh and strident for the role she was playing—was not sufficiently attractive, and, unlike George Stevens, Cukor could not quite make her soft and yielding.

The film was released virtually in defiance of the Independent Theatre Owners' attack on Kate, a fact which confirmed her admiration of Harry Cohn. In order to forestall widespread ill-feeling among the exhibitors, Columbia devised a slogan for all billboards that read, "Is it true what they say about Hepburn—that she's Box Office Poison?" Unfortunately, the plan backfired in Hollywood, where a roller derby was about to open. The roller derby's backers were determined to affect all film attendances and sent men around to write on all the posters for *Holiday*, replying to the question with the words, "Wes Anderson [star of the derby] thinks it's true." Columbia tried to stop the defacement by legal process, but were told by their attorneys, "It's only an opinion —and by a non-expert." The squib affected attendance in Los Angeles.

During the late 1930s, Kate became obsessed with the idea of playing Scarlett O'Hara in Margaret Mitchell's *Gone with the Wind*. In 1936, Lillie Messenger, the RKO talent scout who had directed her in her test, had fallen in love with the manuscript of the novel, sent her by the author's agent, Annie Laurie Williams, and had drawn it to Kate's attention during one of Kate's periodic visits to New York. Lillie Messenger says, "I gave Kate the book to read, and she adored it just as much as I did; she felt she'd be perfect for Scarlett O'Hara. At that time, the studio, following her resignation, was trying to renegotiate a contract for her; she said she would not return to the studio unless she could do *Gone with the Wind*.

"We had a new boss at RKO, a Mr. Spitz, who did not show any interest in the novel. Mr. Spitz called me into his office in New York and asked me, 'How did Katharine Hepburn happen to get hold of the book?' I told him, 'I gave it to her.' He said, rather rudely, 'Did you think this was part of your job?' I had to admit, 'I guess not, but I thought it wonderful, and she should do it.' 'You had no business to do that,' Spitz told me. 'She won't come back to us unless she can play Scarlett. We don't want to do it. So you're responsible for our losing our most important star.' I went home and cried and *cried!* I thought the world had come to an end."

Soon after, Annie Laurie Williams succeeded in selling the book to David O. Selznick. When Selznick bought the book, he resolutely refused to offer Kate the part of Scarlett, despite the pleas of George Cukor, who was going to direct. "She has no sex appeal," Selznick said. Finally, Kate stormed into Selznick's office and demanded to know why she had been refused the role. "Because, my dear, I can't see Rhett Butler chasing you for twelve years," he said. "Well, David," she snapped back, "some people's idea of sex appeal is different from yours."

Despite everything, Kate believed she would eventually play Scarlett. She returned to Fenwick after *Holiday* finished shooting, spending the late summer and early fall of 1938 swimming, resting, enjoying the sun, wind, and water. A hurricane swept along the coast, damaging Fenwick considerably. Kate worked heroically to shore up the collapsing walls. But the remainder of Fenwick had to be pulled down, and was replaced with a new and more elaborate structure.

Shortly before the hurricane, Kate was sitting with her family on the verandah of Fenwick, arguing about politics and eating cinnamon toast, when Philip Barry dropped by unannounced. He walked up to her and said, in front of everyone, "I want to talk to you." "Righto," Kate said. "Let's go on the pier and talk about it." They walked off in the stiff Atlantic breeze.

Phil Barry had become a warm acquaintance over the years. Fastidiously groomed, polished to a fault, he was the nonpareil of dramatists of the rich. Well-to-do himself, his clothes handmade by the finest tailors, he exuded a sense of opulent well-being and confidence. He fascinated Kate, who always felt at home only in slacks and windbreakers. They made an odd pair as they walked along the pier above the blue-grey Atlantic: he, impeccably dressed in a dark suit and tie; she, in an odd jumble of what looked like castoffs, her red hair in its casual topknot straggling in the wind, her wide slacks whipped tight against her slender legs.

As they strolled to the end of the pier, Barry told her in his Brooks Brothers voice that he had begun to work on two plays for her. The first was a rigmarole which instantly annoyed her, and she dismissed it from her mind. But the second sounded attractive: the story of an heiress, Tracy Lord, living in Hepburn-Barry territory, who hates publicity and is descended upon by a *Life*-style writer-photographer team. In many ways, the part *was* Kate, reflecting all her horror of the press, and she warmed to it at once. But there was a stumbling block to her encouraging Barry firmly. "I'd be quite interested in playing Tracy Lord," she said, "provided I don't play Scarlett O'Hara first!"

A few days later, Philip Barry started work on the play, entitled *The Philadelphia Story*, excited by Kate's interest in the material and determined to shape the role of Tracy Lord to suit her personality. When Kate learned that Vivien Leigh had won the role of Scarlett, she was devastated; but now she gave all her attention to Barry's idea, constantly telephoning him at his rented home on an island off the coast of Maine, beseeching him to hurry with the work. She also told Howard Hughes about it, and he promised, if the play was good, to buy the movie rights.

At last, Barry completed the first act and sent it to Kate by special messenger. She read it at once and was very enthusiastic. But the second act, which arrived a few days later, seemed much weaker: the characters didn't really develop, there was a sagging of the construction, and far too much complication surrounding the uneasy relationship of the reporters with the wealthy people of the Philadelphia Main Line.

Characteristically, Kate flew up to Maine in her private plane to talk the problems over, and then returned to Fenwick, leaving Barry convinced she was wrong. He brooded over her ideas, and realized one morning not long after that she was right. He sent her a revised second act. Kate called and said, "It's not quite good enough, but I'm taking it to the Theatre Guild." Barry told her, "No! I don't deal with the Guild now, they made a mess of my play *Hotel Universe!*"*

Kate insisted that the Guild must do the production; she owed it to Langner and Helburn for having closed *Jane Eyre* at her request out of town. Reluctantly, Barry agreed, and Kate drove at once to New York, taking the play with her. She presented it to Langner and Helburn, saying, "It's perfectly fascinating." They agreed, but pointed out that the Guild had little or no money to put the play on. So Kate and Howard Hughes shared in providing half the financial backing.

*This is Kate's version. Mrs. Philip Barry insists that her husband suggested the Guild, and wrote the play for the Langners.

Kate suggested casting: she wanted Joseph Cotten to play C. K. Dexter-Haven, Tracy Lord's heavy-drinking ex-husband, because she had admired him enormously in an Orson Welles production of *Horse Eats Hat*. She wanted Dan Tobin, just back from London, for the role of Tracy's brother, and Shirley Booth as the reporter Elizabeth Imbrie. Kate, Philip Barry, the director Robert Sinclair, Terry Helburn, and Lawrence Langner would sit around the Guild offices, talking to each new arrival who was called in for a reading.

It was Kate's job to sit next to them on the big leather couch and make them feel at ease with a joke or a reference to mutual friends. Very often, an actor or actress was signed up as soon as he had read a few lines; nobody present liked long readings; they could see quality immediately. A typical little scene took place when Dan Tobin walked in to read for the role of the brother. Kate, in slacks, relaxed him on the couch, and Philip Barry came over and looked at him quizzically. "Anderson Sheppard?" he asked. "Yes!" Tobin replied with astonishment. Barry had, with one glance, recognized the tailor of Tobin's very expensive suit.

The moment the company was formed it resembled a club. Sometimes, on previous occasions, Hepburn had stayed a little aloof from the rest of the cast. But she knew at the outset that the play depended on an intense rapport with every actor in it, and she mingled enthusiastically with her fellow players. Even the elusive Maurice Wertheim, one of the major financiers of the Guild, was frequently seen at rehearsals. The changes by Barry during rehearsal, most of them suggested by Kate herself, had hugely strengthened a still straggling and overly expository second act. The third act still needed a great deal of work.

By meticulous observation, Barry had drawn the character of Tracy Lord as close as possible to Kate's own. He brought out all of the elements: the humor, the dash, the aggression, the nervousness, the constant flow of speech, and the quality of vulnerability, fear, sensitivity that showed Tracy to be a true woman. The idea of confronting this family-obsessed, deeply private, ultra-snobbish Philadelphian with a team of reporters was a bright one, crystallizing Kate's whole life up

to that time. She had, after all, even been married to a Philadelphia Main Line husband. It was a part which fitted her
like a chrysalis, releasing her for a witty butterfly actress's
flight.

Just before and during the run of *The Philadelphia Story*,
Kate was faced with two vexing dramas at home. On January
17, 1939, she was sitting and reading in her living room at
244 East Forty-ninth Street when she was shocked to see
smoke pouring from the fireplace, accompanied by a shower
of sparks. She telephoned an alarm, and helped firemen put
out a small chimney fire, meanwhile enduring the ordeal of
having practically every occupant of Turtle Bay turn out to
see the fun.

Shortly after 7 P.M. on June 9, Kate was taking a nap before driving to the theatre for the evening performance of the
play. She woke up with a start to see a man standing near her
dressing table, fingering a $5,000 pearl necklace given her by
Howard Hughes. "What are you doing here?" she yelled. The
man ran to the door. Pulling her dressing gown around her,
Kate ran after him. She grabbed hold of him, and kept shouting loudly as he raced down the stairs. Kate's chauffeur-
major domo Charles Newhill and the cook ran out and
chased the intruder, but Kate had already pursued him into
the street, where he leaped into a waiting car—without the
necklace.

Rewritten over and over again during rehearsal, often with
sharp words between Kate and Barry, but more often with
affection and tenderness and concern, *The Philadelphia
Story* opened in New Haven in February, 1939. Kate had
seen the third act—in which Tracy discovers that she is attracted to the reporter sent to interview her—as very serious
and moving. Kate says, "I was horrified during the third act
when I heard the audience screaming with laughter—it
threw me so much I almost went up on my lines. They
laughed and laughed as I grew more and more solemn, and
crying and crying, and I was fuming inside. I flew off in a
much faster exit than Phil called for, hissing at everyone
backstage, 'They hate it! They hate it!' But everyone back-

stage was ready to hug me, and some of them did. 'No,' my director, Bob Sinclair, said, 'they *loved* it!' "

As it happened, the play almost failed to make it to Broadway. Barry saw it in New Haven and was horrified at the stiff, mannered playing of Kate, Cotten, Dan Tobin, and the rest of the cast. He stamped into a rehearsal the next afternoon and yelled abuse at everyone. Kate yelled back, telling him he had no business to interfere. By the time the play was ready to open in New York, Kate was convinced she had committed herself to a failure, that the play wasn't good enough for a Broadway audience. She begged Langner and Helburn to withdraw it after the Washington opening, but they refused. Barry wrote and rewrote—and rewrote again. Kate was so terrified she didn't go to her home in Turtle Bay when she reached New York. She could not face the distraction of domestic problems. Instead, she took a suite at the Waldorf. She refused to see anyone, cut off the phone, and ate almost nothing. According to Dan Tobin, when she slipped through a side door into the Shubert Theatre to avoid the fans at rehearsal, she said nothing to anyone, except that she would not make an "entrance": if she did, she would be petrified. Tobin says, "The curtain would have to be raised to 'discover' her arranging flowers. She knew that if she received the normal amount of applause, she would be completely lost, so she had the first line of dialogue follow her appearance immediately."

Kate was frozen with stage fright before the curtain went up. To try and forget this was New York, where she had not appeared for several years, she kept repeating to herself, "This isn't New York. It's Indianapolis." She was still muttering "This is Indianapolis" when the curtain went up and she began arranging the flowers in a strange echo of her appearance in *Stage Door*'s play-within-a-film. But as soon as she uttered Barry's first lines, she was totally at ease. All of the stiffness which had horrified Philip Barry at rehearsal vanished, and the audience "picked her up" immediately, responding to her vibrancy and charm. Many lines earned rounds of applause. The rest of the cast, relieved to find Kate was no longer nervous, acted with relaxation and a strong sense of comedy. The final-act curtain was followed by a tremendous ovation, and the critics were ecstatic. Brooks Atkinson of the New York *Times,* who had never been impressed by Kate in the past, said of her performance: "A strange, tense little lady with austere beauty and metallic voice, she has consistently found it difficult to project a part in the theatre. But now she has surrendered to the central role in Mr. Barry's play and she acts it like a woman who has at last found the joy she has always been seeking in the theatre . . . there are no ambiguous corners in this character portrayal. Dainty in style, it is free and alive in its daring expression of feeling."

During the run of the play, Kate began to have a serious problem with her voice. It tended to go up very high, into a shrill scream, when she became excited, and she had to have special training to control it. A friend, the composer Kurt Weill, suggested she take special lessons from the distinguished coach Dr. Isaac Van Grove. Dr. Van Grove remembers Kate clearly: "She called me up when I was on tour with Grace Moore. I agreed to help when I came back to New York. At eleven o'clock one morning, I went over to her house in Turtle Bay. Her chauffeur-houseman, Charles Newhill, opened the door and took me up to the third floor. She had a charming music room there, with a piano. I was surprised. She came in, wearing slacks, looking quite fresh and wonderful, and told me the nice things Kurt Weill had said about me. Van Heflin was there—he was there all the time we worked together—and I got the impression he was fascinated by her, as well as wanting to learn something about voice training himself.

"I knew the moment I talked to her that her voice was forced. In the first instance, Frances Robinson-Duff had spoiled her voice by making it too affected. Then all those shouting arguments at her parents, brothers, and sisters had strained her vocal cords terribly. She had developed a bad 'jump' in the voice—it leaped up without warning. I told her this, and she asked me rather gruffly what I could do. I told her she would have to learn control through singing! She hadn't sung a note except in a picture called *The Little Minister,* and she was timid—more than timid; she was *terrified!* I had her sing Jerome Kern songs at the piano, while I played.

She had a small, sweet voice, and, incredibly, she had memo-
rized all the lyrics instinctively. I got her on pitch, she solved
her problem, and after several weeks she wasn't going 'up'
any more."

Dr. Van Grove's teaching later stood Kate in good stead
when she played the leading role in *Coco*.

It was during this period that Kate had a unique experience. She was invited to lunch at President Roosevelt's home
at Hyde Park, near the Hudson River. Typically, she decided
to have a friend fly her up. The plane landed on the bank of
the Hudson. She trudged up the hill through mud toward the
estate. A guard stopped her, saying, "You can't go in there.
It belongs to the President." "I've been invited to lunch. My
name is Katharine Hepburn," she replied confidently, and
the guard let her through. She spotted a stream, took off her
shoes, and washed her feet clean of the river mud. Farther
up the path, Roosevelt passed her driving in his car. "How
on earth did you get here?" he asked. As he drove her to his
front door, he laughed heartily as she recounted her exploits.

Kate's fellow players, Don Tobin and Joseph Cotten, both
recall that Kate, with a part which was in fact herself, played
with a radiant spontaneity which infected the whole company. The show was a smash hit, and ran for 415 performances, grossing almost a million dollars; the tour which
followed ran 254 performances and grossed $753,538. In
effect, the play saved the Theatre Guild from ruin, and, since
Kate owned a quarter of the production, it made her a very
rich woman.

Six

Following the New York run of *The Philadelphia Story*, Kate felt an overwhelming urge to make it into a film. As owner of the screen rights, Howard Hughes approached studio heads in Hollywood, but all except one refused to take Kate on. Her box-office record, combined with rumors of her imperiousness, and the terror male stars had of being outclassed by her, served to alarm everyone except Louis B. Mayer, head of MGM, who had always been a fan of Kate's, and to whom Hughes managed to sell Kate and the play as a package with the condition attached that she should appear with "two important male stars."

Unfortunately, the "important male stars" who were approached coldly refused to work with Kate, and she was asked to accept two men who were still not in the front rank: James Stewart and Cary Grant. She accepted both with immense enthusiasm. Stewart was a favorite of hers, and she longed to work with Cary Grant again. George Cukor, now under contract to Metro, was the only possible choice as director. Kate's old friend Donald Ogden Stewart wrote a subtly accurate version of Barry, adding two short scenes on the advice of the producer, Joseph L. Mankiewicz, amalgamating two of the characters: Tracy Lord's ex-husband and brother.

Kate supervised a contest of cameramen, in which each of the various MGM cinematographers would be asked to supply a test of her, and she would choose the best. She settled on Joseph Ruttenberg, because he stopped smoking a cigar at her behest and changed to a pipe—she detested the smell of cigars—and because he lit her from above so that a shadow fell over her neck. She had frequently been sensitive about a persistent problem in making movies—what she felt to be her long, prematurely lined, and ugly "gobbler" neck—and this was to become a more serious concern with the onset of age. Ruttenberg disguised the problem, even improvising a special light on a flexible stick with which he walked after her, thus upsetting the union, which forbade cinematographers to do an assistant's, or camera operator's, job.

Filming through July, 1940, was an enjoyable experience for everyone. With his imitation corn-pone drawl, "Stringbean" James Stewart was in particularly good form, running around between scenes with a flowerpot on his head, imitating Carmen Miranda, and making Kate break up with his funny Hollywood stories. Cukor bawled Kate out in the nicest possible way. And she returned to the happy, practical-joking mood of the good old days at RKO.

Joe Ruttenberg remembers, "She used to rush onto the set like a cool breeze on a hot summer night. And many of those nights in the hot summer of 1940 were sweltering. She enjoyed Cary Grant's pushing her through the doorway in one scene so much she had him do it over and over again. She also threw Cary so enthusiastically out the door, bag and baggage, at one moment that he became quite badly bruised. 'That'll serve you right Cary, for trying to be your own stunt man,' she quipped.

"George Cukor always liked a quiet set," Ruttenberg continued. "One morning, he'd become very excited. There was an awful lot of noise, and everyone was chattering, hammering, sawing—it was deafening. You could hear Kate's laughter for blocks! He went off for a short walk to collect his temper. Well, Kate put up her hand and everyone was dead quiet. Then she signaled all of us, the cast, the crew, to follow her up to the flies above the stage, silently. When George came back, the sound stage was completely deserted. He thought he must have gone mad—or wandered onto the wrong stage. The moment he turned to leave, Kate gave another signal, and—she had prearranged this—everyone, all seventy of us in unison, led by Kate, Cary, Jimmy, and me, yelled as loudly as we could, 'QUIET!!!' "

One morning, Kate was driving into the studio when she saw a dead skunk by the road. She hopped out, picked it up, went to a shop and bought a wooden box lined with satin, then presented the little coffin to the script clerk, Jack Greenwood, for official burial within the grounds of MGM. The press picked up the incident and ran headlines like "KATE HEPBURN HAS UNIQUE WAY OF SHOWING MGM PHILLY STORY A STINKER." Even the New York *Times* ran a long article on "High Jinks in Hollywood" based on the episode.

James Stewart remembers a curious little incident which took place during the shooting. "I had learned to fly. I had my pilot's license. It was a Friday, a break in shooting. She said, 'I'll meet you out at Santa Monica airfield. I want you to take me for an airplane ride.' I didn't have a plane of my own, so I rented one for the occasion—it was, after all, a very important occasion. It was a single-engine Fairchild, with a cabin; she could sit in the co-pilot's seat. She was there right on the dot that afternoon. We got in, and I started the engine. She sort of took over; she wanted to know what everything meant on all of the gauges. As I was taxiing, she told me I was taxiing too fast; when I ran up the engine, she said it didn't sound right at all; she questioned a reading I had made on one of the gauges, saying it was quite wrong. I wasn't sure whether she was ready to take off, because she had so much to say that indicated she'd rather not fly with me at all.

"Finally, she said, 'All right, you can go up.' During the takeoff run, she kept talking and *talking*, saying what things were wrong about what I was doing. She'd snap, 'We don't seem to be gaining speed. The airplane will never get off the ground if we go like this.' Finally we did get in the air, and there was a little turbulence which she blamed me for! As we made the first turn, she said, 'No, don't do that; let's just go straight.' Which meant going right out over the ocean! I told her that, and that we had to turn. She said, 'Wait until we get higher, and then we can go out.' I didn't know what she was talking about. She kept coming back to the instruments; she was concerned with the tachometer, which lots of times fluctuates a little—that's the rule rather than the exception. She didn't understand it at all. Its behavior was totally unacceptable to her. Her seat was very uncomfortable; she wasn't able to see enough; she kept saying, 'You can't see anything. You can't see up, you can't see back, it's impossible.' I told her, 'Kate, I think maybe we'd better go back.' She agreed. I was so nervous by this stage that I made a terrible landing; terrible, terrible! We bounced several times, and Kate absolutely had no kind words to say about that at all! Finally I taxied up, and she said, 'Thanks very much. I'll see you at work on Monday.' And left! I was a wreck! I felt I'd been through a terrible thunderstorm and lost the engine. It was a nightmare! I never went flying with her again!"

Cukor loved making the picture. "In the beginning," he said, "the producer, Joe Mankiewicz, had the entire play tape-recorded in New York, so that we would know the lines the audience laughed at. Well, it was rather pointless, really. You see, we had to make the laughs come from visual gags because so much of the wit of Barry was purely verbal, and too many complicated speeches would have slowed things up. Once or twice, I clashed with Kate—she wanted to cry in the last scenes, because she had cried in the play, and [except for *Alice Adams*] she always liked to cry, it had become a kind of stock in trade with her. I said, 'I don't think we'll cry this time round.' She was very unhappy, but she tried to do what I wanted, and then she said, 'All right, I won't cry.' The result was a much stronger scene. She was perfect as Tracy Lord—she was arrogant but sensitive, she was tough, but vulnerable, she didn't care what people thought of her, they had to accept her on her own terms, or forget it. Of course, she was far more polished, more skillful, than she had ever been before."

The picture was finished five days under schedule. On the last day, Hedda Hopper dropped by to interview Kate. She asked her something idiotic like, "Have you changed much during the picture?" and Kate replied, "Yes, I've grown two inches." When the crew presented her with a dozen soap mitts as an end-of-shooting present, Kate said, "Here I've been thinking you loved me. And all the time you've been wanting me to take a bath."

When she saw the picture—which perfectly preserved her enameled performance as Tracy Lord—Kate was overjoyed.

She sent a special note to Joe Ruttenberg: "Dear Joe, I hope my long thin throat has not driven you to drink. But if you please, I hope that these [cut-glass decanters] will give you strength to think of that long string bean you made a queen. The new glamorous Katrink." And at Christmas she sent a card: "Merry Christmas from the new Hartford Belle . . ."

It was fortunate that Kate brought such a steely, airy lightness to the role, that Cukor guided her so limberly through the swoops and soarings of temperament, because she had to conceal the fact that the role of Tracy Lord was metallically heavier than air. Conceived as a series of attitudinizings, the character moved from selfishness to surrender without conviction; yet Kate made everything so supple and fluid it didn't matter whether it convinced or not. In common with other great comediennes of the period—Russell and Colbert and Arthur—she was the protagonist, leading an audience of women into the story, providing a firm buoyant sanity in a crazy world, choosing her mate with the inevitable movement of wings settling on a pistil. The glory of her playing was that it had all the virtuoso excitement of a great violinist, but it was still accessibly human.

Loyal as ever to the Theatre Guild, Kate went on tour with *The Philadelphia Story* on stage as soon as the filming was finished.

While in Toronto, Kate received an offer from John Golden to play in John Van Druten's play *Claudia;* she sent him a long and logically worked out set of reasons from Cincinnati why she could not play the role of a simple, naïve Pollyanna housewife. Later, the part became a great hit for Dorothy McGuire. Kate did not regret the decision, but she did regret turning down George Bernard Shaw's suggestion that she act in his new play, *The Millionairess;* years later, she was to rediscover the material, and make a hit in it.

The tour ended, appropriately, in Philadelphia. Kate gave a touching farewell speech, telling the audience, "The curtain will never be rung down on this play." She and the entire company walked off the stage leaving the stage lights on and the curtain up.

The reviews for the movie were wildly enthusiastic, the audience response was overwhelming, and Kate was nominated for an Oscar, which unfortunately she lost to Ginger Rogers for *Kitty Foyle*. Asked later what she thought of that, she shrugged. "I was offered *Kitty Foyle*, and I didn't want to play a soap opera about a shopgirl. Ginger was wonderful, she's enormously talented, and she deserved the Oscar. As for me, prizes mean nothing. My prize is my work."

It was exciting for Kate to begin a new decade, the 1940s, with a major achievement behind her, with the complete confidence of Louis B. Mayer, a long-term MGM contract, the feeling of belonging to the most powerful studio in the world. She returned East to appear, on September 21, 1940, with Edna Ferber, Robert E. Sherwood, and Booth Tarkington at Hyde Park to make a campaign pledge, broadcast by radio, to the President, who was to be re-elected in November.

The film version of *The Philadelphia Story* grossed $594,000 on its first six weeks' engagement at Radio City Music Hall. On February 15, 1941, Kate answered Eleanor Roosevelt's plea to narrate an Office of War Information documentary, *Women in Defense,* designed to enlist women in science and industry. The story was released just after Pearl Harbor, and proved to be of great value in the war effort.

During this period, Ring Lardner, Jr., son of the famous sportswriter, prepared a screen story suggested by the life of his father and of the columnist Dorothy Parker, and handed it to the director-screenwriter Garson Kanin to show to Kate. Garson Kanin helped Lardner develop a fuller treatment and then referred him to his brother, Michael Kanin. The ninety-page near-final script, called *The Thing About Women,* was presented to Kate in Hollywood, and a series of discussions followed—at Garson Kanin's suite at the Garden of Allah Hotel, Lardner's house in Van Nuys, and Michael Kanin's in Westwood—with Kate driving immense distances to join in. Lardner supplied innumerable accurate details of newspaper life: his elder brother, as well as his father, had been a sportswriter, and he himself had worked on newspapers. Michael Kanin supplied much of the elegant construction of the comedy sequences, and Kate was delighted as the third and fourth drafts came into her hands.

Woman of the Year, as it was finally called, was an account of the relationship of Tess Harding, a Dorothy Thompson-like political columnist, and Sam Craig, a tough sportswriter, who introduces her to the sacred mysteries of baseball, marries her, and then discovers that Tess is more devoted to her career than to her marriage. The parallel with Kate's marriage to Luddy was very obvious. The finale was typically MGM in its sentimental softness. Tess decides to be a good wife. Lardner-Kanin's original script showed the film ending at a prizefight, with the couple starting out in an attempt at a reconciliation which was probably doomed. Louis B. Mayer insisted on the soap-opera conclusion, with Kate donning an apron and settling down to cook, and he ordered a studio contract worker, John Lee Mahin, to make the change. Lardner and Kanin vainly protested, but were at least allowed to give a degree of verisimilitude to the sequence by showing Tess grappling inadequately with her kitchenware. Finally, two versions—the ambiguous and the sentimental—were shot, but the sentimental version was the one used.

Once the script seemed to be satisfactory, Kate immediately took charge of everything. She talked the whole story out to Mayer, who agreed to buy it for the money she demanded: $211,000, a record in that period. She wanted $50,000 each for the writers, $100,000 for herself, plus $11,000 in agents' commissions. Her condition also was that she would select the director and her male co-star. Numb and overruled, Mayer was unable to deny her anything. Almost before he knew it, the contract was signed.

Kate decided that George Stevens would be the perfect man to direct the picture. After their problems during *Quality Street,* they had dated quite frequently, coincidentally with the ending of her affair with Howard Hughes. Many people believed that she and Stevens were in love with each other, but there is no real evidence to support this theory. The differences between them were too extreme to allow for any possible love relationship. Kate's sharpness and aggressiveness were something of an irritation to Stevens, fond as he was of her. His subdued, slightly melancholy, ruminative, and introspective nature found no resting place in this prickly and short-lived friendship.

Kate arranged for Stevens to be borrowed from Columbia, where he was currently under contract after leaving RKO, and asked for Spencer Tracy as her co-star. She ran all of Tracy's pictures and was convinced he would be the perfect choice. Though she had never met him, she had always deeply admired him, particularly in *Captains Courageous*, in which he played a Portuguese fisherman, and she had wanted to play the good and bad women opposite him in *Dr. Jekyll and Mr. Hyde*, her other favorite film of his.

She says of her feelings at the time, "I had always known something remarkable about Spencer, something which had impressed me more than anything else: he had always wanted to play Jekyll and Hyde without makeup. I thought, there is *proof* of a great actor. He wanted me to play the sweet girl who loves Jekyll, and the prostitute who consorts with Hyde. He could have changed from evil to good with the flicker of a glance. Wouldn't it, I felt then, and I felt now, be fascinating to do it that way? People are so enormously sexually complicated . . . you would show him creating, out of his own imagination, a whore in the place of a very innocent and sweet young thing whom he was expected to marry. Well, Mayer and the others at MGM laughed at the idea.

"Spencer was unforgettable in *Captains Courageous*. Even today I never can face the end without weeping so! He's sinking under the waves, struggling with the mast . . . oh dear, dear, dear . . . He didn't know what kind of accent he was going to use for the film. They told him he'd have to have a Portuguese accent, so he said, 'Well, get me a Portuguese fisherman.' They brought a Portuguese fisherman, and Spencer started talking with his words stretched out— 'Leetle feesh,' he'd say, and the fisherman asked him what on earth he was talking about. 'You mean little fish?' he would ask—he spoke English perfectly! Spencer gave up, he used a bogus accent anyway, and it sounded very good . . ."

Kate was devastated when she was told that Tracy would not be available to play the role in *Woman of the Year*—he had left on location in Florida for a film called *The Yearling.*

But she was lucky: Tracy, who always disliked location shooting when swamps and severe heat were involved, became fretful during the shooting, there were numerous problems on location, and the film was canceled.*

Tracy returned looking for a pleasant, relaxing comedy to be shot in the well-ventilated studios of Culver City, and *Woman of the Year* proved an ideal choice. Joseph L. Mankiewicz, the producer, remembers, "I was walking into the commissary one day when Kate and Spencer met for the first time in the corridor. Kate said, 'I'm afraid I'm a little tall for you, Mr. Tracy.' I turned to her and said, 'Don't worry, Kate, he'll soon cut you down to size.'"

It was an immediate attraction of opposites. Kate was edgy, assertive, brilliant, stylish; Tracy was a subdued, slow-moving, retiring grizzly bear of a man—impatient with fuss, simple, direct. Kate's acting style was revealed in constant movement, a dazzle of feverish activity; Tracy's was interior, suppressed below the surface, with deep, half-hidden reserves of feeling. Kate was intensely feminine, he was intensely masculine. They proved to be the most extraordinary acting team ever to be seen in motion pictures.

Kate describes the first day she and Tracy worked together. They were playing a sequence set in Bleeck's, the old *Herald Tribune* bar in New York. They had been to a baseball game, and their feelings for each other were developing. Kate says, "I accidentally knocked over a glass. Spencer handed me a handkerchief, and I took his handkerchief and I thought, 'Oh, you old so-and-so, you're going to make me mop it up right in the middle of a scene.' So I started to mop it, and the water started to go down through the table. I decided to throw him by going down under the table, and he just stood there watching me. I mopped and mopped, and George Stevens kept the camera running. Spencer just smiled. He wasn't thrown at all."

Stevens says, "The sequence was based on something that had happened when I was going out with Kate in 1939. I took her to a ball game—she had never been to one—and she was

_____
*It was resumed four years later, with Gregory Peck in the Spencer Tracy role.

terrified of being recognized. She always used to be climbing out of trains backwards through a window with a tennis racket. Photographers would shoot her skinny backside. She did the goddamndest things to escape attention, when all you have to do is sit still not to attract notice. After the ball game, walking across on Forty-ninth Street, I said, 'Let's take a walk down Broadway.' She said, 'My God, that's an awful idea. Broadway? I can't do it. They'll mob me!' I told her, 'Without the tennis racket, nobody will recognize you.' We walked two blocks down Broadway and nobody noticed her. I saw Jack Dempsey's bar and said, 'Let's go in here and have a drink.' She whispered, 'In *there*?' I told her, 'Yes. There won't be any trouble.' We walked in and I said, 'Two bourbons.' She told me, 'This is going to be a very unpleasant evening. I'm going to be mobbed in here.' I told her, 'Only if you create a scene, then they'll really focus on you.' Nobody even looked up as we walked in.

"She was so nervous, she reached for the drink and tipped over the chaser. I said to her, 'You broke the rules. Let's get the hell out of here. If you're going to tip over glasses, how are we going to escape trouble?' She told me, 'I didn't do it on purpose.' I said, 'Don't tell me that.'

"As we walked out, I delivered a parting shot: 'You upset a glass, didn't you? But where were the mobs of people? You see, it's all in your mind.' But I think she never got over her terror of her public."

Stevens says, "I saw Spence and Kate's friendship developing right under my eyes. They were such unusual people. I became terribly fond of them. They responded amazingly to the script, which was perfect for them.

"Mayer told me Spence was difficult, that he drank, and I said to him, 'I never found anybody I couldn't keep up with. It's all right, so long as it's not on the set.' Well, he was fine. And they fitted the parts so well: Kate the articulate woman, Spence the inarticulate GI Joe who was too old to be drafted.

"She was the rarer beast of the two. Spence would come over before work to my little office and sit and talk, or I'd go in his dressing room. All of a sudden, there'd be a knocking on the door. The door would open, and it was Kate. She'd say, 'What are you two conspiring about?' He would say, 'Kate, I like guidance about things, and this man is our director.' She said, 'And what about *my* guidance?' Spencer said, 'How could I be such a damn fool as to get into a picture with a woman producer and *her* director, how can I be such a dumb bastard as that?'

"From the beginning of the picture, and their relationship, Spence's reaction to her was a total, pleasant, but glacial put-down of her extreme effusiveness. He just didn't get disturbed about doing things immediately; she wanted to do a hundred and one things at once; he was never in a hurry. She loved to rehearse, to do everything except hang the arc lights; he loved to do nothing except 'be' the part, if possible on the first take. She 'worried the bone'; he just took it and padded off with it. Slowly."

Woman of the Year won an Oscar for best screenplay, Kate was nominated, and the movie was a major success in the major metropolitan centers. The reviews noted Kate's increased maturity and polish. William Boehnel of the New York *World-Telegram* echoed everyone's sentiments when he wrote: "The title role is played by Kate with such humor, resourcefulness and contagious spirit that I think it is even better than her performance in *The Philadelphia Story,* and that was just as fine as anything could be."

Everyone agreed that the Tracy-Hepburn team was incomparable. Kate said later, "We balanced each other's natures. We were perfect representations of the American male and female. The woman is always pretty sharp, and she's needling the man, sort of slightly like a mosquito. The man is always slowly coming along, and she needles, and then he slowly puts out his big paw and slaps the lady down, and that's attractive to the American public. He's the ultimate boss of the situation, and he's very challenged by her. It isn't an easy kingdom for him to maintain. That—in simple terms —is what we did."

Once they fell in love on the picture, Kate and Spencer were faced with a problem which would have defeated many couples. Spencer, a devout Catholic, was married and had two children. He had rejected Loretta Young years before because divorce was against his religion. Kate knew from the outset that he could never marry her. The gossip columnists made a great deal of this fact, causing Kate acute distress. But it seems clear now that even if he had been free, there would never have been a marriage. Kate still believed that marriage was not suitable for an actress, and she would never have wanted to separate him, even to a small degree, from his children. She accepted the situation from the beginning, enjoying the freedom which the non-marital, deeply intense, but not finally binding relationship gave her. Still the free-thinking Fabian, she had no religious scruples about the matter. In a sense, she was living out her mother's unfulfilled precepts: no children, no husband, free, idealistic, selfless love.

Referring to the relationship, Kate said years later, "As for marriage, it's a series of desperate arguments people feel passionately about . . . that's what Spencer and I felt when we acted . . . The trouble is everybody wants to take care of his sexual life first. It's a force of life, sex; you can't deny the thrill of riding high, wide, and handsome with someone you love. The only thing is that age doesn't bring any sexual wisdom. You're just as confused forty years later as you were when you first heard about it. My Dad admitted he knew less about it at eighty. It's totally confusing, and you can't put it down in black and white the way the researchers want you to; you can't describe the magic, you can't compute it . . . A tiny thing about Spencer: he made the best cup of coffee in the world."

She added, "You can't have the whole bargain. An actor should never marry, not even another actor. You're too involved with yourself, and your work is too demanding, to give the necessary amount of attention to another human being. Inevitably, that person feels left out. And becomes unhappy. We must never make people unhappy. Life's too short for that."

Their relationship was remarkable from the outset. Spencer's health had been permanently damaged by his constant drinking. Kate, very much the doctor's daughter, with enormous sweetness and kindness devoted herself to nursing him when he was sick, finding him when he was lost in various places and could not be found by MGM, bringing him home and feeding him. Although to the casual visitor he sometimes seemed cruel to Kate, his "put-down" humor was in fact a front for an overpowering admiration and affection. He might call her "a bag of bones," but he deeply adored her as a woman.

Their badinage, affectionate yet humorously cruel, was a constant wonderment to their friends—the writer-director Garson Kanin, George Cukor, the writer-producer-director Chester Erskine, and many others. Kate sometimes literally sat at Tracy's feet when they went out to visit; she always was metaphorically at his feet. He was the only man apart from her father she completely trusted, respected, and admired. He was not only her adored companion but also her trusted adviser, whose word on whether she should play a particular part was law.

What fascinated her most about him was his incredible directness and cleanness of spirit. He said and did exactly what he thought. He didn't play with a role, he lived inside it. His love for her was as deep as hers for him, but it was not as openly and vibrantly expressed in words. He lived his love for her, rather than talked about it; it was as ingrained as his talent, in the very marrow of his bones.

Kate always insisted that Tracy was strong and fearless. But these were adjectives inspired by love. The truth was that she was by far the stronger of the two. Tracy was intensely Irish: melancholic, wry, bitterly ironical. He suffered from a piercing sense of inadequacy; he tended to despise the fact that he was an actor; he was ridden with guilts and anxieties. Yet it would be wrong to say that life with him was miserable, because he had a sharp, entertaining sense of humor and an inspiriting feeling for fun, which released his friends from the burden of sharing his private despair.

Kate sustained him with her Puritan discipline, energy, drive; with her innocent's love of life, which he could not really share; and with her concern for every living thing. She taught him that a fascination in the seasons, in weather, in birds, animals, and strange, intriguing, original human beings would allow him to escape from the prison of himself.

And he helped her: he allowed her to escape from the

prison of her actress's egotism. Finally she threw away the
last vestiges of her early sophomoric snobbery. The directness of his pain made her stop posing. He cut to the quick of
her nature, and she discovered herself as a woman. She
learned that woman is the stronger sex; that it was her finest
role to challenge, excite, and support him; and that her brand
of true women's liberation came with freedom from self-
preoccupation—releasing her own anxieties at last by concerning herself as deeply with another's. She was not a saint:
she often quarreled bitterly with Spencer. But she never
quarreled in support of her own ego, only out of a need to
improve the strength of his.

The attack on Pearl Harbor took place shortly after
Woman of the Year was completed, and Kate told Roosevelt
she would do anything she could to support the war effort in
Hollywood and in the East. She became fascinated by the
idea of co-starring with Spencer in a version of I. A. R. Wylie's
novel *Keeper of the Flame*, which pointed to the dangers of
Hitlerite fascist movements operating in the United States.
Since both Roosevelt and his Inter-American Affairs chief
Nelson Rockefeller—frequently conferring with Hollywood
bosses in those days—were concerned about possible Nazi
incursions in America, Kate felt that the movie would be a
valuable assistance to the war effort. George Cukor was
brought in to direct, with Victor Saville producing.

Before proceeding, Kate answered a plea from Lawrence
Langner and Theresa Helburn to appear in a tour of a new
Philip Barry play, *Without Love,* opposite the slender and
insipid Elliott Nugent. She agreed, largely because the play
served a topical purpose: within a comedy about a couple
who foolishly embark on a Platonic marriage, there was contained an urgent plea for Eire to enter the war with the
Allies. The husband, played by Nugent, was an Irish-American politician, bent on securing his country's cooperation in
the war effort.

Problems arose from the moment Kate arrived in New
York to rehearse. Langner says, "The problem was in the
casting. We approached many big stars, but they refused to
play second to her, despite the great success of her last play,

The Philadelphia Story. Elliott Nugent and Kate Hepburn
were about as well mated as a cat and a dog. You could never
think of them being deeply in love—liking each other,
friends perhaps, but not ever going to bed together. It was
absurd, it could not have been. It was a tragedy Tracy didn't
play the role. Nugent was a charming man, but without sex
appeal, and sexual charm was the essence of the role Phil
Barry wrote. The play never jelled, and as a result of Kate's
feeling about Nugent's not 'working' with her, she over-
played too extremely, trying to make up for his deficiency,
his inadequacy, and her whole performance failed to soar. No
matter what she did, she couldn't 'fix' the problem. When we
went on tour, we all knew it was a blunder. It was very hard
on poor Elliott."

Audrey Christie, who acted a supporting role in the play,
says, "Kate was miserable throughout the tour. Elliott Nugent was drinking because he was aware of his inadequacy,
and she hated that. But she concealed her feelings beautifully
and was always considerate to Elliott. She used to drive her
car out into the country in various places and scream to get
her frustrations out, decades before anyone thought of pri-
mal-scream therapy. During the tour, Kate used to wear
newspaper hair curlers. One day, her dresser came up to her
and Kate said, 'I don't like these curlers.' 'What's wrong with
them? I did them the way you asked,' replied the dresser.
'They're Hearst newspapers,' left-wing Kate declared."

Spencer went along on the tour to keep her company,
staying at a different hotel to deflect the gossips, reading the
script, which he liked, of a picture called *A Guy Named Joe,*
about a dead pilot who returns to earth. This was a case of
Kate's needing Spencer's support, because she was quite
aware that she was playing a role in a comedy that was
earning only a lukewarm response from audiences.

Despite her dissatisfaction with the play, Kate decided to
take it to Broadway after she had finished work on *Keeper of
the Flame* in Hollywood. In her absence, Donald Ogden
Stewart had prepared an accomplished screenplay for *Keeper
of the Flame.*

Victor Saville, the producer, has vivid memories of its

preparation. "At the time we made this picture, there were two ladies at the studio who read stories to Louis B. Mayer: they were known as Scheherazade One and Scheherazade Two. One day, amongst the properties was I.A.R. Wylie's *Keeper of the Flame.* Scheherazade One asked me to go with her while she told Mayer the story. We went to see Mayer, who said, 'Make it.' He didn't grasp that the portrait of the fascist was based in part on William Randolph Hearst, one of Mayer's closest friends. I hired Donald Ogden Stewart to write the script, George Cukor to direct, and Kate and Spencer to co-star.

"After Stewart finished the script, we had a meeting. To my amazement, Hepburn stood up and told a long, elaborate version of the story which had nothing to do with the script at all! We heard her out, and when she had finished, I broke the silence and said, 'If the picture is going to be done that way, then I resign. It's not the way I want to do it.' There was a long pause. Spencer Tracy got up and said, 'Well, let's go to work with Don's script.' Kate was shocked, but it went ahead according to plan. When the studio found out the picture had a lot more to do with fascism than any executive had realized, the production boss, Eddie Mannix, tried to kill the picture. America was not in the war, and he felt it was unjustifiable. Then Pearl Harbor happened. Eddie came to me and said, 'Now that we're at war, there's no reason to make *Keeper of the Flame.* The public doesn't need to be warned of fascism.' I said, 'We do need to be warned—of possible fascism in our own ranks.' He let us proceed."

Donald Ogden Stewart adds, "It was an anti-fascist picture at a time nobody knew very much about fascism. It was of great concern to Kate, with her left-wing ideals—later on in the forties, she spoke up for Henry Wallace for president, and he certainly wasn't what you might call the people's choice."

Keeper of the Flame contained a scene weirdly reminiscent of the play-within-a-film of *Stage Door.* Kate, as the widow of the fascist boys' club leader Robert Forrest, enters a living room carrying a large bunch of lilies. Her movement, the cradling of the lilies in her arms, her grief were all exactly identical with the earlier dramatic gestures but with an important difference: this time the scene was unfelt.

Kate at age four (1913)

During lunch break on *The Little Minister* (1934), Kate with long-time friend, Laura Harding (COURTESY OF EDDIE KILLEY)

On the golf course (about 1933)
(COURTESY RKO RADIO PICTURES, A DIVISION OF RKO GENERAL, INC.)

With her drama coach, Frances Robinson-Duff (1935)   (U.P.I.)

The fascinating faces of Hepburn

With Fred MacMurray in *Alice Adams* (1935)

Cary Grant, Kate and James Stewart in *The Philadelphia Story* (1940)

Kate and Robert Taylor in *Undercurrent* (1946)

With Humphrey Bogart in *The African Queen* (1952)   (U.P.I.)

Kate's greatest performance: an anguished confrontation with Sir Ralph Richardson in Sidney Lumet's *Long Day's Journey Into Night* (1962) (DENNIS STOCK—MAGNUM)

With Tracy between scenes of Stanley Kramer's *Guess Who's Coming to Dinner?*, their ninth and last film together (1967) (U.P.I.)

During a shooting break on ABC-TV's *The Glass Menagerie* (1973) (U.P.I.)

Kate appeared for the first time with Henry Fonda in
On Golden Pond (1981)

The resplendent Katharine Hepburn

Tracy, by contrast, was at his best in the picture. Subdued, cool, he conveyed the ruthlessness of the reporter sent to investigate Forrest's death without seeming to try. He was ideally cast in the role, grimly and skeptically exploring the secret of the dead boys' club hero who was in fact a rampant fascist. He also liked George Cukor, and later rented a cottage on the Cukor estate in West Hollywood which he and Kate often shared. Sometimes he good-naturedly sided with Cukor against Kate. One day, referring to a scene in which her cottage catches fire, Kate said, "We don't need dialogue explaining how people saw the fire. They'd smell the smoke first." Cukor said, "It must be wonderful to know all about acting—and even more about fires." Spencer broke up laughing.

Cukor recalls, "It was Kate's last romantic glamour-girl part, and she acted with some of that artificiality she'd supposedly left behind at RKO. That first scene, floating into a room in yards and yards of white draperies with these lilies —well, it was all far, far too much. I don't think I really believed in the story, it was pure hokeypokey, and her part was phony, highfalutin. She tried to make something of her haughty lines—'I had visioned,' and so on. But it was very much a *Christopher Strong* performance; she was always coming on in something glittering in that one and delivering long theatrical speeches, and now she was doing it again.

"I didn't like the 'glamour' side of Kate; I loved the fresh, natural Kate when she forgot to be a movie queen. The subject brought out the movie queen in her, and that wasn't good. And we should have done the picture on location. We did it on the sound stage, fir forests, mansions, lodges in the grounds, mysterious gates.

"Everyone looked like a waxwork in Madame Tussaud's. And when an old woman went mad, we had a raging artificial thunderstorm, prop room lightning. One of my few good memories of the picture was that we had Percy Kilbride as a crazy, funny cabdriver. He played Pa Kettle later on. I suppose that confers some kind of immortality on the picture."

Kate, too, felt that the movie was pretentious and unconvincing, though she was happy that Spencer co-starred with

her so expertly in the role of the investigative reporter.
There can be no doubt that Donald Ogden Stewart never
really licked the problems presented by the material. *Time*
wrote: "For Hepburn and Tracy, it was a high point of significant failure."

Kate returned to New York in the late fall of 1942 feeling
that her career was about to slip again. *Without Love* opened
at the St. James Theatre on November 1 to a lukewarm
audience response and a devastating review by Brooks Atkinson: "As the unloved wife, Miss Hepburn is giving a mechanical performance that is not without considerable
gaucherie in the early scenes. In both the writing and the
acting, *Without Love* is theatre on the surface of a vacuum."
The play flopped. It was to be eight years before Kate returned to the stage.

Seven

In those early years of the 1940s, Tracy was still battling against the alcoholism which had plagued him during the latter part of the previous decade. Kate made it her bounden duty to break him of the habit. She evidently met his alcoholism as a challenge, drying him out by 1943. Sometimes she had to find him in remote parts of the country where he had hidden after collapsing in the wake of a monumental binge. Tracy became her erring father, and she his adoring daughter, and this fact caused many of the tensions in their loving friendship.

The tragedy was that by the time Kate cured him of his drinking, his health had already deteriorated. His kidneys and liver would never be healthy again. Though still in early middle age, his early forties, he was physically on the point of being an old man, his digestion poor, his nerves weak. His streak of hypochondria kept him in the hands of doctors, but he needed them anyway.

It appears that Louise Tracy, his wife, accepted his relationship with Kate with detached stoicism. She evidently realized that her love relationship with him was long since over, and since the Roman Catholic Church would not permit a divorce, she saw no reason to become antagonistic to him at this stage. Sweet-natured and kind, preoccupied with work on behalf of deaf children because their son, John, was born deaf, she never struggled with Kate over Spencer.

The relationship among the three was not so much an armed truce as a tripartite agreement. It can best be illustrated by one tiny, significant detail: when Tracy was ill, the two women sat beside his bed in shifts, exchanging notes on

115

the patient's progress as they passed each other in the doorway of his hospital room.

In those years, Kate's routine remained virtually unchanged. She still rose early each morning, was always first on the set, involved in every aspect of making a picture, and was always home last at night. Kate remained as private as ever, rarely giving an autograph. On one occasion, some fans begged her. She refused. A fan said, "How dare you refuse? We made you what you are today." And she replied, "Like hell you did."

She always wore the same military student's cap, which she had picked up on her trip to Europe with Luddy in 1932, and an old army fatigue jacket which her brother Richard had left behind on a visit years before. She had a succession of dogs, which she adored, taking them with her on walks around the Hollywood and Beverly Hills reservoirs. She told a friend, "I always wear slacks because of the brambles and maybe the snakes. And see this basket? I keep everything in it; it's wonderful—no, it's not full of groceries. I have odd items of clothing in it, books, papers, new scripts, you name it. So I look ghastly, do I? I don't care—so long as I'm comfortable."

She always refused to eat out. She said later, "Whenever I eat out, I pass out—sounds funny, but it's true. I've only been to a restaurant five or six times in my life, and each time I've passed out. My nerves are terrible—if people are watching me, I gobble my food, and then I get sick. So I always eat at home."

During the years she was working for him, Kate grew to admire Louis B. Mayer. She told Louella Parsons in 1963, "I get so mad at some of the things they say about Mayer. In all the years I was a star at MGM, I never had a written contract with him—just a verbal one. But he lived up to it. 'Mr. Mayer' —I always called him that—understood the agonizing vagaries an artist has to go through. He didn't get angry at his stars when they got drunk or did things they shouldn't."

Kate followed her pattern of moving from house to house each year, or sometimes twice a year, returning East at every possible opportunity, and concerning herself more deeply with Fenwick and her homes in Hartford and New York than with anything that went on in Hollywood. She did, however, take an interest in the Stage Door Canteen, in which stars helped entertain or serve the troops, and she made a brief appearance in Sol Lesser's movie, *Stage Door Canteen,* based on the famous place. She was shown giving moral support to a hopeful young actress when the girl's lover sails off to war.

Still concerned with supporting the war effort, Kate accepted an invitation from her old friend Pan Berman, who was now a producer at MGM, to make a picture about the Chinese peasants' struggle against the threat of Japanese aggression. The film was *Dragon Seed,* based on the novel by Pearl Buck, in which Kate was to play Jade, a militant girl in a farming family. The kindest thing to say about her performance is that the role of a Chinese peasant was not meant for her.

Both the Nationalists and the Communists put enormous pressure on Pan Berman to make him use their uniforms and insignia in all of the scenes of revolt against the Japanese. Berman detested both groups and kept the uniforms anonymous.

The picture, budgeted at three million dollars, involved the largest construction task in the entire history of Metro. The farm was set up at a 120-acre section in Calabasas in the San Fernando Valley, a thirty-six-mile drive from Los Angeles. Fifty acres of hills were terraced; twelve-inch pipes were laid over one mile so that five million gallons of water could flood the area; rice paddies were laid down, with barley standing in for rice; and ten farm buildings were erected under the supervision of art director Cedric Gibbons.

Kate was fascinated by the realistic look of the "Chinese" location. She read the novel several times, and studied everything available on China that was in print. Full of enthusiasm, still like an eager young girl at the age of thirty-two, she would drive out each day, while the majority of the company were trundled out by bus. She enjoyed making the movie, but was seriously concerned about the health of her director, Jack Conway. Suffering from tuberculosis, he was running a temperature most of the time and frequently took to his bed with high fevers. To protect the picture, Pan Berman assigned another director, Harold S. Bucquet, to watch every move Conway made, in case he should have to take over in an emergency. The decision was fortunate; finally, to Kate's consternation, Conway collapsed and retired from the shooting, and she had to make a painful adjustment to a new director.

Pan Berman says, "Kate was just as big a louse when I worked with her in her struggling days. I don't mean that literally—I was still fond of her. But, God, she was tough! She was difficult—but even when she drove you mad, you had to admire her spunk, her guts. She got exactly what she wanted —wouldn't work any later than she thought she should, wanted triple overtime—but when she was on the set, she toiled like a bridge mender."

Kate took a great interest in *Dragon Seed*, sitting in on script conferences with the writer, Marguerite Roberts, who was busily reconstructing an original script written by Jane Murfin. A great pleasure of those weeks was renewing her friendship with that strong associate of the 1930s at RKO, Pan Berman's assistant Jane Loring. She often lunched with Jane, or dropped by her office for preparatory discussions on the picture.

Hurd Hatfield, who played Kate's brother in the picture, says, "Making it was a horrible experience. I remember the location in the valley, the endless addressing of everyone through loudspeakers, and the way everyone had to do 'bits of business.' The very first scene I played, Kate had to do some washing, Aline MacMahon was picking her teeth, and I had to ride a buffalo playing a flute—and I'd never ridden so much as a horse before that! To come out and ride a buffalo my first day in Hollywood, and then have Katharine Hepburn step out and watch me! I fell off! A few days later, I introduced her to my parents. My mother stammered out something silly like, 'You were wonderful in *The Philadelphia Story*.' She hadn't seen it. And Kate said, 'The film or the play?' with a terrible air of challenge."

Hatfield adds, "The dialogue in *Dragon Seed* was incredible. I'll never forget Kate saying the line 'I don't want my baby teethed on Japanese bullets!' It was unforgettable! She

was very kind to us beginners, though I think my own shy-
ness and insecurity irritated her."

Shortly after finishing *Dragon Seed,* Kate visited the set of
The Picture of Dorian Gray, where Hatfield was appearing
in the title role. "I was terrified," Hatfield says. "When she
appeared in the middle of a take, everything stopped. I stood
there, looking quite foolish, in my nineteenth-century costume, not knowing what on earth to say to her. She strode
up to me, looked me hard in the eye, and said, very loudly,
'They say you're absolutely marvelous in this part. ARE YOU?'
I was much too frightened to reply."

Around the time she made *Dragon Seed,* which was only
moderately successful critically and commercially, Kate became obsessed with making a film of Eugene O'Neill's
Mourning Becomes Electra, with Garbo as her mother, Cly-
temnestra. Whenever she mentioned the idea to Mayer, he
looked blank, so she asked her old colleague Lillie Messenger, who had directed her in her screen test and was now
Mayer's storyteller, to recount the plot to him. At first, Mayer
was intrigued, but after two hours, Lillie Messenger mentioned that the story included incest. "No!" Mayer yelled.
'Disgusting! Filthy! We'll sully the nest! Lillie, get out and
find me another Andy Hardy story!"

During the making of *Dragon Seed,* Kate was pleased to
learn that Mayer, who had bought the rights to *Without Love*
soon after it opened in New York on the recommendation of
the producer Lawrence Weingarten, had decided, despite
the play's failure, to make it as a film. The Irish political
element was eliminated, and Pat Jamieson, the Irish politician, became a scientist who was unable to proceed with his
experiments because of the Washington housing shortage, an
element which was introduced because of Weingarten's admiration of George Stevens' housing-shortage comedy, *The
More the Merrier.* Kate adored the gentle, considerate,
rather professional Lawrence Weingarten, and they became
lifelong friends. Donald Ogden Stewart wrote the script, and
Tracy was cast as Pat Jamieson. George Cukor was unavailable to direct the picture, so Kate recommended the diminu-

tive Harold Bucquet, whom she had grown to like on *Dragon Seed.*

Lawrence Weingarten says, "As always, Kate was 'into' everything on *Without Love.* I remember one charming experience. We were building the sets and dressing them when the set decorator, Ed Willis, came up to me in a fury and said, 'I quit.' I asked him, 'What's the matter?' He said, 'She doesn't like the set—she wants it like it was on the stage.' I said, 'Oh, come on, now, calm down.' Kate came in that night ·—she used to come in all the time—I used to say to her, 'Even looking at photos of you makes me tired!' I didn't know what to do to resolve the problem. I couldn't say to her, 'Keep your nose out of this, it's not your business.' As she was leaving, late at night, after sniffing her disapproval of everything down to the cushions, I said to her, 'Kate, if you've got time before you go, go down and see Buddy Gillespie in Special Effects to see how the miniatures are coming along.' She got the message. She didn't interfere any more. People always said to me, 'She's trying to do everything.' And my reply was, 'The thing I'm afraid of, and you should be afraid of, is that she *can* do everything.' Producer, director, cameraman! That's what she was! Her idea of everything was always better than you could ever have envisioned."

Once again, Kate's and Tracy's comedy timing was highly effective in *Without Love.* They prepared the picture in Kate's home so perfectly that they scarcely needed to work when they came on the sound stage.

Harold Bucquet said later, "Directing Mr. Tracy amounts to telling him when you're ready to start a scene. He hasn't let me down yet, and if he does, perhaps we'll get acquainted. Miss Hepburn requires direction, for she tends to act too much. Her acting is much less economical than Mr. Tracy's but his style is rubbing off on her. The important thing is that I don't coach them on their scenes together. No one should do that, for they do a thorough job by themselves, and know exactly what they want to accomplish when we begin a scene."

During the picture, Kate suffered a grief reminiscent of the loss of cameraman Henry Gerrard during the 1930s. Harold Bucquet was stricken with cancer. A devout Christian

Scientist, he refused to be operated on, and would not even
acknowledge his own symptoms. Kate was bitterly shocked
by his early death.

The picture was a great success. Weingarten says, "It was
the first time people had heard T. S. Eliot quoted on the
screen, and the first time someone played 'Clair de lune'
properly, not the vamped-up version. I ran the picture for
the studio staff, and everyone applauded. The previews were
tremendous. And the picture was a big hit."

A favorite novel of Kate and Spencer's during the early
1940s was Conrad Richter's *The Sea of Grass*, a story of Colonel James Brewton, New Mexico cattle tycoon, obsessed with
the grasslands of his family estate, and Lutie Cameron, the
strong-willed young woman who marries him. Kate and
Spencer decided at once that they should play the roles, even
calling each other "Colonel" and "Lutie" at home and in
front of friends. They persuaded Mayer to buy the rights
from Twentieth Century–Fox, and brought over the young
director Elia Kazan, who had made a hit with *A Tree Grows
in Brooklyn*, from Twentieth as well. Pan Berman produced,
and Marguerite Roberts rewrote the Fox script by Vincent
Lawrence, with Kate a vivid presence at all of the original
discussions. Kate and Jane Loring supervised some changes,
and Kate told the cameraman Harry Stradling, to "watch out
for my neck." Stradling recalled later, "Kate said to me, 'I
like to have a baby spot* under my chin at all times.' And I
replied, 'Baby, you already have one.' "

Kazan regretted the entire venture from the outset. "I had
been interested in the novel," he says. "I wanted to do it
realistically, staging it on location in New Mexico, and using
rough, homespun clothes for the characters. But as soon as I
got to Metro, I found out what the score was: that the whole
picture was going to be done in the studio. Today, I would
quit if any such idea were handed to me. But I was young and
green and so I went ahead. I was a damn fool to do it at all.

"I went in to discussions: Tracy was full of funny Irish
stories, and Kate was laughing at them. She sat at his feet and

*A small spotlight.

worshiped him, and I felt out of place. It was as though I were entering a private club of which I was not, and never would be, a member. It wasn't that they weren't gracious to me, but . . . Well, let's say they did their best to make me feel at home. Unsuccessfully.

"And I was scared of Kate—I was overpowered by her. After all, she was 'royalty.' And MGM was overpowering, too. Cedric Gibbons, who laid down the law in everything, made the sets too grand, and the costumes were too pretty . . . and then there was the policy of 'star treatment,' to which I was entirely opposed. I hit the MGM machine, and was shredded.

"Quite simply, the whole point of Richter's novel was thrown away by the treatment. A rather spoiled, protected woman comes into a background that is rough, hostile. It frightens her and she tries to adapt . . . It should have been like a Russian picture, you should have almost smelled the land. You should have got the stink of horseshit. Instead, it was a miserable picture." Another participant in the picture, who wishes to be anonymous, says, "It was one of those pictures in which, every time Kate went to the bathroom, she came back in a new costume."

If *The Sea of Grass* was a disappointment, then *Undercurrent*, which Kate made after it, was a disaster. All of the trappings of which Kazan complained—the glossy MGM costumes and sets, the painted backdrops which replaced locations—were welcomed by Kate's director Vincente Minnelli, with the result that the picture was wholly artificial. The casting of this melodrama about a girl married to a psychopath, played by Robert Taylor, was based on the absurd supposition that Kate could play someone defenseless, when anyone could see at a glance that no problem in the world, least of all a difficult husband, would have been beyond her solution. She played the part mechanically, to an elaborate musical score "borrowed" almost in its entirety from Brahms.

During the making of *Undercurrent*, Kate became very friendly with Vincente Minnelli's wife, Judy Garland. Kate forced her to get up early and take morning walks, relieving Judy's insomnia by distracting and relaxing her, to try and stop her from drinking and taking drugs. In future years, as

Judy's health declined, as she systematically destroyed herself, Kate did her best to provide moral support.

In June, 1945, Kate traveled East with Spencer to give him aid in a new venture: he was to make his first stage appearance in fifteen years in a play called *The Rugged Path,* by Robert Sherwood. He acted the part of Morey Vinion, a journalist enlisted in the Navy. Garson Kanin was engaged to direct. Spencer was terrified. (Kate said later, "Any actor worth his salt is petrified all the time. He's three times more petrified if he has to go on the stage.") Spencer became ill before the out-of-town opening in Providence, Rhode Island, and ran a high fever, but he still insisted on giving a performance. Kate stood in the wings through the whole evening, held his head between the acts, and cleaned him off when he vomited. Gradually, his health improved; but his nervousness did not.

In Washington, Kate, Spencer, and Kanin quarreled miserably over details of the rehearsals. Spencer struggled through performances, devastated by the bad reviews, constantly threatening not to continue in Boston. Kate compelled him to appear in Boston, but by the time he reached New York he was again ready to quit. For Kate, the whole experience had now become a nightmare. She invaded the Plymouth Theatre, sweeping Spencer's star dressing room, scrubbing the bathroom floor until it was spotless, and making sure that Spencer was as comfortable as possible at her house in Turtle Bay.

Kanin found it impossible to work with Spencer, who grumpily refused to take advice on changes in his performance. Kate did her utmost to keep the peace between all parties, but it was useless. Opening night was appalling. Spencer began well, with Kate watching him in the wings, ready with towels and medication, like a second in a championship boxing match. But halfway through the play, his tension and accompanying sickness got the better of him, and he faltered badly. The standing ovation after the last act was a display of sentimental homage rather than a true expression of the audience's feelings.

After the show, Mr. and Mrs. Robert Sherwood gave a

party for Kate, Spencer, the Kanins, Spencer's brother Carroll, and several other friends. Everyone was in a good mood until the reviews arrived. Spencer's performance was well received, but the play was not. He withdrew from social circles for the rest of the run, declined all interviews, and spent most of the time with Carroll and with Kate. After ten weeks, he closed down the play and went home.

In the mid-1940s, Kate's career had sunk as low as it had in the mid-1930s. But she was so buoyed up by her mutually adoring relationship with Spencer, and by the massive MGM studio machinery, which gave her a feeling of enormous confidence, that she never allowed her weaker vehicles to depress her. She did not even balk at an incredibly complicated and foolish script by four writers, *Song of Love,* based on the private lives of Clara Wieck, Robert Schumann, and Johannes Brahms, and directed by Clarence Brown.

Brown says, "Kate was the most amazing human being I have ever known. It was agreed with Mayer that Kate would simply bang away, more or less correctly, at a wooden piano as Clara Schumann, while Artur Rubinstein would match her exquisitely in the MGM recording studio, with the MGM orchestra. All Kate had to do was give a rough approximation of the correct fingering. I told her this when we had our first script discussion.

"She hit the roof! She said, 'Nonsense!' 'What's nonsense?' I asked her. 'The idea that I'm going to pound away at some goddamned keyboard. I'm going to play a real piano. Rubinstein can carry the bulk of the works, but I'm going to lead in with the first few bars, and I'll bet nobody knows the difference!' Well, she sat down and trained and trained with a pianist for weeks, and goddamn it if she didn't come up at the end playing perfectly. When we went into the matching, Rubinstein said to me, 'If I hadn't seen it and heard it with my own eyes and ears, I wouldn't have believed it! That woman is incredible! She actually does play almost as well as I do! And when she ends and I begin, only I in the whole world could tell the difference!'"

Pace Brown, Clara Schumann was among her wost performances.

Shortly after she finished *Song of Love*, Kate received word that her house in Turtle Bay had very nearly burned down. Charles Newhill, her chauffeur–major domo, had accidentally knocked over a lamp while applying a flammable cleaning fluid to the floor. A spark from the lamp socket had ignited the fluid, and flames had completely engulfed the room. Newhill just managed to escape in time, and summoned the fire department, but rugs and furnishings were permanently damaged and had to be replaced. Kate rushed back from Hollywood by plane, and supervised all of the cleaning up and redecoration with manic energy.

In the summer of 1948, Frank Capra, the celebrated director of *Mr. Deeds Goes to Town* and *Mr. Smith Goes to Washington*, bought the successful Broadway play *State of the Union*, by Howard Lindsay and Russel Crouse, as a vehicle for Spencer. Capra had liked the play's central character, based on Wendell Willkie, a rich industrialist who runs for president with ideals held high. After making a series of pictures in which the central figure was a kind-hearted common man, Capra welcomed the chance to make one in which he dealt with a good millionaire. The man's wife, who sees through the ruthless politicians trying to use her husband, was a fascinating character also. Capra drove up to Tracy's house in Hollywood one afternoon and gave him the play. Tracy was impressed, and accepted at once. But MGM would only make him available if the picture were made at the studio and released through its distribution outfit, Loew's, Inc. The deal was concluded, and Claudette Colbert cast as the wife.

Then, on a Friday, with a $15,000 wardrobe fitted, and Colbert scheduled for the first scene, she arrived in Capra's office and told him her doctor had forbidden her to work past five o'clock each day, as she became tired (her doctor was her husband). When Capra protested, she said that her agent also did not want her to work late (her agent was her brother). Capra told her, "This is ridiculous. I can't give you that privilege. Five o'clock quitting time, with everyone else on another quitting time. I can't do that." She said, "Then I won't do the picture." So Capra shouted, "Well, get the hell out. Check in your wardrobe and go home."

"It was an enormously dangerous thing to do," Capra says. "The picture starting on Monday, and no female star. My partner Sam Briskin was frantic. He called Louis B. Mayer, who suggested we call Spencer Tracy, so he wouldn't read it in a column and walk out himself. I talked to Spence, and he said, 'What the hell happened?' I told him. He said, 'Goddamn you, I'm going to report you to the Actors' Guild.' Then he laughed. 'You told that Frankie Froggie Colbert to go to hell, did you?'

"I said, 'Jeez, you know any actresses? You got any friends?' And he says, 'The *Madam!* I've been rehearsing my part with her, she's taking Colbert's role, at home here.' I said, 'My God, do you think she'd do it?' And he said, 'I don't know. She's kind of nutty that way, about people being in trouble. She's "theatre," you know.' He put her on the line. Kate said, 'Sure! What the hell? When do we start? . . . What clothes do I wear on Monday?' And she hung up. I was amazed. No contract, no talk of agents, money, billing—nothing. She worked day and night, all through that weekend, with the costume designer, Irene. She came to my house in Brentwood on Sunday, in her little tiny open car, her hair flying in the wind, in a pair of slacks and a funny high-necked sweater, washed so often it was loose, and pinned together with a giant safety pin at the neck. She undid the safety pin and the whole thing flopped open. She came in, took her clothes off in the bedroom, and tried on the costumes, some of them ready made and slightly altered for her shape. That's sheer professionalism—she knew we were in a jam, and she helped out. I don't know anybody in the business who wouldn't have held us over a barrel for money—and we would have paid anything to save the picture."

Making the picture was a very real problem, because it came at the height of the first inquiries into communism in Hollywood by the House Committee on Un-American Activities. The script took a strong anti-conservative stance. Kate was infuriated by the ill-treatment of many left-wing figures at the time, and narrowly escaped investigation herself. Moreover, Kate, as a highly liberal, liberated woman in the

picture, was not only up against the reactionary Adolphe
Menjou—cast as a rearguard politician—in the script. Off-set,
they barely spoke to each other, and Kate despised him for
naming names at the House hearings. George Cukor still calls
Menjou "the late, unlamented A. M." Capra says, "Kate and
Spencer may have hated Menjou, but it never showed. They
were far too professional for that. However, I think some of
the scenes when Kate collides with Menjou were played with
unusual sharpness, even for her."

Capra recalls, "They detested each other, but they played
beautifully together. Here was Tracy, head of the 'Irish
Mafia,' Menjou, head of the right-wingers, and Hepburn, the
bell-ringer of the left. What a parlay! But it worked. I had to
keep the reporters constantly off the set because they kept
trying to make a controversial story about the clash between
Hepburn and Menjou, and they kept trying to steam one up
against the other."

State of the Union contained many rather cruel stabs at
President Harry Truman, but Truman enjoyed it enormously. Capra says, "We thought he would regard it as sedi-
tious, but he ran it over and over on the presidential yacht.
Later, Truman's campaign manager told me that the picture,
which showed how a President can fight corruption in his
own ranks, gave Truman the impetus to run for another
term.* His support undoubtedly saved all of us—the writers,
Kate, Spencer, myself—from going before the House Committee. But despite his approval, I became known to right-
wing elements as a security risk. The columnists damaged my
career, and I never was quite as 'on top' again after that."

All during the shooting of the picture, Kate conducted a
campaign against the House Un-American Committee. She
issued a statement to the press: "J. Parnell Thomas, head of
the House Un-American Committee, engages in a personally
conducted smear campaign of the motion picture industry.
He is aided and abetted in this effort by a group of super-
patriots who call themselves the Motion Picture Alliance for

_____
*Kate was in support of Truman's rival, Henry Wallace, in the presi-
dential race.

the Preservation of American Ideals. For myself, I want no part of their ideals or those of Mr. Thomas . . . The artist, since the beginning of time, has always expressed the aspirations and dreams of his people. Silence the artist and you have silenced the most articulate voice the people have."

While *State of the Union* was being edited, Kate—rightly pleased with her sparkling performance—went to England to be with Spencer during the making of a George Cukor production, *Edward, My Son,* based on the play by Robert Morley. Spencer and Cukor stayed with Laurence Olivier and his wife, Vivien Leigh, while Kate stayed at Claridge's. It was not a comfortable period: the script was weak, the picture was floundering from the beginning, and Spencer was miscast in the part of the pompous rags-to-riches tycoon in which Morley himself had been a great hit, playing his own leading role on the stage. The film subsequently flopped.

By contrast, despite a somewhat mixed reception from the critics, and a not wholly successful career at the box office, *State of the Union* further cemented the Tracy-Hepburn team. Louis B. Mayer wanted another MGM/Weingarten/Cukor/Tracy/Hepburn comedy as soon as possible, and the result was that the angular, witty Punch and Judy team of Garson Kanin and his wife, Ruth Gordon, came up with a funny idea for a picture about a couple, both lawyers, who take opposite sides in a case. The title of the script was *Man and Wife,* later retitled *Adam's Rib.*

Kate recalls that the idea for the story had been born in the winter of 1947, when Kanin and Gordon were motoring from New York to their weekend cottage in Sandy Hook, Connecticut, along the Merritt Parkway. Ruth mentioned that when the Raymond Masseys had broken up, the Masseys' friends, the attorney William Dwight Whitney and his wife, Dorothy, not only helped arrange the details of the divorce but split up themselves and married the divorced partners. The Kanins altered the story somewhat in rewrites: Amanda Bonner (Kate) is a militant feminist who defends a dumb blonde (Judy Holliday) when the blonde shoots her two-timing husband (Tom Ewell), against the attempts of district attorney Adam Bonner (Tracy) to pin the guilt on the accused.

The script was perfect. Weingarten says, "It was the first time in thirty years the studio had ever seen a screenplay that was ready to shoot immediately, without changes." The characters were designed by the Kanins, who knew Kate and Spencer very well, to mirror every detail of the Kate-Spencer relationship. The public had the delicious feeling of seeing a love affair acted out in front of their eyes, with all of the tensions, the divisions of opinion, the intense intellectual give-and-take that marked a magnificent relationship. The legal details were extremely careful. Garson Kanin had known a judge, and modeled the character on him. Kate and George Cukor attended a murder trial in Los Angeles and observed how the accused woman looked brassy and overly made up on her first day in court and then, acting on her attorney's advice, became more and more modest and subdued in subsequent appearances.

Cukor says, "We took pictures of the accused, and watched very carefully what happens in a courtroom. I gradually understood what a judge does—he can listen to the law and interpret it, and make sure the jury makes the right decision. He *directs* the jury—I hadn't known that. It was fascinating. Then I wanted the couple in the picture to have the right kind of home. I picked up oddments from the apartments of people I knew, and put things in."

At the end of the picture, Kate delivers a speech which could well have been made by her mother: "An unwritten law stands back of a man who fights to defend his home. Apply the same to this maltreated mother. We ask no more. *Equality!* Deep in the interior of South America, there thrives a civilization, older than ours, a people known as the Loreanoes,* descended from the Amazons. In this vast tribe, members of the female sex rule and govern and systematically deny equal rights to the men—made weak and puny by years of subservience. Too weak to revolt. And yet how long have we lived in the shadow of a like injustice?"

One of the great pleasures for Kate of making *Adam's Rib* was that it was shot on location all over New York, sometimes within walking distance of her own home in Turtle Bay.

---

*Presumably, the authors meant the legendary Orellanas.

Lexington Avenue, East Fifty-second Street, and Bowling
Green Park were happy and attractive venues. Kate watched
from the sidelines those scenes in which she was not involved; and she took a particular interest in the work of the
young Judy Holliday, who played the angry wife in the story.
Miss Holliday, who was acting at night in Kanin's *Born Yesterday,* was nervous and unsure of camera technique; Kate
gave her moral support, encouraging her, trying to overcome
her extreme, frozen nervousness, and begging everyone at
Columbia when she returned to Hollywood to let Judy
Holliday play *Born Yesterday* on the screen.

Lawrence Weingarten says, "I'll never forget Kate's un-
selfishness to Judy Holliday. There was a scene when Kate is
talking to Judy at a table. Kate insisted George Cukor focus
the entire scene on Judy, so all you saw of Kate was her
shoulder. I never knew such kindness in a star. It was incredible. Kate was wise in the ways of film. She knew that the
supporting cast would give her strength."

Kate managed to persuade Cole Porter to write a song for
Adam's Rib, "Farewell, Amanda." She adored this brilliant
man whose life was spent in agony after a fall from a horse.
Kate says, "I was at his house, I remember, at a dinner party.
He had a lovely house, lovely things, but the curtains were
sort of cockeyed. One of them was pushed in a rather unfortunate direction. I walked over and straightened it, right in
the middle of the meal. Cole called to me, 'You're worse than
I am.' I said, 'Oh?' He said, 'Yes, I'm always fiixing things. But
I'll tell you when you're in real danger. When you walk down
a path and you straighten out your footsteps behind you!' "

Adam's Rib was an enormous success, more than justifying
Kate's faith in the script, and her playing, like Tracy's, was
inspired. When the publicity was prepared for the picture,
Spencer insisted on first billing ahead of Kate. Garson Kanin
said to him, "Spencer, didn't you ever hear of 'ladies first'?"
And Spencer replied, "This is a movie, not a lifeboat."

During the late 1940s, Kate's greatest excitement was seeing the famed Laurette Taylor in *The Glass Menagerie* on

the stage. Kate says, "She was so brilliant I would swoon. The play opened in Chicago. Terry Helburn wanted me to come along to it, and I said immediately, 'Yes.' We saw her before the play started. We went backstage. I was far too awestruck to speak at all. She was hefty, round, with very, very fine hair, done up in rags, sitting at a dressing table. She had funny little pots around her; she was making up. I sat, not speaking, just *watching*. Intently. She was wonderful in the part. She never 'drove' it, or any part, she just sort of 'let it happen.' She and Spencer were the most gifted actors I ever saw. If she had to dial a telephone, she didn't actually dial, she just *indicated the movement*. You would have to have enough brains to catch on. She sketched the scenes. I thought, 'What a fascinating technique!' " Influenced by Laurette Taylor and Spencer, Kate's playing became far quieter, more subdued and subtle in subsequent years.

Ever since *The Philadelphia Story*, Kate had been pressured by Terry Helburn and Lawrence Langner of the Theatre Guild to appear in Shakespeare. She had been horrified by the idea, feeling she was "nowhere up to it," as she told Miss Helburn. Langner told her she must extend her range as an actress. Then, finally, with additional pressure from her beloved Armina Marshall, she yielded to Langner's idea of her playing Rosalind in *As You Like It*, intrigued also by the notion of showing off her legs in the scenes in which Rosalind undertakes the impersonation of a boy. In late 1949, she signed a contract with the Guild to appear in the play, and, once *Adam's Rib* had finished shooting, started to memorize the role.

She had sharp feelings of regret over the decline of MGM at the time. Following an anti-monopoly campaign conducted by a series of attorneys general, the studio had been compelled to divest itself of the various theatre holdings of its parent company, Loew's, Inc., and the threatened onset of television as the mass medium of the 1950s further undermined the studio. Kate, in common with almost all of the great MGM stars, was soon to be let go. Spencer was not, but left two years later. Meanwhile, he was able to take leave of

absence to travel East with Kate, and to go with her on
out-of-town tours with the production.

Just as she had been before, Kate was largely responsible
for the casting. She chose William Prince as Orlando, Cloris
Leachman as Celia, and Jay Robinson for the two roles of Le
Beau and Sir Oliver Martext. Michael Benthall was brought
from England to direct. Kate found him very sympathetic,
highly talented, a mentor as well as a friend. She also asked
her dear friend Constance Collier to coach her in the role of
Rosalind, and she worked with Constance three hours a day
for eight months.

The show went into rehearsal at the Cort Theatre in New
York in November, 1949, traveled to various cities for nine
weeks, and opened at the Cort on January 26, 1950. None of
the cast ever saw Spencer, who was smuggled in and out of
tour hotels in the freight elevator because he and Kate were
determined to keep their loving relationship a secret from
almost everyone.

Kate played Rosalind with a startling vitality and attack.
She involved herself, as always, in every aspect of the production. Indefatigably athletic, she continued her regime of
playing tennis, golfing, walking early in the mornings. She
ran several miles around Central Park every day, with her
chauffeur Charles Newhill following her in the limousine,
and she skied every weekend, with as much energy as she
applied to everything else. During rehearsal, she made herself an authority on Shakespearean costumes and interiors,
nearly driving the designer, James Bailey, mad, but exciting
and even inspiring him at the same time. When she arrived
in a new city, she found out the names of the best local
doctors and dentists and pinned the list up in each dressing
room. She discreetly—or indiscreetly—put pots of deodorant
in each room when the players sweated through their heavy
period clothes.

Constance watched details of Kate's acting with the aid of
a powerful pair of opera glasses, making suggestions in her
wonderful croaking voice. She never missed a performance.

Actor Jay Robinson remembers, "If any of us got sick, Kate
would say, 'Oh, come on, get up and out of it.' She'd never

tolerate weakness. It wasn't that she wasn't kind—she just didn't understand how anyone could *yield* to an illness.

"And if one dressing room was the least bit dirty, she'd sweep it out herself with a broom."

Shortly after the run of *As You Like It,* on March 17, 1951, when Kate was forty-one, her mother died in her sleep at the age of seventy-three. Kate had deeply adored her, and it was painful to realize that this brilliant woman was gone. When Dr. Hepburn married Mrs. Hepburn's nurse, Madelaine, Kate shrugged and accepted the situation. But she was bitterly disappointed when they decided not to retain the house in Hartford and presented it to Hartford University. Kate says, "I've never been able to go down Bloomfield Avenue again."

Eight

While Kate was appearing in *As You Like It*, the director John Huston, whose father, Walter Huston, she had always deeply admired, decided to make a screen version of C. S. Forester's novel *The African Queen*. It was the story of a missionary and a riverboat captain who fight the Germans in Africa during World War I. Huston cast Humphrey Bogart as Alnutt, the Cockney captain, changing the part to a Canadian to account for Bogart's accent, and they both agreed Hepburn was the only person in the world to play Rose Sayer, the tough but kindly missionary. She fell in love with the part at once.

Bogart described his feelings about Kate at the time:* "John and I went to see her, entertaining righteous skepticism. We had heard the stories about her. How she drove hard Yankee bargains with producers . . . that Hollywood was only a necessary evil to her, her real interests being the stage and her home in Connecticut; that she wouldn't sign autographs for film fans and detested publicity. We knew, too, that she had been fired from plays because she tried to direct them, and today insists on editing and cutting her films. If she chose, she could be difficult.

"Then there was the zany side, which we figured threw the lie at her shy, publicity-hating nature. Like the five baths a day she took because, she said, they helped her think; like the story that she couldn't sit without propping her slack-clad legs almost as high as her head. She'd say, 'yah' for 'yes,' 'rally' for 'really,' sweetened tea with strawberry jam, shined her freckled face with rubbing alcohol; wouldn't use makeup

Coronet, April, 1952.

except on her lips, or wear stockings, and had never used jewelry or perfume."

Huston called Kate and asked her out to dinner to discuss the story. She said, "I never eat out, because I get nervous indigestion and have to lie down after eating restaurant food." Instead, she asked Huston and Bogart up very early the next morning. They went over to see her at her latest house, a monstrosity perched on the side of a hill. She almost at once said that she liked the idea of the film, would adore going to Africa, and had dozens of ideas for adapting the material. She announced her intention of writing her autobiography, and said that Africa would make a "colorful chapter." John Huston said, "For posthumous publication, I presume?" Later, commenting on a remark she had made that "plain women know more about men than beautiful ones do," Bogart said to Huston, "Since she's a crow, she should know."

Humphrey said later, "You wonder whether the man was pulling your leg—or is she pulling it? Here is either a twenty-four-carat nut or a great actress working mighty hard at being one. You wait for the laughs he promised, but you can't stand the dame. She won't let anybody get a word in edgewise and keeps repeating what a superior person she is. . . . Later you get a load of the babe stalking through an African jungle as though she had beaten Livingstone to it. Her shirttail is carefully torn for casual effect and is flapping out of her jeans. She pounces on the flora and fauna with a home movie camera like a kid going to his first Christmas tree, and she blunders within ten feet of a wild boar's tusks for a close-up of the beast. About every other minute she wrings her hands in ecstasy and says, 'What divine natives! What divine morning-glories!' Brother, your brow goes up . . . is this something from *The Philadelphia Story*?"

Kate in her turn adored Bogey from the outset: "He was a real man—nothing feminine about him. He knew he was a natural aristocrat—better than anybody." His leathery rough exterior, whisky-sour personality, and impression of a thousand midnights did nothing to conceal his warmth and consideration. Kate's feelings about Huston were ambiguous: looking at the tall, loping, giraffelike figure, the long, hang-

dog, humorous face, she felt she detected a certain pretension, a posing as a Hemingwayish big-game hunter among
men.

"He couldn't hit a tin can with a peashooter," she says, "But
he liked to give the impression he could kill an elephant."
Despite the fact that she felt Huston was something of a
put-on, as well as a hard taskmaster with a sadistic streak, she
learned a deep appreciation of his talent both during script
discussions and later, on location.

Kate left for London in April, 1951, staying at Claridge's
and alarming everyone by appearing in slacks at the front
door. Told that slacks were not allowed in the lobby, she used
the servants' entrance from that moment on. Since Spencer
was busy in Hollywood preparing a picture called *Father's
Little Dividend,* Kate took Constance Collier as her companion. The New York columnist Ward Morehouse was in London and reported an interview with her: "She sat on the floor
in front of a roaring fire in beige sweater and slacks, saying,
'It's quite a venture, this African jaunt, and thank God
Lauren Bacall is coming along. We'll be shooting on a thirty-
foot boat for weeks, moving miles and miles down a river. I
don't play the African Queen—I play a missionary and I'm
very upright. Bogey is a wretched creature . . . I don't know
what they'll think of my accent in Africa. They'll find it queer
as hell everywhere . . . I wish Constance were going with
me . . . If anybody's looking for me, the name is Kate Hepburn, Belgian Congo.'"

Kate said later, "That was a difficult experience—in London. Sam Spiegel, who was producing the picture, kept bor-
rowing bits and pieces to keep us all—and the picture—
going. I kept thinking, 'My God, suppose he can't pay my
hotel bill!' Here am I and Constance Collier living it up at
Claridge's, which costs a *fortune,* and heaven knows whether
he'll be able to pay. Me, with my New England tightfisted-
ness—the very idea a bill might go unpaid! I *certainly* wasn't
going to pay it! I left never really certain if he'd paid it or not.
I guess he had, or we'd have worked in the kitchen!"

While Kate was in London, Huston had concluded a
twenty-five-thousand-mile series of plane journeys scouring

locations at Nairobi, Entebbe, and finally at a place called
Ponthierville, on the Lualaba River in the Belgian Congo,
where he refitted an appropriate riverboat. He returned to
London, where he and Bogey played darts and drank in the
pubs while Kate scoured various houses and museums col-
lecting a missionary's wardrobe.

The whole group flew to Rome on the first lap of the journey at the beginning of May. Kate was horrified when she
saw the airport floodlit with kliegs, *paparazzi* swarming, and
a bedlam of eager fans. She locked herself in the plane's
washroom for most of the stopover. When one reporter
managed to intercept her on the way to the washroom, she
hit him with her umbrella.

Arrived in Ponthierville, Kate insisted on a full-length mirror and a dressing room. Huston arranged for the construction of a bamboo dressing shack, which was built on buoyant
oil drums and pulled along the Lualaba River for each new
location. She refused to start work until it arrived. The prop
men had the task of buying up every piece of mirror from
tribesmen around the area, gluing the pieces together, and
making a frame for them. They finally presented her with a
fragmented monstrosity laced with join lines, which she accepted like royalty. At first, she acted with a ridiculous hauteur, until Bogart shook her and said, "You ugly, skinny old
bag of bones! Why don't you come down to earth?" And she
growled, looking him right in the eye, "Down where you're
crawling? All right!" She laughed, everyone laughed, and
from that moment on she behaved herself.

Kate's dressing room was not an idle self-indulgence. It
gave her a focus, something to work on, and from, and a
refuge at the end of a stifling day's shooting. She filled it with
marvelous flowers in water jars hung from the ceiling, African drums, and spears, and kept telling Bogart everything
was "divine" until he could willingly have killed her. Bogart
got plastered night after night, groaning about the insects,
the humidity, and the sheer misery of trying to sleep in a
jungle alive with strange sounds.

He wrote later: "While I was griping, Kate was in her glory.
She couldn't pass a fern or berry without wanting to know its
pedigree, and insisted on getting the Latin name for every-

thing she saw walking, swimming, flying, or crawling. I
wanted to cut short our ten-week schedule, but the way she
was wallowing in the stinking hole, we'd be there for years."
One day he saw her, loaded with cameras, fly swatters, recording instruments, and butterfly nets, going through the
jungle. She was so laden she could barely move. Bogart said,
"Would you mind carrying my makeup kit?"

Another time, Kate asked Bogey, "Can you help me?"

"To do what?" he growled. "Swat flies?"

"I'm trying to find a bamboo forest, Humphrey."

"What the hell for?"

"To sit in and contemplate," she answered.

Kate was fascinated by Ponthierville, but the humidity was
so extreme it mildewed her clothes, covering them in green
mold. The river was infested with crocodiles and a disease
called bilharzia, which could destroy the health of anyone
who came in contact with it. Finally, an infestation of red
soldier ants, an inch long and moving in formation, moved
into the river basin by the millions and made the continuing
of shooting far too difficult. So the entire unit, Kate, Bogey,
Bacall, Huston, had to shift to new locations at Entebbe,
Uganda, and at the foot of the Murchison Falls, to complete
the story, and the boat the *African Queen* had to be dragged
1,500 miles across country.

Severe rains affected shooting, Kate came down with dysentery, the cameras were ruined and had to be replaced, and
Huston was restless and difficult to work with. Feeling ill and
exhausted most of the time, Kate kept on doggedly. She and
the Bogarts became deeply attached to each other during the
shooting.

Cameraman Ted Scaife says, "Both Hepburn and Bacall
were like a couple of Florence Nightingales, making sure
that members of the unit had their anti-malaria tablets, their
'stoppers' and 'starters.' The unit used to set sail downriver
each morning in Sam Spiegel's 'fleet,' which consisted of a
towing vessel pulling the *African Queen*, followed by a gen-
erator, lights, and reflectors, a camera raft, another raft with
props and sound equipment, and finally Kate's loo—a float-
able toilet she insisted on. The whole collection was the

strangest sight at first gleam of morning in the middle of the Congo!"

Huston said later, "She took to Africa like a duck to water. In fact, Katie, who first regarded me as something of a murderer for my big-game hunting during off times when we were waiting for additional equipment to catch up with us, turned into my staunchest hunt companion. She didn't do any shooting, but she carried a gun and a camera, and I have seen her stand fast when the elephants were stampeding, and advance with only a 16 mm. camera in her hands on a forest pig which stood four feet at the withers and could lay a man wide open with a little thrust of his foot-long tusks."

Kate says, "It was a dream. I would walk to the locations —I adored them all, Stanleyville, Ponthierville, Entebbe, the Murchison Falls, Lake Albert—it was a most interesting experience. I would love to have gone back and done more work there. We were working in a wild-game preserve at the Murchison. I walked a lot. Wonderful flowers there! The crew brought me such great flowers—thrilling!"

On one occasion, she received an invitation to see a large tree cut down, a major event in the area. She says, "I wanted to go, desperately, but I was sick with dysentery and half a dozen other things, I was wasting away, and I had to lie down. John and Bogey were very annoyed. Well, they went, a huge storm blew up, and a lightning bolt hit the tree. The branch fell off and nearly killed them all! I was grateful for the dysentery!" She adds, "And the reason I got dysentery was my temperance! I was so busy complaining about Bogey and John drinking hard liquor I tried to shame them by drinking water in their presence at mealtimes. Well, the water was full of germs! They never got sick, and I had the Mexican trots and was in bed every day for weeks! I thought I was going to die—and in the Belgian Congo!"

Cameraman Ted Scaife recalls an episode at the foot of the Murchison Falls. "Kate had to go into the water to release the *African Queen*, which was stuck in the reeds. 'Oh!' she said, when Huston asked her, deadpan, to do this. 'The river's full of crocodiles!' And of course it was. Huston said, 'Don't worry, I'll have my prop men fire a few rounds of ammunition into the water. You'll find the crocodiles get scared by the noise, and they'll vanish.' Kate thought about this for a while and came back with, 'Yes, but what about the deaf ones?' She went in anyway."

The English crew was magnificent, and Kate was fascinated by the way they overcame technical problems. Areas of jungle growth had to be chopped away by hand; many of the crew actually stood and arranged lights when they were shaking and sweating with severe attacks of malaria. Kate often walked unsteadily from her own sickbed to observe a new composition by cameramen Jack Cardiff and Ted Scaife.

Finally, the sickness among the crew became so severe that the entire production had to be transferred to London. It was impossible to tell when one location ended and another began, or where the "English" sequences occurred. Kate, though feeling ill, enjoyed the trip home, her bags stuffed with souvenirs and a film record of the experience. "I felt like a tourist," she says. "Bogey hated Africa, but for me it was a glorious adventure."

As soon as Kate saw the film in rough cut, she knew that it would be a great hit, and she was right! The combination of Bogey, as the tough little Canadian boat captain, and Kate, as the scrawny, haughty, but vulnerable lady missionary, was brilliantly original and exciting, and James Agee's script, full of wry wit—much of it supplied by Kate and Bogey themselves on location—was more than matched by the inspired, carefully modulated direction. Bogart grew deeply fond of Kate, and learned to admire her approach to living: "She was a true eccentric," he said later. "And I found that no one is sexier than Katie, especially before a movie camera, and you remember she has legs like Dietrich's. The twenty years since I saw them on the stage in *The Warrior's Husband* hadn't hurt them at all. You learn to brand as rank slander the crack that you can throw a hat at Katie and it'll hang wherever it hits."

Robert Morley joined the unit when it returned to England, playing the role of Rose Sayer's missionary brother. He remembers, "I had never met her before, and I was always nervous of her, because she seemed a formidable lady. She knew a good deal more about the business than I did. She was the sort of lady who, when you were doing a scene with her and you weren't very clever about getting into the right position, or were about to fall over one of the cables, would continue with her performance, impeccably, and at the same time manage to push you into the right place with a friendly shove and pick up the cable as well! When I used to be making up in my chair in the morning, she would, with only about three minutes before she was due on the set, snatch a pencil out of somebody's hand, make a quick mark with it on her face, not looking any different after she'd done it, and say, 'I'm made up now,' and go on the set ahead of all of us! She fascinated me: *she kept to her course.* She was one of those curiously lucky aristocrats to whom life comes easily."

The African Queen turned out to be the greatest success of Kate's career, and earned her the finest notices she had ever received. By daring, at forty-two, to look more like fifty-five, haggard, worn, shiny-faced, ferociously freckled, a spectacular rag, bone, and hank of hair, and by playing with a completely open, raw, brave directness and lack of fuss, she achieved greatness. Leaving the lacquered world of Hollywood movies may have been painful for her, but her sojourn in Africa deepened her as a woman and as an actress.

The immensity of the continent, the sheer force of the jungle, overpowered Kate and humbled her. Her passion for nature, hitherto expressed in the modest pleasures of climbing hills around the Beverly Hills Reservoir, or exploring the estuary of the Connecticut River, was fully unleashed. Even more than the reviews, the enthusiasm of her friends, and the beauty and truth of the movie itself, her discovery of a greater world was deeply significant in her life.

Next year she would be released from Metro-Goldwyn-Mayer; next year she would become a more truly international figure than she had ever been. It was to be the greatest experience of her career: moving into middle age with the exhilarating knowledge that she was also moving into her full maturity as an actress, that she would now be able to travel, to expand, to discover places she had never seen before. But her joy was not unqualified: her absence in Africa had been an agony for Spencer, who had started drinking heavily to ease his loneliness, and she had the abiding concern that if she left him for a long period again, his health might seriously deteriorate.

Back in New York in late 1951, Kate spent several weeks resting and recovering. She met with the Kanins, who had been working on a new story for her and Tracy, *Pat and Mike*, about an athlete, Pat Pemberton, who takes up golf, has trouble playing properly because of the attentiveness of her fiancé, and falls in love with sports promoter Tracy-Mike. For Kate, who played tennis so constantly and still had a very good handicap at golf, the part was a natural, and she was enchanted by the idea.

Loaded with souvenirs of Africa, Kate accompanied the Kanins on the train to California. She recalls that she kept her companions happy on the journey with excerpts from her diary of Africa, entered in a small red book given her by Constance Collier. It was a devastation to her that the book was mislaid while she was moving into an imitation French château once owned by Charles Boyer in Beverly Hills.

Kate continued to rest in Hollywood, breaking the isolation occasionally by showing slides of Africa to friends. But she soon recovered, and began preparing for *Pat and Mike* by getting plenty of practice at the Beverly Hills Hotel tennis court, and at the Lakeside golf course. George Cukor was brought in to direct, and there were marvelous script conferences, with Tracy effortlessly acting the role of the promoter, his spectacles perched on the end of his nose. The entire picture was shot at the Riviera Country Club, with a number of women pros corralled for the occasion. "Gorgeous" Gussie Moran, Babe Didrikson Zaharias, Alice Marble, Betty Hicks, and others were all engaged. The Kanins' script was brilliantly funny, in the spirit of Damon Runyon. The producer, Lawrence Weingarten, says, "Gar had written a line in which Spencer said of Kate, 'She's pretty well stacked.' I said, 'Do you know the meaning of this word? Kate is not well stacked. She has a small bust.' I pressured him, George pressured him, and he came up with another line, 'There ain't much meat on her, but what there is is cherce!' It got the biggest laugh in the picture."

George Cukor says, "The reason this comedy, and its pre-

decessor *Adam's Rib,* worked was that none of us took ourselves very seriously during the writing and preparation. We
batted ideas around like tennis balls, we all *felt* the lines and
situations without any kind of ghastly solemnity. If we all
laughed, a line went in. I remember there was a scene in
which Spencer massaged Kate's leg. No sex implied, but it
was very sexy. You sensed the empathy between these two.
We had wonderful fun working out that scene."

Perhaps the most inspired sequence in the picture was one
in which Kate, made nervous by her fiancé, who is watching
her, gradually loses the game: the net becomes as high as a
wall, her tennis racket shrinks to the size of a soupspoon, her
opponent looms like Goliath. Bill Tilden, the great tennis
player, had said to Kate, the Kanins, and Cukor one day,
"That's the way it feels when you lose. You turn into a
midget." They adopted the idea, and it worked effectively.

Kate's second lead, the gravel-voiced newcomer Aldo Ray,
says, "There was a scene in which I had to carry her off a golf
course, all the way into the clubhouse and up the stairs. I did
it, the camera followed us in one take, and I deposited her
on a couch as the scene ended. Then I whispered in her ear,
'I'm going to FUCK YOU!' She said, shaking her head like a
schoolmistress, 'You'll do no such thing! If you do, I'm going
to call Spencer!"

Directed with irresistible energy by Cukor and played
with the skill of champions by the stars, *Pat and Mike* was not
only a classic portrait of sporting people in action, but itself
had the appeal of a good tennis match. The thrust of the
Kanin-Gordon lines was perfectly delivered by Kate and
Spencer, both at their peak. The reviews were uniformly
warm, Bosley Crowther saying in the New York *Times:*
"Katharine Hepburn and Spencer Tracy, who lost their amateur standing years ago so far as their popular rating as theatrical entertainers goes, are proving themselves equally able
as a couple of professional sports in *Pat and Mike.*" The picture was a great success, even in the Middle West, where Kate
had never exerted a strong appeal, and Kate was delighted
with her appearance in the picture, looking ten years younger
than she had in *The African Queen,* and getting a rare
chance to show off her legs in short white tennis skirts.

Early in the 1950s, Kate became obsessed with the idea of playing the role of Epifania, George Bernard Shaw's outrageously spoiled, madcap heiress in *The Millionairess*, on the stage. Kate told me, "I adored *The Millionairess*. Everything kept saying, 'Why do you want to do it? It's such a bad play.' Well, I thought it was fun, and I still do. It portrays a wonderful character. My mother worshiped Shaw. She knew everything he'd ever written. Backwards. So did my father. A great deal of Shaw was read out loud at home. He was sort of a god. In 1939, when I was doing *The Philadelphia Story*, Gabriel Pascal, who was going to produce it on the stage, wrote to me and asked if I would do it. Donald Ogden Stewart would have done the script. I read the play out loud to the whole gang at home. We thought the first act was great, the second act was less, and that it fizzled in the third act. I said 'No.' I was so stupid, and so doltish. I should have said, 'Well, maybe, but perhaps I could go to England and talk to the old boy.' I could have met him! It was like the time I said to Mary Pickford, 'I don't go out to dine'—a compulsion to give a very quick, very firm answer, which I've struggled to learn not to do. You cut yourself off from an awful lot of fun.

"Then, ten years later, when I was rehearsing for the road tour of *As You Like It*, I was sitting one night at home in Turtle Bay, all alone in the house with the fire going, with that marvelous edition of Shaw, the one with huge print, which is wonderful when your eyesight is starting to fail and you have to reach for the glasses, and I read *The Millionairess*. Suddenly I thought, 'I know how to do this. This could be marvelous!' I gave it to Michael Benthall. I said, 'Read this play.' He said, 'It would be absolutely sensational!'

"After the tour of *As You Like It*, Michael and I took it to 'Binky' Beaumont of H. M. Tennant in London, who had been after me to do something. He asked us to dinner, and it came to the coffee. He said, excitedly, '*What have you got?*' And when we said *The Millionairess*, he nearly died! He had done it with Dame Edith Evans, and it had not succeeded. But we talked him into it."

Kate traveled to London with Constance Collier to do *The Millionairess*. When Hugh Beaumont refused to send an extra ticket for Constance's companion, Phyllis Wilbourn, Kate cashed in the two air tickets for three tickets on a cheap ship. She, Constance, and Phyllis were hopelessly seasick most of the way across.

Epifania, the protagonist of *The Millionairess*, was a spectacular part for Kate. She was in almost every scene, wild, commanding, screaming with rage at her subordinates, tackling her fellow players head on—sometimes literally—cracking bizarre jokes, yet finally disclosed to be a sensitive and lovable human being as well as a sacred monster. It was as though Tracy Lord in *The Philadelphia Story* had grown older, more arrogant, more outrageous, and had not been "broken in." Epifania was also a cross between Katharina in *The Taming of the Shrew* and Susan Vance in *Bringing Up Baby*. Kate read and reread the play, and reread it again, convinced that although it represented the less attractive side of her character—the bossy, overpowering, crotchety side—it would release her wonderfully on the stage.

Luckily, Hugh Beaumont saw her point of view, and understood that the play had possibilities. He arranged to tour it through the British provinces from the North of England to Brighton before the London opening, and Kate welcomed this chance to polish the playing in front of the warm and considerate British audiences. The sophisticated and debonair Cyril Ritchard and the saturnine Robert Helpmann appeared, respectively, as Kate's stooge and her Egyptian doctor.

Although Kate lost her voice on tour, and had to send notes to everyone to save herself for the actual performance onstage, she managed to give a wonderful show, at once horrible, absurd, and touchingly comic.

Her London opening was a triumph, and was ecstatically received by Kenneth Tynan, the most influential critic of the time, in the *Observer*. In a review notable for its barrage of similes, he compared her with—among other things—a fire, a branding iron, and Adolf Hitler. This review, and others which were equally enthusiastic, insured a successful run.

The only trouble was that Kate's enthusiasm tended to exhaust the other players, and in a scene in which she was supposed to break Cyril Ritchard's leg, she very nearly succeeded in doing just that. Ritchard says, "She threw me over in a kind of jujitsu movement. She had to get me by the ankles and tip me backward, then as I struggled to my feet, she grabbed me again and made me roll over. Later she chased me down some stairs—it was offstage, but you heard the clatter as I fell. A policeman and a policewoman taught us how to do the scene. One night during the London run, she tipped me over and I *heard* the muscles go. I was in agony—I don't know how I came back on the stage—but I did manage to get through the part each night, even though I was on crutches. I don't *think* people noticed me hobbling before the scene! I was never allowed to mention it again.

"I gave her a Christmas present soon after—one of those leather bags she likes to carry over her shoulder. She was so angry she almost hit me with it. She explained, 'I don't like Christmas presents!'"

During the play's run, Kate was joined by Spencer, who flew in to be with her. She had enormous trouble with the fans on this visit. Her leading British fan, John Marven, says, "She signed a couple of autographs in books, then ripped them out. One of the fans turned nasty and was going to hit her; Tracy intervened, and for a moment it looked as though he were going to smash the fan. The fan fled. Hepburn was totally uncooperative. I went to see her and waited for hours around the back entrance of her hotel. Finally, she came out, saw me, and jumped down my throat. She said, 'I don't do that kind of thing in the street, I have no intention of doing it,' when I asked her for the autograph. Three days later, she came walking along—on a Saturday morning. She'd been to Shepherd's Market, she had a string bag with carrots and cabbages and parsnips, and I asked her again. She said, 'Is there anyone else around?' I said, 'No.' So she just snatched the book and signed it, shut it hard, so it was smudged and wet and useless, and slung the book at me.

"I saw her again, years later, on her next visit to London. I had a beautiful picture of her, and waited and waited to see her. About ten o'clock one Saturday morning, she came out of the hotel with Gorgeous Gussie Moran and went to her car, a broken-down Ford with a shattered window at the back. Robert Helpmann was sitting in there with the chauffeur—she was on her way to Wimbledon. She looked at me coldly when I approached her and said, 'I've done one for you before. I won't sign a picture in the street.' I asked her, 'Why won't you do it in the street?' She replied, 'It's not in my nature.'

"I told her, 'Nature is what we're put in this world to rise above.' It was a line from *The African Queen*. She gave me a particularly filthy look, then up with the tennis racket and she rapped me across the shoulder with it! She jumped in the car, and it moved up, only to stop at a traffic light. I saw a hand come out—hers—beckoning me. She said, 'Give me the picture!' She signed it—right across the face, ruining the photograph! I still have it to this day.

"Gorgeous Gussie Moran and Mr. Helpmann were in the back of the car, killing themselves with laughter! I never asked for her autograph again. She hasn't changed. I was backstage at *Coco* when a fan asked her for her autograph, and in the rush of people he pushed her. She yelled at him, 'Don't push me! You're pushing the wrong person. I'll push your head off!' "

The Millionairess ran for a successful limited season of twelve weeks in London, but its New York run (for the Theatre Guild) was a flop, partly because of reviews which accused Kate of storming, fuming, carrying on excessively in the play, and partly because she lost her voice again at dress rehearsal at the Shubert Theatre and had difficulty making herself understood on opening night.

Despite this failure, Kate was determined to turn *The Millionairess* into a film. Because the play had not succeeded in New York, everybody in Hollywood turned it down. Kate's agent, Abe Lastfogel, of the William Morris Agency, finally called an independent producer, Lester Cowan, and interested him in the idea. Cowan told me, "By all the laws of show business and practicality, filming the play was something that couldn't be done. But Kate convinced me I should get involved, despite the fact that Shaw had never been successful at the box office. In his will, Shaw left a stipulation that nothing was to be changed in his plays. Of course, this was absurd. Finally the Estate allowed us to change 20 percent. But we had to *tabulate* the words first. It was a real headache.

"She was a hypnotist! I went ahead, with the gravest doubts. I felt a great respect and awe for Kate. We often met at her home in Beverly Hills; Abe Lastfogel literally delivered me to Kate like a parcel from a mail delivery service. When Kate looked at me, her will penetrated my whole being, and I knew nothing would stop her. I admired her so! The project *had* to happen. I was her cheerleader or accessory. I told her, 'There's only one man who can match Shaw's wit on the screen pictorially. That man is Preston Sturges.' "

Noted for his brittle, inventive comedies about the rich—*The Lady Eve* and *Unfaithfully Yours* had been masterpieces of stylized romantic elegance—the accomplished writer-director Preston Sturges was in a steep professional decline that year. But Kate saw the wisdom of Cowan's choice: Sturges came from a wealthy background, and had known women like Epifania; he could improve Shaw's somewhat weak and straggling construction; he could render complicated verbal jokes effectively visual; he could re-create the whole *mise en scène* of Epifania's extravagant life to perfection. She advanced Sturges $5,000 out of her own pocket to bring him to New York to work with her. Once he arrived, she regenerated him. She told him she expected nothing short of total discipline and dedication from him. He hadn't been up early in the morning since childhood; he had drunk heavily; and he was in very poor physical shape. Kate installed Sturges at the Waldorf Towers, and forced him to get up each morning and walk to her house in Turtle Bay. He responded by writing more vigorously than he had in years. Inspired by her, he created some of the most amusing scenes of his career under her authoritative guidance.

Kate worked with Sturges every day for seven weeks, refusing to allow him to drink before 5 P.M., and then only in extreme moderation. As a result of this rigorous discipline, he produced an inspired script. When it was finished, Lester Cowan dropped by for some very minor suggestions. "Without Kate, Sturges couldn't have written anything," Cowan says. "She plucked him out of the grave. She gave him the mental therapy of writing. She acted out scenes for him even as he wrote them.

"Then came the harrowing business of trying to sell the darned thing. We discussed deals with Alex Korda in Britain, and with J. Arthur Rank. Part of the deal would be that we got someone very big to play the role of the millionairess' Egyptian friend. We finally did make a deal based on our getting Alec Guinness. But he discovered he had to do another picture, *The Prisoner*. Sturges and I went to Ireland to see Guinness on *The Prisoner* location in a jail; they got along, but Guinness finally decided not to work with us."

Kate says, "We had one of the funniest scripts that was ever written. But we couldn't sell it. Preston was over the hill, my career was in the trembles, and people wouldn't finance us. We'd be on the verge of getting the deal worked out, but we just weren't strong enough to set it up. It was heartbreaking —shattering. Certainly it was the greatest disappointment of my life. I still read the script today; it's just wonderful. Preston had eight million ideas every minute. I'd sit with him as sort of a producer, not as a writer, and he was like a wonderful, wonderful fountain. But he didn't know the difference between the good ideas and the bad ideas at that time. The failure of that project killed Preston. He died of neglect."

Luckily for her peace of mind, Kate had an interesting offer in 1953 from a director she admired, David Lean. She had liked his Dickens adaptations, *Great Expectations* and *Oliver Twist*. He had decided to film a version of Arthur Laurents' stage play, *The Time of the Cuckoo*, retitled *Summertime*, in which Shirley Booth had been a great hit on Broadway. It was the story of a lonely Ohio spinster, Jane Hudson, who goes, equipped with camera, to Venice, a city she has dreamed of visiting all her life. She falls in love with Renato di Rossi, an antique shop proprietor (Rossano Brazzi), and they enjoy an idyllic interlude on the island of Burano. But Jane—painfully aware of their differences—returns to America alone. Reminiscent of Lean's own *Brief Encounter*, the film was a touching, fragile evocation of doomed love. And Kate was born to play the part of Jane,

with all of its tenderness, love of beauty, open warmth and
honesty, deep sensitivity and awareness of pain, final rejection
of an unworkable situation, and brave acceptance of loneliness and defeat.

Kate was deeply impressed with David Lean—military,
dark-skinned, intensely disciplined—but making the picture
in Venice proved to be something of a mixed pleasure. The
humid heat of the summer of 1954 seemed more intense than
Africa's. Kate liked the *palazzo* on the Grand Canal which
the producer, Ilya Lopert, had rented for her, and the company of Constance Collier and Phyllis Wilbourn. But she had
a constant battle to keep the *palazzo* up to the standards of
cleanliness she demanded, and, to her great annoyance, she
became a kind of one-woman spectator sport, attracting not
only what seemed to be the entire population of Venice but
every tourist from every hotel in the city. When she tried to
visit art galleries and museums, she was followed everywhere, and curtly brushed off requests for autographs.

Making the picture was excruciatingly slow. David Lean
was even more meticulous in matters of detail than George
Cukor, seemingly choreographing every pigeon down to the
last feather and arguing with his cameraman, Jack Hildyard,
on angles of the camera or effects of sunlight. He coolly swept
aside many of Kate's most urgent suggestions. She admired
him deeply, and was aware of his fierce poetic response to the
material, but often there was an awkward state of armed
truce.

The technical problems were endless. The Italian crew
members were often slow and inefficient. All of the equipment had to be floated on launches and barges, and could not
be moved without the currents and beyond the rigorous
canal speed limits. Crowds, police, and noise often ruined
key sequences, which had to be completely rerecorded in
England. The sound truck carrying all the recording equipment was seized when it entered at an illegal entry point on
the Italian border on its way from Paris. A customs strike
prevented the rushes from being processed in London, so
they had to be processed in Rome.

Always a vivid embodiment of the life force, Kate found
filmmaking in the golden city exhausting even for her. She

had not entirely recovered from the dysentery she had con-
tracted in Africa, and sometimes she felt weak and ill and
fretful. But there were compensations in wickedly witty, enchanting Constance; in her co-star, the suave and elegant
Rossano Brazzi; and in the inspiration of David Lean. And
the character of Jane constantly intrigued her: she added
touches of piercing observation throughout the shooting.

The most difficult sequence in the picture, and the most
famous, was the one in which Jane, photographing an antique shop, backs too close to the edge of a canal and falls
over into it.

Kate says, "I knew how dirty the water was, so I took all
kinds of precautions—even washed my mouth with antisep-
tic, put special dressing on my hair, wore shoes that wouldn't
waterlog. But like an idiot, I forgot my eyes. When I fell in,
I had a startled look, with my eyes open . . . Well, the water
was a *sewer!* Filthy—brackish—full of trash! When I got out,
my eyes were running. They've been running ever since. I
have the most ghastly infection—I'll never lose it till the day
I die. When people ask me why I cry such a lot in pictures,
I say, mysteriously, 'Canal in Venice.'"

When she saw *Summertime*, exquisitely photographed by
Jack Hildyard, bathed in a golden Venetian light, filled with
bells chiming, fluttering pigeons, dark echoes, ringing sheets
of green water, gondolas gliding, Kate was enchanted. She
told David Lean she adored the picture. As in so many other
films, her playing was defenselessly free, deeply felt, reveal-
ing the spirit of a woman who had never lost her sense of
innocent wonder, whose vulnerability was worn like a
wound, whose defense of bossy efficiency could in a moment
crumble into tears of adoration or despair. Venice in the
picture became a symbol of life: of sunlight and noise and
sexuality flooding in waves through the cool, scrubbed clois-
ters of a virgin's soul.

Kate understood Jane Hudson deeply, giving a raw realism
to what might have been little more than an accomplished,
glossy romantic fantasy. Her odd, stiff-backed spinsterish
stride, her stern, bony face melting into tender concern, her
air of agonized loneliness, her harsh, flat, insistent voice fall-

ing into pallid decrescendos of surrender: she had not lost the
touch that had made young Alice Adams so adorable. Critics
and public alike fell in love with the performance, and the
picture was a great success. One journalist, Art Buchwald,
even got carried away to the point of saying, "Her bones are
the greatest calcium deposit since the white cliffs of Dover."

Back in London from Venice—where Spencer had been
able to visit her briefly during the shooting—Kate had pleasant visits with Noël Coward and "Binky" Beaumont, among
other friends, and began discussing with Michael Benthall an
exciting venture: a tour with the Old Vic Company to Australia, a continent she had always wanted to visit. She and
Benthall spent the last weeks of the summer of 1954 selecting
three Shakespeare plays: *The Taming of the Shrew, The Merchant of Venice,* and *Measure for Measure.* Kate supervised
the sets, costumes, and arrangements for the tour, bringing
to the task all of her subtle skill and experience and her
lifelong dedication to Shakespeare's texts. The productions
were to be staged in Sydney, Brisbane, and Melbourne in
collaboration with the venerable Australian theatre management company of J. C. Williamson's. Kate was very excited
by the idea of traveling this far afield so soon after her trip
to Africa, and still more excited by the idea of appearing with
Bobby Helpmann again. He would play Shylock to her
Portia, Angelo to her Isobella, and Petruchio to her Katharina.

The really serious problem was in leaving Spencer for a
long period. It was impossible for him to travel to Australia
because of motion picture commitments in Hollywood, and
Kate feared that without her tender care he might experience a sudden decline in health. But she could not resist the
opportunity of the tour: deeply as she was committed to
Tracy, she was, like most stars, even more committed to
herself and to her career, and Tracy also could not renege on
his obligations. They uneasily accepted the separation, just as
they had accepted the separation when Kate went to Africa,
even more painfully aware than before that they were not
like ordinary people, that they had to face the difficult challenges of the roles they had chosen in life.

Kate, with Robert Helpmann, Michael Benthall, and the members of the Old Vic Company, left for Australia by Qantas Airlines at the beginning of May, 1955. Despite her worry over Spencer, Kate was in an excited mood, and Robert Helpmann, an Australian who had not been back for almost a quarter of a century, broke down and cried with joy as the plane circled over Botany Bay before landing in Sydney. To Kate's relief, only a small group of 150 fans was at the airport to greet her; her films had never been "big" in Australia. She stepped off the plane wearing sand-colored gabardine slacks, polo-necked white sweater, oxfords, and a cream poplin raincoat; she was swept by the twinkling, rotund Harald Bowden of J. C. Williamson's into a waiting limousine, and driven as quickly as the speed limit allowed through the ugly, depressing factory suburbs between Mascot Airport and the city. To Bowden's dismay, she looked at all this squalor with the rapt eagerness of a tourist looking at the Taj Mahal. She was fascinated by Sydney itself, with its turquoise-blue harbor, rich parks, narrow, crowded streets, suntanned bustling people, and feeling of a cheerful frontier at the edge of the world. The Hotel Australia, where she had been booked, had a Bostonian pomposity and dowdiness, and she rather liked its faded charm.

That night, she gave one of her very rare press conferences, expertly fielding some very shrewd, and often sharply rude reporter's questions. When someone asked her why she didn't dress up, she said, "Dorothy Gish once made a remark that sums up everything I feel about dress. She observed, 'I'm paid to dress up in my working hours. Why should I bother in my free time?' "

Asked what she ate, she said, "I eat a huge breakfast—I don't diet." When do you have it? "Pretty damn early." Vitamin pills? "No, I'm a doctor's daughter." Clothes? "Must be comfortable. Rough-surfaced materials. Better for spilling food and drink on." On smoking: "Never smoke in the daytime. It's not my throat I worry about, it's my brain. Smoke fogs it. It affects your vitality—or what I like to think is my vitality." She said she hated refrigerators because they made so much noise; and air conditioners, too. She joked about her summer home of Fenwick: "We're so close to the water that the tide rises three feet on the first floor every year since the hurricane of 1938. Funny for a Noël Coward comedy, but not very convenient." Toward the end of the conference, she grew impatient, and her joking spirit emerged. Asked about her legs, she said, "I wore tights onstage in *As You Like It*. Why don't I show them in films? I'll tell you why, sir. I like to keep them a secret. I *adore* looking at them myself." She concluded the conference with a neat slap. Someone challenged her: "Are you temperamental?" She told him, with a ghastly grin, "I'm charming. See how charming I am. Of course, I may drop dead at any minute."

Next day, Kate and Helpmann attended a civic reception. The Lord Mayor of Sydney declared pompously, "I am delighted to welcome Mr. Hepburn and Miss Helpmann to our fair city." Kate and Bobby could not repress their laughter; later, the same gaffe was repeated by the Lord Mayor of Melbourne.

Kate had a good time rehearsing with the company at the echoing, run-down Tivoli Theatre. She walked all over the city, tan gabardine slacks flapping in Sydney's high southerly winds, coat flying from her armpits. She and Helpmann explored the handsome Botanical Gardens by the harbor, hunting for four-leaf clovers. She came up with several; Bobby dismayed her by holding out a clenched fist and saying, "You're going to hate me, but—" He opened his hand and it contained a six-leaf clover.

The limited season performances of the three plays were sold out, despite mixed reviews by Lindsay Browne and Josephine O'Neill, the most powerful local critics, and some unfavorable comparisons by theatre buffs of Kate with Vivien Leigh, who had appeared in another Old Vic Shakespeare tour three years earlier. Most critics agreed that Kate lacked the variety and richness Vivien Leigh had brought to her playing, and they objected emphatically to the American intonations of her speech. The productions were very striking. Helpmann played Shylock with a raw racial pride and bitterness, memorably expressing his contempt of the corrupt anti-Semitic society of Venice; Kate was gay and charming in the early scenes as Portia; severe, subdued, and austere as the young lawyer. In *Measure for Measure,* staged on Leslie Hurry's stark dun-colored sets, Helpmann was a pallid and poisonous Angelo to Kate's vehement, overpowering, and exhausting Isabella; in *The Taming of the Shrew*, she was a funny, bewitching, exasperating Kate to Helpmann's jaunty, forceful Petruchio, against Peter Rice's evocative sets of arches against dark blue sky.

The limited season was a complete hit, and the audiences were spontaneous, quick-witted, unsophisticated, and adoring. The nine-week run ended with a great occasion: the crowd threw colored streamers onto the stage, and Kate and Helpmann made speeches. Kate spoke of the clover-gathering contest against Bobby in the Botanical Gardens, and of her delight in Sydney Harbor and Bondi Beach. Next day, she and the company left for Brisbane, Queensland, where they enjoyed another successful stay.

Unfortunately, the Melbourne season got off to a bad start. Kate has a vivid memory of her whole experience in the southern city: "On the front page of a Melbourne paper, there was an article which read, 'We have no idea why Miss Hepburn chose to come to Melbourne, except that it was quite obvious her career must be over as a motion picture star. And Robert Helpmann's is certainly over as a dancer!' An *insulting* review! Awful! But Australia was a fascinating country—as fascinating as Africa—and we had a wonderful time. It was while I was in Melbourne that I had the most thrilling experience of my entire life.

"After that terrible review, I decided I'd better supply myself with more happy interests. I decided to look around. Bobby wasn't so interested in going around; I always am, in seeing what the country has to offer—flowers, animals, and birds. I went with a driver to Sherbrook Forest, which is about twenty miles out of Melbourne, and found it was a huge rain forest. I'd heard it was difficult to find your way out; I didn't want to get lost, and not be able to get back for the performance. I had to be very careful about what I was doing. I had been given a little map of the place so that I could feel my way along; there's a stream that goes through it, so I was fairly safe, I could use that as a guide. I went to a spot in it, and sat down on a picnic table. Some kids came along through it, I suppose nine or ten years old. I listened to the birds with them: the kookaburra, which imitates everything, and the lyrebird, which imitates the kookaburra. I said to one little boy, 'Have you ever heard a lyrebird?' He said, 'Yes, I have.' I asked him, 'Is that one?' He told me, 'It could be.' I told him I was going to track it. And he came with me.

"We finally reached a spot in the woods and there in front of us was a mound of pulverized dirt. And on it was this extraordinary bird. About the size of a guinea hen, with powerful thigh muscles and extraordinary long-clawed fingers, doing a dance, and sending forth sounds you couldn't believe. I stood there with the little boy for about an hour and a half just watching it, dancing in a pattern, a thrilling, rib-tingling experience. It was like a very sexual, exciting play. A wonderful musical! I finally had to quit watching because I had to get back to town and curl my hair. I got to the theatre, walked into Bobby's dressing room, and said, 'You've missed the great experience of my life.' I told him, 'I'm absolutely transported—I don't think I'll be able to remember a goddamn thing tonight.' Bobby became very anxious to go. I began to find out a lot about lyrebirds. I found that lyrebirds mark out a territory—they have a *lot*—and you don't cross their individual marked-out areas. They keep the chicks with them—they lay one egg—and keep it until it's four years old, which is very unusual, and then it's sent forth into the world. If the wife dies, the male goes off and lives with the other males. Never mates again. The female never dances on the mound built by the husband—the husband will take the male chick and teach it to dance on the mound. The mother will also teach the male bird to dance, but only on the limb of a tree or on the ground. Bobby and I had to see this, so we went time and time again. And he never saw anything. He said, 'I don't believe you ever saw anything.' I insisted I had. I loved going back to the rain forest—the curious green-brown, with a weird light filtering through it—but no sign of the lyrebirds. Finally, the last day we were there, I said to Bobby, 'It's the wrong kind of weather for it,' but he was determined. 'Let's go anyway,' he said.

"We went. And it was as if they knew that it was our last day, and that we had made this tremendous effort to see them. Stravinsky told me later that much the same thing happened to him. We saw not one but it must have been fifty birds! They were all dancing, dancing on the boughs, moving around, walking around—it was extraordinary! The same broken rhythm, the spine-chilling quality of Stravinsky's music. The sound they made was fantastic, a strange pattern of cries.

"Bobby did a lyrebird ballet later that was dedicated to me; he wouldn't have known much about them if it hadn't been for me. He had a dream, Bobby did; he dreamed that I had deliberately lied to him and that I was keeping the lyrebirds away from him. That every time I went out to the rain forest, I would shoo them off. And that one day he went alone, and escaped me. He crawled up the hill in the dream, and there I was at the top, naked, in a bower, with lyrebirds all dancing around me. That was what gave him the notion that he should do a ballet!"

Nine

During Kate's absence in Australia, Spencer had suffered acutely. He needed her more and more as a support; to build up his ego, relax him, give him a sense of his own worth, nurse him when he was sick, and keep him away from drinking. He had embarked on a picture called *Tribute to a Bad Man*, shot in the Rockies by the director Robert Wise. Lonely, fretting at her visit to a remote country he found hard to reach by telephone, he began drinking again, and vanished from the location for a week. The patient, considerate director did his best to be supportive, but it was useless. When Spencer, who had found difficulty in breathing at high mountain altitudes, broke down one day during the shooting and wept, Wise immediately stopped production, and the studio fired Spencer. Kate, hearing the news so far away, and committed to her tour, was desolate.

Her anguish increased because she had long since committed herself to another picture immediately upon her return from Australia: a comedy called *The Iron Petticoat*, in which she played a Russian airwoman. Her distress was intensified when, during the production of *The Iron Petticoat*, Tracy went to Mont Blanc to make a picture called *The Mountain*, in which he played a mountaineer. Tracy again suffered terribly from the altitude, and on one occasion he was stranded for hours in a cable car with Robert Wagner and other members of the cast, gazing miserably into the chasm below.

Kate decided that the ideal director for *The Iron Petticoat*, which had been written for her by Ben Hecht, would be Ralph Thomas. As a doctor's daughter, she had laughed uproariously at his comedy *Doctor in the House*, which ex-

plored all the amusing, entertaining mishaps that mark a
doctor's life. Ralph Thomas remembers, "I was making a
picture in Greece with Dirk Bogarde and Brigitte Bardot. I
got a telephone call in the middle of the night from Venice.
They said it was Katharine Hepburn on the line; I didn't
believe this at all. She'd always been my idol, and it had
never occurred to me that she would wish to make a picture
with me.

"We got to England and started work. Bob Hope was
added to the package as her co-star; I think she liked the
challenge of acting with a professional comic. She was marvelous to work with. I wish I had made the picture when I
was a little more experienced, because of the problem of
handling these very diverse personalities. Really, they were
playing in two different pictures: she was a mistress of light,
sophisticated, romantic comedy, he was much broader, and
eventually I didn't so much direct the picture as watch them
in action, with a strong bias in her favor. She understood all
the problems, she gave everything she had, she is the most
cooperative person that ever breathed, and even when it was
obvious the picture wasn't working out, that we were headed
for disaster, she never lost her spirit. She played with total
truth, but it was very difficult for her to perform with someone whose stock in trade was telling funny stories.

"She did a great deal of good by stealth. She doesn't like
it to be known, but she helped the crew in all kinds of ways.
If she saw that someone looked sad, she had a knack of tact-
fully finding out what was the matter, and putting it right.
She could have done anything she wanted—she could oper-
ate the camera beautifully, knew how the tracks work, could
light a set better than almost any cameraman around. She
didn't interfere, but if things weren't right, she had an enormously succinct way of saying how it should be done. She
spent most of her time on the set when she wasn't on call. She
became my favorite person in the world."

Though she liked Ralph Thomas very much, Kate was very
disappointed with the picture, and told Thomas so. "She's a
marvelous loser as well as a good winner," Thomas says. His
wife, the producer Betty Box, adds, "She was a great example
to me as a woman, not only in her work but in her life, the

way she cared about other people. It was the first time I had
found any deep concern for others in *any* actress. I felt that
Bob Hope was very uncertain and insecure, whereas Katie
was very certain and direct and sure. *She* was tremendous,
but *he* was trying to do too much, he was doing his television
shows at the same time. She had extraordinary resources of
inner strength. He insisted on top billing. She didn't care; she
didn't think it was important.

"She was always against publicity. There was a marvelous
woman journalist called Nancy Spain who was later killed in
a plane crash; Nancy badly wanted to interview Katie, she
admired her so much. We persuaded Katie to see Nancy and
told her that Nancy would treat her very well and that anyway Katie would want to meet her. Finally, Katie did. Nancy
had a marvelous interview. Two days later, Nancy called up
and said, 'I want to do something for you in return. A friend
of mine, Ian Fleming, is quite unknown, but I think you'd like
the story he's done.' Our reward for letting Nancy see Katie
was that we got the first James Bond. And then we sent it
back and said it wasn't quite what we wanted!"

Despite her great care in learning a Russian accent for the
role of the airwoman, and some amusing self-parody in the
comedy scenes, there can be no avoiding the fact that Kate,
like *The Iron Petticoat*, was a disaster. It was the worst moment in her career since she had been labeled "box-office
poison" in the 1930s.

In the spring of 1956, Kate traveled with Spencer to Cuba
to make *The Old Man and the Sea*, from Ernest Hemingway's novel. Kate's old beau Leland Hayward had long since
ceased to be her agent, and had become a celebrated producer—of such hits as *South Pacific, Carousel*, and *Call Me
Madam*. In 1953, he had obtained the rights to Hemingway's
famous story, and in 1955 Spencer had been cast in the central role of the aging fisherman who has an epic struggle with
a huge marlin in the waters off Cuba. Leland signed the
German-born Fred Zinnemann to direct.

From the beginning of the Cuban adventure, everyone
was deeply dissatisfied. Hemingway disliked the small boy

chosen to play the old fisherman's companion, calling the lad "a cross between a tadpole and Anita Loos." He also felt that Tracy was "too fat, rich, and old" for the part. He was not particularly warm toward Spencer. The shooting proved difficult: weather conditions were changeable, and Spencer, compelled to play many scenes in an open boat, was feeling his age and felt that Fred Zinnemann drove him relentlessly. Kate and Spencer grew to dislike Zinnemann's approach to the shooting, and Zinnemann became restless over Spencer's recalcitrance. The whole experience was a disagreeable ordeal for everyone, but Kate managed to slough off some of the misery she felt by painting some wonderful sun-washed, sparkling sea-and-skyscapes of Cuba, filled with white walls, crescent moon-shaped beaches, glimpses of distant sails.

While she was in Cuba, Kate closed a deal to make a movie for the Paramount producer Hal Wallis, calling him frequently by long distance in Hollywood to discuss the matter. She was to play the lead role of Lizzie Curry, in a film version of N. Richard Nash's well-known Broadway play, *The Rainmaker*.

The director chosen was the shy, reserved, deeply subdued, and endearingly self-effacing Joseph Anthony, who had also guided the stage production. Lizzie Curry was an unhappy spinster character, struggling to look after her father and brothers in a depressing small town. Lonely and afraid of life, she meets an apparent con man, Starbuck. His physical assurance and powerfully masculine charm break through her protective shell. Starbuck promises to bring rain to the parched soil of the southwestern state, and his promise is metaphorically fulfilled when he enriches Lizzie's sterile and sexless existence.

The theme was similar to that of *Summertime,* in a different setting, and Lizzie was an ideal part for Kate. During the adaptation from stage to screen, Anthony had added many touches of delicate and tender humor to Lizzie's character. Geraldine Page had played the part in the theatre, acting it with a somewhat plaintive air. In an attempt to curb her mannerisms, Anthony had tried to urge her to the kind of forthright, positive directness, covering a nervous vulnerability, which seemed to him to characterize Lizzie, but instead Miss Page had acted in a fluttery, ZaSu Pitts–like manner which was her specialty, all limp wrists and eyes turned up to heaven. Anthony had her distractedly straighten objects all through the production, but he was never quite satisfied with the playing. "What we strove for with Gerry we had with Kate," he says. "It was very available and wonderful."

The aggressive, truck driver–like Burt Lancaster was cast as Starbuck. "He was very difficult from the outset," Anthony says. "He was anxious to get out of his contract to Hal Wallis; he was terribly antagonistic on the telephone before we met and at our first meeting; he told me, 'This play is a bunch of crap. The writer doesn't know anything about country life, or what it means to be in a drought, with the cattle starving.' I told him the drought was just a symbol of Lizzie's parched soul, but he dismissed the idea out of hand. He was grumbling, disagreeable, plainly rude. I decided if he stayed I would not. Later, he apologized, to the limited extent of which he was capable, but it wasn't a very happy way to start a picture. I didn't think highly of him. I still don't.

"He was not much fun to work with. He had to work himself up to scenes; he had no natural command of himself at all; and he was butting into other people's business all the time, half directing, suggesting things to the cameraman, insisting on key lights, interfering. He had to be completely in charge of everything or he wasn't satisfied.

"My rapport with Kate was, by contrast, total. She called me at the very outset of negotiations on the telephone from Cuba, and said how happy she was she would be working with me. I had a sense of immediate, direct, simple pleasure, and a feeling of trust in me that came over the wire. It was wonderfully encouraging.

"I finally met her in Hollywood. She drove up to the studio in a battered Ford roadster, hiked over, and ran into me on the way into Hal Wallis' office. We went to lunch in the commissary with Hal and his entourage. I was silent, and I felt shy; I was rather startled when some youngster came over with her mother or aunt and asked for Kate's autograph. She was abrupt in her denial almost to the point of rudeness.

She was quite firm that she was having lunch with people, talking about work, and that was not the time for anybody to be silly and gushing. She just said, 'I never give them!' and the child and mother made a rather awkward retreat. What she was saying was, 'Don't join this parade of nonsense, this intrusion of privacy.' If it cost her professionally or in terms of her public, she was willing to pay the price."

Kate had an instant rapport with Anthony. He respected her need for privacy in thinking out the details of her role. Along with the cameraman, Charles Lang, Jr., he protected her most "difficult" area, her neck, with the special use of shadows. He saw that in playing Lizzie Curry she wanted a clean and uncomplicated approach to character, avoiding all the "bunk," as she called it, which cluttered up the approach of so many actors. She even gave Anthony a sketch, of Lizzie running to a barn to her prospective lover, which said a great deal about the character's release from inhibition. She wrote in a corner of the drawing, "But Joe, what is my motivation?" in an ironical comment on the then fashionable Method system of Lee Strasberg. Anthony's problem, he remembers, was to reduce Kate's enormous energy, aliveness, animation by an appropriate amount to balance the more subdued, rough, and earthy playing of her fellow players. He made endless takes in an effort to force her to look exhausted, as Lizzie would have been after a day of toil. He had to remind her to play more realistically, not to "color" scenes excessively, not to be too "clean," too simple and clear-cut in her approach. Their discussions were deeply searching. The only serious problem lay in Kate's accent: Lizzie was a Southwesterner, and Kate was still very distinctively New England. But everyone decided it would seem strained if she spoke differently.

Unhappily, like *The Sea of Grass* before it, *The Rainmaker* was shot almost in its entirety in Hollywood. This was a vexation to Kate; and she was not entirely happy with Lancaster. She came to the first reading knowing her part from beginning to end; Lancaster had been used to a system in which lines were learned the previous night for the sequence to be shot the next day. He was somewhat unsettled by her total efficiency, while Kate, despite her personal reservations, acted most considerately toward him.

During the shooting, Anthony, who had enjoyed visits with Kate at her house for lunch or afternoon tea, invited her out to dine. He says, "She replied, 'I can't go anywhere. I can't do anything. I can't appear in public; people would follow me, I'd never be able to rest . . . I can't go to the movies, or walk down the street.' I realized then what it meant to be a star. The loneliness . . . What it meant to be a public figure, to have to live as a recluse . . .'"

On another occasion, Anthony called Kate on a Sunday and suggested dropping over for half an hour. "She said, rather sharply, 'Oh! That's unexpected! I don't think so! I don't think so!' I said, 'Fine,' and she hung up. Ten minutes later, she called and said, 'I'd be enchanted if you and your wife would come to lunch.' And then she wouldn't let us go! I think she had a moment of regret that she had turned me down, that she had acted a little impetuously. She didn't want to feel she was being 'used' by her guests inviting themselves over, but really she was lonely, she wanted friends, and once they arrived she wanted them to stay with her. Her graciousness, her warmth and pleasure in entertaining were unforgettable."

At the preview in New York, Kate ran down the balcony stairs to the lobby and told Anthony she enjoyed the movie very much, calling it "a darling pickshah!" "So objective!" Anthony says. "As if she had nothing to do with it!"

The movie was quite well received by the critics, but its public reception was not exceptionally warm. Bosley Crowther wrote in the New York *Times:* "Even though [Miss Hepburn's] manners are quite airy for the Corn Belt and her accent suspiciously Bryn Mawr, she holds her own better than even with a bunch of voracious clowns."

Kate's performance as Lizzie Curry was not quite right—she seemed too New Englandish and schoolmistressy to convey the rough awkwardness of a southwestern farming woman—but her acting gleamed like bronze. In many scenes in which she entered the spirit of this wise, virginal woman of the soil struggling for happiness, she was reminiscent of

Jane Hudson in *Summertime*. In others, she seemed actressy
and self-conscious, out of touch with the material. Much of
the picture turned out to be a "midcult" version of farming
life, making Burt Lancaster's criticisms of its unreality seem
most reasonable in retrospect. But the picture displayed all
of Kate's formidable technical armory quite unimpaired by
time.

On the last day of shooting *The Rainmaker*, Kate said to
Hal Wallis, "I'd like to direct a picture for you." And he said,
"Sure. You can direct the next Martin and Lewis picture!"

While Kate was making *The Rainmaker*, Spencer was un-
dergoing the disagreeable ordeal of reshooting most of *The
Old Man and the Sea* in the studio tank at Warners. John
Sturges had taken over as director, and Spencer found him
more congenial than Fred Zinnemann, but it was still difficult for Spencer to put up with hours spent in the bobbing
tank water, whipped by artificial storms. His health suffered
severely from the stress of shooting, and at the end of each
day Kate was shocked to find him utterly exhausted.

What Kate and Spencer needed desperately was a comedy,
a pleasant, relaxing diversion in which they could appear
happily together, without the separations that different locations entailed. The perfect subject proved to be a trifle called
Desk Set, written by Henry and Phoebe Ephron.

Almost as sophisticated and amusing as the Kanins, Henry
and Phoebe Ephron had become established as a producer-
writer team at Twentieth Century–Fox. Toward the end of
1956, they were casting around for an appropriate property
to adapt as a CinemaScope comedy. They ran into the producer Charles Brackett on the lot, and he mentioned that he
had obtained the rights to William Marchant's Broadway
play, *Desk Set*. Ephron dropped by Brackett's office and
picked up two copies of the comedy. He liked it at first
glance, remembered Shirley Booth's great success in it on
the stage, and recalled that Shirley Booth had also been the
precursor of Kate in *The Time of the Cuckoo/Summertime*.
He called Phoebe at home and asked her to come in to the
studio and read it. She liked it equally, and said, "It's contem-

porary, it's funny." *Desk Set* was the story of Bunny Watson, a murderously intelligent woman in charge of a TV network library who can answer the most abstruse questions immediately. She is threatened with dismissal when an engineer, Dick Sumner, invents a computer called Emmy. Emmy can answer questions even faster than Bunny, and the amusing complications spring from the clash of woman and machine.

Ephron called Buddy Adler, head of production at the studio, and said he wanted to go ahead; Adler gave him the green light. The Ephrons went to New York to note where the laughs came in the stage production. They returned to Hollywood and wrote the screenplay in about three months, making deft changes in the structure and dialogue. They decided Kate and Spencer would be perfect for the leading roles, but did not tell them so until the script was finished. On a Sunday, two days after the screenplay was first circulated at the studio, it was sent over to the home Spencer rented from George Cukor on St. Ives Drive in West Hollywood.

Kate and Spencer adored the script the moment they read it. On Monday, Kate called her agent, Abe Lastfogel, and told him very firmly, "We want to do it." That same afternoon, Walter Lang was written into the project as director. Henry Ephron says, "Walter's face fell when he heard that Tracy was going to be in it. He had just seen him in *The Mountain* and he said, 'He looked like Santa Claus. He can't play love scenes.' We said, 'You can't fight that kind of talent. He and Kate will be great. Nobody else can play those parts.' " Lang reluctantly surrendered.

Kate asked for a rewrite in which Spencer's part would be made more important than it was in the existing material, and the Ephrons agreed. Kate enjoyed a series of conferences with the couple, making extensive suggestions, and accepting almost all of theirs. During the six weeks of rewrites, they became friends; Henry Ephron says, "We got to know those inevitable man's shirts, those inevitable slacks, which were dry-cleaned so often they had faded to nothing, and the inevitable sea bircuits she ate for lunch while we went off to the commissary. We told each other funny stories, and gossip, to refresh ourselves, and had a great time.

"Finally, the work was over. Kate took the script home on

a Saturday, and Spencer read it. On Monday, she arrived
looking woebegone, and said, 'Spencer doesn't want to do
the picture.' I already had had a feeling this might happen,
because I had talked to Albert and Frances Hackett, co-
authors of *Father of the Bride,* in which Spencer had appeared, and they said, 'When he hears a starting date, he gets
nervous, and tries to withdraw. Watch out!' I found out that
Spencer had read a review that Sunday by Edwin Schallert
of the Los Angeles *Times.* Not a review of one of Spencer's
new pictures. But it contained an unfavorable reference to
his playing in *Dr. Jekyll and Mr. Hyde* sixteen years earlier,
and it had upset him violently. I went down with Walter
Lang to talk to Buddy Adler. We were all quite desperate:
Kate had suggested doing the picture with Fred Astaire.
Adler snapped at us, 'Look. If it comes down to that, I don't
even want Hepburn. I want Hepburn and Tracy or I don't
want either one of them.' I said, 'I'm absolutely sure I can talk
Spencer into it.' Adler told us to convene a meeting with
Kate and Spencer and find out what Spencer's problems
were. 'New York wants the picture. We've got to have it,' he
said.

Kate, Spencer, the Ephrons, and Walter Lang all met that
afternoon. Spencer was besieged by a barrage of flattery.
Everyone told him, "It's nothing without you." Finally he
came around. "I glanced surreptitiously at Kate when Spencer said 'Yes,' " Ephron remembers. "I saw a tear appear in
her eye. She was, I think, a little disappointed. It's paradoxi-
cal, she needed him for the part, but she realized that he
wasn't as strong as she thought, that he could be persuaded
so easily. She loved him so goddamned dearly!"

With Kate and Spencer both signed, the project went full
speed ahead. In the CinemaScope era, locations became very
important, and the Ephrons decided to shoot much of the
picture in New York. Remembering the happy experience of
making *Adam's Rib,* Kate was all for this idea. The Ephrons
wrote a scene in which the engineer tries to unsettle the
bluestocking by asking her questions like 'What is a palindrome?' It was planned so that it could begin outside IBM's
building on Fifty-seventh Street and continue down Sixth
Avenue; they stop at a sandwich shop on the way. Henry

Ephron and Kate went to New York to scout the correct line
of camera movement in the scene, to find an actress who
could play Peg Costello, Kate's warmhearted and adorable
close friend in the picture, and to cast some young New York
girls as secretaries. They found new locations, and when Joan
Blondell came up to Henry's suite to read for the part of Peg
Costello, both Kate and Henry fell in love with her sweet,
sunny personality. Ephron says, "Joan was plump, very
gemütlich, a marvelous foil for Kate." She was chosen in
preference to Thelma Ritter, whom Henry and Kate had
seen previously.

No sooner had the locations been picked out and Henry
Ephron returned to Hollywood than Spyros Skouras, president of the company, arrived from New York and announced
at a Twentieth Century–Fox company dinner that the picture would be too expensive if it had to be shot in New York.
He also declared that "a picture starring Hepburn and Tracy
will not be commercially successful." He pointed out that
their pictures did not make money in the Middle West and
the South. Ephron screamed at Skouras at lunch, "You bring
us all the way up to the altar and then you say it's going to
be a bad marriage! Where were you when we first arranged
to do locations? What the fuck is the matter with you?"

Kate and Spencer heard that Henry Ephron was in trouble, and Spencer called from New York to find out what was
going on. Ephron told him. Spencer said, "Jee-zus! Forget
New York. We don't have to walk down Sixth Avenue in a
scene. If we can't play that scene in front of a backdrop, we
shouldn't be getting paid."

Production went ahead in Hollywood with Skouras' reluctant approval. "Kate and Spencer were wonderful," Ephron
says. "They did not just 'bring the body.' They worked out
everything between them. It was a happy set. They got along
will with Walter; he wasn't their idea of a director as Cukor
was; but they accepted him."

Walter Lang's direction was smoothly efficient, discreetly
self-effacing, and Spencer and Kate were at their best. Just
before shooting, an amusing episode took place.

Ephron says, "Kate was in every aspect of the picture—at
times a real pain in the ass. But you had to love her. She came

down to the set the day before shooting and mentioned the big plant we had curling all over the office set in the picture. It was mentioned in our script as being a philodendron—the long word got a laugh when she wrapped her tongue around it. 'Henry,' she said, 'Henry, *that is not a philodendron!*' Walter Lang moaned, 'Jesus Christ, Katie, will you please go home?' I told her, 'Katie, will you get the hell outa here? It's three o'clock already, and we have to line this thing up for a shot at nine o'clock tomorrow morning. Go home!' Katie stood firm. 'It's not a philodendron!' she said. Walter and I yelled, 'Get the studio gardener!' We *got* the studio gardener. 'That's a philodendron,' he announced. She insisted, 'It's NOT a philodendron!' We ordered her off the set. As she walked off, she growled, 'I'll show you what a philodendron is. You're a bunch of idiots!' Which was a common exit line for her. We finished preparing the set at a quarter to five, and Walter and I went to Walter's office for a five-o'clock drink. All of a sudden, Hepburn appeared with a thirty-five-foot philodendron which weighed ninety pounds—she had carried it up three flights of stairs when she couldn't get it into the elevator—put it down in front of Walter and me, and said, 'THAT is a philodendron!' The gardener admitted he was wrong—and we replaced the plant we had."

Making *Desk Set* proved to be a comfortable experience, and the movie, though not an unqualified hit, recouped its costs and enjoyed moderately good reviews.

Kate was prodigiously funny as the know-it-all research librarian who immediately can describe the difference between a palindrome and a palimpsest without consulting a dictionary, and Spencer visibly enjoyed himself in the role of the shrewd, quiet engineer who finds that she is more than a human computer. They played together with all of their old, exhilarating give-and-take, showing they had lost nothing of the skillful comedy timing of *Adam's Rib* and *Pat and Mike*. In a fine humor, intensely happy to see Spencer relaxed again after the ordeal of *The Mountain* and *The Old Man and the Sea,* Kate characteristically chose not to proceed to another romantic comedy, but instead returned to her first love, the stage, in order to help the struggling and demoralized nascent American Shakespeare Festival company at Stratford, Connecticut, under the direction of John Houseman and Jack Landau.

Yielding to a suggestion of Lawrence Langner, who had founded the company, she agreed to play for only $350 a week, and the free use of an extremely humble, uncomfortable shack on the edge of the Housatonic River. Kate agreed to play Portia to Morris Carnovsky's Shylock, as well as Beatrice to Alfred Drake's Benedick in *Much Ado about Nothing*.

She had a series of discussions with the solemn and dignified John Houseman at Turtle Bay. Houseman says, "I can only speak good of Kate. Jack Landau, who was my associate up there, and who was not as strong as I was, but was extremely talented, worked very closely with her. I thought that it was better for him, rather than me, to handle her, knowing she is a bossy character anyway, and she had already played Portia for the Old Vic and had very strong views on the acting of the role. I was the producer, the heavy; we all three existed in a constant state of tension, but I was really very fond of her. She had the highest standard of professional behavior, which transmitted itself to the rest of the company. Not at all the lady star condescending to lend her presence to us. Rather, she was almost a Girl Scout cheerleader, the chief of the 'boosters.'

"I'll never forget how she used to have the local fishermen on the river up for coffee and breakfast at her little house before they left for their pre-dawn fishing. We were all filled with alarm because she used to swim in the very swift, dangerous currents each morning. We'd see her come riding in on her bicycle, hair flying in the wind, or running along a bridle path in army fatigues, breathing hard. Wonderful!

"Her presence, her name helped everything enormously. Business had been very bad, the theatre had only been going for a year. I found her as exhilarating as when I had first seen her—years before, at Stockbridge in *The Admirable Crichton*. She had learned from Constance Collier that the actress must have one major scene in which she justifies the description of 'star.' In *Much Ado* it was the church scene, in *Merchant* the court scene, and she acted both very finely.

"She was kind, thoughtful, generous to the other players. She never upstaged the young girls or pushed them out of the limelight. She was always present thirty minutes before everyone else, and always last to leave. She was an inspiration to everyone, an ideal team worker. She hated people 'yessing' her, she challenged everyone to fight her, and if they didn't, she wasn't at all pleased. But given the challenge and the conflict, she was excited and she was happy."

Houseman recalls, "Alfred Drake, who played Benedick to her Beatrice, was used to being a musical leading man, and having the ladies throw themselves at his feet. Kate was a different cup of tea, and he was inhibited by her. After the first day's rehearsal, he wanted to quit. He was never at ease with her—his ego was a little impaired."

Alfred Drake says, "I had met Kate years before. In 1946, I had accepted a movie contract from Harry Cohn at Columbia, and had drinks with her, Lawrence Langner, Spencer Tracy, and Jimmy Cagney in New York. Kate said, 'Where are you going to live?' I told her the agents had arranged something. Well, they hadn't. When we reached the Coast, nothing was ready. I called her, and she offered me her house, the old Eleanor Boardman house high up in the hills. My wife and I accepted, and we stayed there for ten days.

"I didn't see her again until ten years later, when John Houseman asked me to work with her. I found her difficult to work with. If there's any single thing you can say about Kate the first time you meet her, it's that she's certainly a rugged individualist. She checked on the sets, the costumes, the direction, the lighting.

"Kate's initial attitude toward Much Ado was almost dictatorial. We already had two directors, but she was used to being in charge, and now we had a third! I always put my faith in my director: I feel he's God the Father out there in the dark. I don't like to be directed by my co-star who's talking through the director to me. On one occasion, we were rehearsing in Much Ado and I saw her out front whispering in Jack Landau's ear. I said, 'Katie, don't do that. If there's something you want to say to me, come up and say it directly. We'll see if it works or doesn't work.' She didn't much like that from me. We did not *begin* as friends.

"Kate had seen a production of *Much Ado* in England with Peggy Ashcroft, and had adored it; she thought it was perfect. She felt our production must be totally free of comparisons with something that was unbeatable. She had insisted it be done in Spanish California settings. As a result, she wanted to change the text, and substitute certain words, like 'gun' for 'sword.' Which was not necessary because, though they did have guns in California later, they also wore swords. I happen to be a stickler when it comes to Shakespeare, and I don't want the text to be rewritten by anyone. 'Additional dialogue by' strikes me as being the height of *chutzpah*, and I don't want any part of it! We had arguments about that. I remember one occasion I *boiled*. She had cut one of Beatrice's most beautiful speeches, and I told her, 'Don't you realize that's a wonderful thing, the finest thing Shakespeare ever wrote for a woman onstage? How dare you cut that! Are you afraid of it?' The next day it was back in. She did it magnificently—it was a joy to hear!

"She's so Spartan, so disciplined, I accused her of being something of a Jesuit. I remember how she hated people smoking near her—I smoked—and she had an obsessive hatred of dirt. One of the most startling pictures I've carried in my mind is something that happened at early rehearsal one day. She was sweeping the floor of the Masonic Hall, where we were rehearsing, with a broom!

"Another time, we quarreled and she stormed off the stage. Three minutes later, she came back. She had a prepschool humor—she adored the humor of insult. To me that's a bore. Luckily, I'd read *Tom Brown's Schooldays*, so I was more or less equipped to deal with it. On one occasion I remember, she came storming into my dressing room out of the blue and said, 'You know, the trouble with you, Alfred, is that you haven't dealt with a co-star in a long time. All you've had is leading ladies.' And my reply was, 'Well, at least they've been ladies.' She got flustered and said, 'There's nothing you can say to me that Spencer hasn't said to me much more!'

"After the run at Stratford, we went on tour. Both at Stratford and thereafter, I should have taken my bow before her. That was normal, as she was the top star. She said, 'Oh, no, I'm not going to have that, we'll take our bows together.' The reason she gave was curious. She said, 'I'm not going to take a chance on your getting more applause than I do,' which was a lie, obviously. *Of course* Katharine Hepburn is going to get more applause than Alfred Drake! But she insisted, and that was very generous of her.

"I had to leave the tour because of another engagement. I gave a company party, and she insisted on giving it with me, and paying for half of it. She said, 'I've no talent for giving parties. You'll have to do all the arranging.' I did all the arranging, and we had a delightful party, with performers from local supper clubs. I made a lethal punch with a champagne base, brandy, and soda water and so on. I filled her glass eleven times—she drank every drop, and she was stone-cold sober! She was the last to leave.

"Next day, she said, 'Why didn't you ask me to dance?' I said, 'For God's sake. I catered this thing, I worked on it, I never got a chance to dance with anyone!' She said, 'You didn't dance with *anyone?*' I said, 'No.' She said, 'Very well, then, it's all right.' On my last night, she spoke a beautiful farewell to me to the audience, and presented me with an absolutely exquisite oblong silver cigarette box from Tiffany's, with all the names of the cast inscribed on it.

"I hurried back to my dressing room to get out of makeup so I could go and thank her. When I arrived at her dressing room, her maid said, 'She's gone. But she left this note for you.' I still have that letter, and it's one of the loveliest letters I have ever had from anyone. It was utterly gentle, generous, and kind. When she made her musical debut in *Coco,* I sent her a telegram. 'Welcome to the illegitimate stage.' "

During the Shakespeare tour, Kate was sticken with pneumonia, and played many performances with a temperature of 103. Weakened by this illness and never satisfied with the production as a whole, she declined, to everyone's disappointment, to take them to Broadway. Instead, she decided to make another film, and began reading scripts.

In these late years of the 1950s, Kate retained the habits of twenty years before. She continued to run around Central

Park or along the country paths of Connecticut; she played tennis obsessively at Fenwick or at the Beverly Hills Hotel court, where people often used to stand and watch her, unsettling her with remarks like "She's not as quick as she used to be." She read Shaw and Shakespeare assiduously, constantly returning to favorite passages; and she continued to rent the homes of the great silent stars in Hollywood, reliving her childhood dreams. Her relationship with Spencer was still marked by the humorous put-downs, amusing collisions, the mingling of despair and joy that had marked it from the beginning. Aware that he would need constant attention, and aware that she must dedicate herself to him like the doctor's daughter and nursing sister she was at heart, Kate began to think seriously in 1957 and 1958 of retiring from the screen for good.

Kate retained the friends, the loyalties, of earlier years: Laura Harding, Lawrence Langner, Terry Helburn, Armina Marshall. She also had become very close to Samuel Goldwyn's wife, Frances, an exquisitely beautiful woman; Lawrence Weingarten; and John Ford, whom she had grown to admire deeply. "Very few people know he saved my life," she says. "On *Mary of Scotland*, I was riding—I had learned to ride sidesaddle—at a full gallop, and suddenly he yelled, 'DUCK!' I did, and if I hadn't I'd have been killed instantly. There was a branch I hadn't seen." Kate still showed a sisterly concern for Judy Garland, aiding her during her frequent breakdowns; she continued to be very close to George Cukor; she constantly saw her family; and she painted her delicate, precise landscapes of both coasts.

For Kate, in middle age—she turned forty-nine in November, 1958—life became more and more a discipline, less and less the madcap, eccentric jaunt of her youth. She had come to understand her own nature, had come to terms with her faults, and accepted herself frankly. "Stone-cold sober, I found myself absolutely fascinating," she said years later. Her terror of life, of people, of facing an audience or a camera increased with the onset of age, but it was counterbalanced by a warmer humor and a greater concern for others, which she knew was the way to happiness. She also learned some-

thing she had not learned in her youth: that she couldn't have
everything, that she couldn't have the life which society had
laid down for women—marital security, children, domestic
toil—as well as the joy and release of her work. As her private
life grew more painful, she enjoyed making movies more
completely; it became increasingly a release into a fantastic
adventure. She saw more pictures herself, and again found
release simply in watching them.

Above all, she retained a fundamental simplicity, honesty,
and innocence, which at once exasperated, irritated, cleansed,
and refreshed her friends. For all of her shrewdness, piercing
wisdom, fundamental striking home to the truth, she was still
a child at heart. She returned to childhood fairy tales, by
Grimm, Hans Andersen, Andrew Lang, and loved to reflect
on the carefree days at Bryn Mawr, her first madcap adventures on the stage. Her secret as an artist was that she
never lost her sense of wonder. She had managed to pass
through adolescence and young adulthood with her spirit
unspoiled. Each day, greeted very early, was at once an adventure and a challenge. Each person she met was utterly
intriguing, and it took a real clod to defeat her passionate
interest.

Her experiences with the flora and fauna of Africa and the
lyrebirds of Australia had enhanced her feeling that she must
know everything about nature. She never gave up her long
walks in Hollywood or Beverly Hills, often following the
same paths she and Laura took. She knew the squirrels, herons, sparrows; she knew the migratory habits, construction of
the nests, the whole pattern of life in the vanishing wilderness. It was as though she wanted to drink in the whole of life,
measure it, control it, absorb it utterly before she lay in the
earth at last, hands folded in sleep.

It was in the midst of this period of reverie, of delving
continually into the past, that Kate decided to reunite herself
with two old and valued associates, Sam Spiegel and Joseph
L. Mankiewicz, for a version of Tennessee Williams' play,
Suddenly Last Summer, adapted by Gore Vidal. Originally,
the play had been a modest one-acter, produced with another, *Something Unspoken*, under the general heading of

The Garden District. Kate was asked to play the part of Mrs. Venable, a monstrous, bloodsucking caricature of an American mother, whose homosexual son, Sebastian, has been cannibalized by youths. In order to conceal the secret, she has Sebastian's cousin Catherine committed to a sanitarium, and insists upon the girl's having a lobotomy of the brain to destroy her memory.

From the beginning to end, the making of this elaborately pretentious and guilt-ridden homosexual fantasy was a nightmare for Kate. Certain doubts about her suitability for the role of Mrs. Venable became overpowering during the production. For the first time since she had played Mary Queen of Scots—whom she always thought of as somewhat of a ninny, a despicable and spineless weakling—she thoroughly disliked the woman she was playing. Worse, the picture was made for reasons of economy in England, and Spencer was in Hollywood, in uncertain health, committed to making a movie for their mutual friend John Ford, *The Last Hurrah.* Her separation from him was an unsettling and anxiety-producing one, as always.

Kate had problems with everything and everyone on the picture. Elizabeth Taylor, playing the tragic cousin Catherine whom Mrs. Venable victimizes, was rather cold and distant. Her other co-star, Montgomery Clift, his jaw shattered in a recent auto accident, was deteriorating under the influence of drugs, and was frequently confused and almost inaudible in dramatic scenes. Absurdly miscast as a psychiatrist, when he looked far more the tragic patient, he suffered from insomnia, blinding psychosomatic headaches, a feeling of desolation which ruined his performance. He was ineffective, dying on his feet. In most shots, he looked shockingly ill.

Kate was kindness itself to him. She tried to help him to sleep regular hours without pills, to face up to the physical effects of his injury, but her brisk no-nonsense New England doctor's daughter's common sense was useless. Mankiewicz threatened to close down production. Mankiewicz, who had produced *The Philadelphia Story* and *Woman of the Year,* and had made the heartlessly brilliant, coldly sentimental *All about Eve,* was not a sympathetic person, and Kate grew to hate him. Mankiewicz says, "She felt I was being brutal to

Montgomery Clift, but we had a real problem making the picture work, he was always late—it was horrible. Finally, on the last day of shooting, Kate came up to me, looked me hard in the eye, and *spat*. On the floor. Then she went into Sam Spiegel's office and spat on *his* floor. She never worked with either of us again." According to the actor Gary Raymond, who played a supporting role in the picture, "Actually, it was quite different. It's true she was angry with Mankiewicz's treatment of Clift, but what happened was this: on her very last day on the set, she went up to him in front of the whole cast and crew and said to him, 'Are you absolutely through with me?' He said, 'Yes.' She went on, 'I have nothing more to do with you or with the film?' He said, 'No.' And then she spat—right in his face!"

Tennessee Williams was pleased with Kate's acting of the role of Mrs. Venable, while she herself hated it. This was in fact one of the most awkward and artificial performances she ever gave, suggesting all too clearly her discomfort on the set. Soon afterward, Williams wrote *Night of the Iguana*, about a beaten-up hotelkeeper in Mexico, especially for her, but by that time, fond as she was of Tennessee, appreciative as she was of his talent, she disliked his plays except for *The Glass Menagerie* and one or two others. They were infused with destructiveness and a hatred of women. She wanted to construct. She loved women, believing them to be superior to men. Distressed by the trend that pictures were taking—toward grotesquerie and perversion—she returned to the stage for a brief and only moderately successful season at Stratford, as Viola in *Twelfth Night* and Cleopatra to Robert Ryan's Marc Antony in *Antony and Cleopatra*.

The 1960 Stratford season was marked by a bizarre little incident. One afternoon, she was out fishing on the Housatonic when she remembered to her horror that she had to play a matinee. She managed to get her boat moored, ran up a bank, and slipped and fell in the mud. When she reached the theatre, she was dismayed to see the entire audience wandering over the lawn in front of the theatre, dressed up in style, waiting for the doors to open. She had no alternative but to run right through them, wet, bedraggled, and covered with mud from head to foot, splashing several women accidentally as she waved her mud-soaked arms. "Disgusting!" "What does she think she's doing?" several people said, until they realized that this muddy river urchin was none other than the leading lady they were about to see.

After the return to Stratford, Kate devoted herself religiously to looking after Spencer, but she made it a rule never to appear on the sets of his films. In *Inherit the Wind*, the story of the Scopes "monkey" trial of the 1920s, Spencer played the role of a lawyer, based on Clarence Darrow, who has a passionate concern for justice. Kate at once stimulated and infuriated the director, Stanley Kramer, with a stream of suggestions on twenties clothes and hair, and even courtroom procedure, based on her customary massive research before the picture started.

When Spencer made *The Devil at Four O'Clock*, in Hawaii, she went along for the trip, watching him work every day. She broke her usual rule of not watching Spencer work because of the rugged character of the location in various jungle areas: it was necessary to see that Spencer retained a reasonably healthy condition despite the heat and constantly changing food and water.

After returning from Hawaii, Kate and Spencer read and were deeply impressed by Stanley Kramer's script for *Judgment at Nuremberg*, based on the story of the Nuremberg trials, in which Kramer wanted Spencer to play an American judge. Spencer accepted the challenge immediately: both he and Kate felt it was the most important, serious, and adult script either of them had ever read. The problem was that the picture had to be shot in Germany, and Spencer, following a particularly bad flight to Cuba for *The Old Man and the Sea*, was terrified of flying. Kate went along on the trip to bolster his courage. They left from New York; Spencer was approaching the plane at Idlewild when he became seized with panic and could not go aboard. Luckily, Kate, with a few whispered words and a kiss on the cheek, gave him the strength to continue.

The flight was smooth, and Kate and Spencer reached Berlin after a brief stopover in Munich, looking reasonably comfortable. The German publicity representatives met them at the airport and drove them to the Berlin Hilton. Two blocks from the Hilton, Kate told the driver to stop the car, jumped out, and walked around the streets until she found the back entrance of the Hilton, making her way to the suite by freight elevator. She traveled to Nuremberg for the shooting, enjoying portions of Marlene Dietrich's coffeecake and strudel between scenes. Spencer told Stanley Kramer one day, "The Kraut pretends she baked those cakes herself." Spencer winked. "She didn't, of course."

Kramer says, "I wanted Spencer to go to Berlin for the world premiere, and Kate didn't want him to go. I said, 'How can you tell him not to go? The trip wouldn't hurt him, and you said you'd go with him.' She replied, 'It seems such a stupid thing to do. What do you want to flaunt him in front of the Germans for?' I said, 'I'm not flaunting him. Willy Brandt's invited us. Let's go.' She was reluctant, but finally she agreed."

In the early months of 1962, Kate and Spencer remained in Hollywood, feeling badly hurt by an article, which appeared in *Look* magazine, discussing their relationship openly for the first time. As protective of her privacy as ever, Kate felt that the author of the article, Bill Davidson, had overstepped the mark, and he quickly was crossed off certain Hollywood invitation lists. Spencer was badly hurt by the article also, consoled only by the pleasant, undemanding task of narrating the elaborate Cinerama epic *How the West Was Won* at his old studio, MGM. His crusty voice was ideal for relating this saga of suffering and triumph of the early pioneers.

Unknown to Kate, that spring and early summer plans were afoot in the East to bring her back to the screen. The man behind the scheme was a sharp-witted, roly-poly television boss named Ely Landau, one of the few men in America capable of making business out of culture.

In his role as head of Channel 13 in New York, Ely Landau had been the creator of a television series entitled "The Play of the Week." Among his most successful productions had been a version of *The Iceman Cometh*, with Jason Robards, which Eugene O'Neill's widow, Carlotta, had felt was the

definitive version of an O'Neill work on the screen. When
Landau sold the station, Mrs. O'Neill suggested that he should
take over all the unproduced O'Neill properties. He agreed,
and decided to proceed at once with a motion picture of *Long
Day's Journey into Night*. Landau and his partner, Jack Drey-
fus, felt that Kate would be perfect for the role of the drug
addict Mary Tyrone, the wife of an unhappy actor and mother
of a struggling writer, whose tragedy is explored in the course
of an afternoon and a night in Connecticut in 1912.

Landau decided to take his courage in both hands and call
Kate in Hollywood. "She knew all about the 'Play of the
Week' series," Landau remembers. "She knew there had
never been a greater role for a woman. But she said, 'I
couldn't do it—it's too big and demanding.'" Kate knew and
admired Landau's work; she also knew that Mary Tyrone was
one of the greatest parts for a woman ever written by a
dramatist. But she was terrified by the demands the play
would make on her and the long separation from Tracy that
would again be necessary. She said she couldn't take the job
on. Landau urged her to at least agree to a conversation, and
she reluctantly assented. Landau flew out to Hollywood. In
the meantime, Kate read the play two or three times, knowing in her heart she would be perfect for the role. She discussed it at great length with Landau and then drove him
back to the airport.

Landau says, "On the way to the airport, she stopped the
car in the midst of a passionate discussion, and we got out and
began walking along a canyon street. She suddenly burst into
tears, and said, 'I don't know whether I can do it. It's so
demanding. I want to do it. I'm fascinated—but I'm terrified!
It's so great!'"

Kate's emotion of fear was entirely new for her. Up to this
stage in her life—she was now fifty-three—she had attacked
every role with crushing confidence. Her dislike of her appearance and portrayal in *Suddenly Last Summer* accen-
tuated her concern that she might not succeed in the role of
another tortured woman with a grown-up son. But she came
to realize that, unlike Tennessee Williams' Mrs. Venable,
Eugene O'Neill's Mary Tyrone, based on his own mother,
was observed with an intense heterosexual sympathy. After

numerous new rereadings, she at last saw how her playing in
the role could prove appealing to her vast public.

Shortly afterward, Ely Landau returned with his director,
the driving, earnest Sidney Lumet, for further discussions.
Lumet regards his experience with Kate as the most tremendous event of his life. "It was the most totally creative, marvelous time I've ever had," he says. "It couldn't have begun
worse, however. As I walked across the room with hand out-
stretched, I didn't even have time to say 'How d'you do'
before she snapped, 'I hear you want to start rehearsals on
September 19.' I told her, 'Yes, Miss Hepburn.' She continued
sharply, 'Well, I can't start until the twenty-sixth.' 'Why not?'
I asked her. 'Because if we start on the nineteenth, you'll
know more about the play than I do.' I thought, 'Oh, *oh*,
there's going to be trouble.'

"As we left, Ely said, 'That didn't go too well, did it?' I told
him, 'I don't care. There may be blood, but I won't do the
movie without her. If it's going to be hell, it will have to be
hell.' We had another meeting with her later that day, and
things were a little more relaxed. I wanted Spencer to play
Kate's husband Tyrone in the play. It would have been very
good casting. She said, 'Then why don't you come to breakfast tomorrow morning, and I'll have him read the play tonight.'

"I came to breakfast. It was extraordinary to watch her
with Spence. She was a totally different person. She turned
really submissive—it's the only word I can use—and hardly
opened her mouth, other than introducing us. She smiled,
laughed at everything he said—which, by the way, was quite
justified; he was the most charming man I've ever met in my
life—and finally when we got down to business, I explained
to him, 'I don't have to tell you what it would mean to have
you.' He replied, 'Look, Kate's the lunatic, she's the one who
goes off and appears at Stratford in Shakespeare—*Much Ado*,
all that stuff. I don't believe in that nonsense—I'm a movie
actor. She's always doing these things for no money! Here
you are with twenty-five thousand each for *Long Day's Journey*—crazy! I read it last night, and it's the best play I ever
read. I promise you this: If you offered me this part for five
hundred thousand and somebody else offered me another

part for five hundred thousand, I'd take this!' And Kate exclaimed, 'There he goes! No! It's not going to work!' And we just went ahead and had a charming breakfast.

"Well, he didn't play it, and Sir Ralph Richardson was our second choice. Within a week of rehearsal, I knew I was lucky to be living at the same time that lady was. I found her an incredibly creative spirit. I don't think she knew how good she was."

While Kate's agent, Abe Lastfogel, worked out the details of the contract, Kate studied and again studied the part, talking to Tracy at length in order to deepen her understanding of the Irish character of the Tyrone family. Meanwhile, in New York, Ely Landau found a wonderful old house on City Island in the Bronx which ideally reflected the characters' moods. The interior was authentically designed by Richard Sylbert. The entire production was rehearsed and the interiors shot at the Production Center Studios on West Twenty-sixth Street.

Once she had overcome her initial fear, Kate was utterly involved in every aspect of the production. She was enchanted by the fact that her husband was to be played by Sir Ralph Richardson, a bold step on Landau's part, since many people felt the role should be acted only by an American. She was sensitive and considerate of the young Dean Stockwell, who was overawed by her.

Sir Ralph Richardson has very happy memories of making the picture. "I found Katharine enchanting," he says. "It was the only time I worked with her. She frightened the life out of me. I smoke a pipe. She wouldn't let me smoke. The first time we met, she said, 'Take that beastly pipe away.' We had canvas 'retiring rooms' on the set; mine was next to hers. I would go to my room secretly to smoke my pipe. I would light it, and she would know immediately and shout, 'You're at it again!' She's a great Puritan. I would stop smoking my pipe—I think she did me a lot more good than I realized at the time. Her energy was extraordinary. There would be long periods of work on the set—so long and exhausting we would be sent away to rest. I would go to my canvas room and lie down. As I did so, I would hear Katharine in her room

reading aloud to her companion, Phyllis*—she was completely tireless. All I can say is that I am overcome with
admiration for her."

On the first day of shooting at City Island, the weather
became icy and a grey drizzle sprinkled the house and the
scruffy lawn. The script called for a sparkling summer day.
But Kate was already shivering with cold when the shooting
began. She told a visiting reporter, Eugene Archer of the
New York *Times,* "I look terrible in this play—you know, I
progress to the nether reaches of insanity in the course of a
day—but I've never had such a part. It even has humor in it
—dark, macabre humor. You'll see it when we play it. You
know, I don't think the play is about dope at all—it's something else that's been lost. In the case of this wife, it's religion
—but we've all lost something, haven't we?—and that makes
it universal."

Sidney Lumet, after initial misgivings, was overwhelmed
by Kate. He says, "It was the culmination of a lifetime of
self-exploration; she found depths of feelings in herself that
surprised and even shocked her. The work went marvelously
—even in things that were in a way a *violation* of her. She's
not a *physical* actress, she doesn't like to touch people, handle people. It's not her style. In the third act, when Edmund,
her son, played by Dean Stockwell, says, 'Momma, I'm going
to die,' I said, 'Katie, I'm going to have to ask you to do
something here that's going to come as a great shock. When
he says, "I'm going to die," I want you to reach back and haul
off and sock him across the face like you never hit anybody
in your life before.' She immediately knew the sense of that
—the emotional sense—but she was absolutely terrified. It
was horrifying, a terrible thing for her to do, there was nothing in her that could ever manifest itself in that kind of
violence. But she knew how right it was for the character, she
knew the sense of it. She asked, 'Let me do it tomorrow,' and
the following day she did it after thinking about it all night:
Whap!

"I invited her to see rushes of the film. She told me, 'I've

---

*Phyllis Wilbourn, whom she had inherited after Constance Collier's
death.

always gone to rushes, and I'm good on them, but I'm not going to come to these.' I asked her, 'Why not?' She made the most remarkable observation. It was, 'If I go to rushes, all that I'm going to be able to look at is this'—she pulled the flesh under her chin—'and this'—she took hold of the flesh under her arms. She said, 'I can't have all that distraction. I need all of my energy just to play the part.'

"She went on, 'I know the way you work—honestly. I know you can't protect me photographically. Boris Kaufman [the cameraman]—he doesn't do filters. If I come out ugly, I don't want to see that.' Such a devotion to her craft! Such self-knowledge of her own talent. I fell in love with her . . . it was just one glorious day of work after another.

"She never left the set. She said to me, 'It's a tough picture. If you can, try to get my difficult scenes early in the day. I get tired.' Often I was able to do what she wanted. One scene I didn't get to until four in the afternoon—the only time in the picture we had more than three takes—and she was very exhausted, her tempo varied from take to take, and she fell off the chair in a scene in which she is talking to the maid. She played the rest of the scene on the floor! Her exhaustion was appropriate. She didn't want us to stop, and we didn't, even though we weren't prepared at all . . ."

Lumet recalls the tender concern Kate had for Dean Stockwell, who was drinking heavily. "Dean would come in with a bottle of vodka, and Kate at first almost did what she did to him in the movie—struck him. She was so angry at him —out of love. But she was tender to him. The first day of work was cold, and he had forgotten to bring an overcoat. The next day, there was a coat in his dressing room; she had gone out after shooting and bought him one. She always had an enormous affinity for heavy drinkers—maybe because of Tracy. We had many drinkers in our crew, and she was good to them all. One man came in late after being off the picture three days. He showed up looking like something the cat had dragged in, and she took him to her dressing room, cleaned the vomit off, and washed him so gently. She knew exactly what to do from experience."

At the end of the picture, Kate gave Ely Landau a hand-

carved boat with three passengers in it marked "Faith, Hope
and $400,000," a reference to the production budget.

Kate's performance as Mary Tyrone was extraordinary,
among the most formidable virtuoso displays of her career.
It was a part against her nature: she moved toward sunlight;
the character of Mary Tyrone moved toward the dark night
of the soul. Kate personified clean, shining, positive efficiency, all warmth and quick, stabbing intelligence; Mary
was filled with self-pity, desperate, hopeless, dragged down
constantly into death. What Kate had to do in acting the role
was strip away her natural buoyancy, her confidence, her
arrogance, and meet her own suffering head on. The pain of
life was a fire she quenched with showers of common sense.
In playing Mary, she had to let the fire consume her. It was
a case of inspired miscasting. Her innate nervousness—the
fluttering of the hands, smiles tremulous through tears,
words rushing forward in a torrent or decelerating into a
painfully squeezed out, monotonous slowness—was marvelous for comedy; here the gestures proved equally perfect for
tragedy. She reached the apex of her art in the scenes in
which Mary's drug addiction is disclosed: she becomes a
gaunt, famished figure with long grey hair, spinning on the
carpet of the Tyrone house like a Kabuki lion. Here all of
Kate's early struggles, her pain over Tracy, her suffering over
the death of her mother and of several friends, emerged with
a force so intense that it was almost unbearable to watch.
Like a student observing a brilliant operation, one was forced
by her to see.

Though the picture was only a moderate commercial success, it received very enthusiastic reviews, even from the
irascible Dwight MacDonald, who wrote in *Esquire:* "Katharine Hepburn's face—that terrible smile, those suffering eyes
—was especially worth watching. I have never been an addict of Katharine Hepburn; she struck me usually as mannered, to say the least; but here, stimulated by O'Neill and
Lumet, she emerges as a superb tragedienne." She and the
other players shared the acting award of the Cannes Film
Festival, and she received her ninth Academy Award nomi-
nation for her role.

After the strain of making *Long Day's Journey into Night*, Kate at fifty-three felt tired, drained, as near to beaten as she had ever been; and she was faced with the severe problem of her father's physical decline. It was an ordeal for her, on visits home from New York during and after the shooting, to see his noble spirit flickering like a spent candle in a glass. In a way, it was almost a blessing when he died, completely exhausted by a long life dedicated to medicine and to intellectual probity. She wrote to Leland Hayward on November 22, 1962, "Your flowers are beautiful—we took them out to [her sister's] farm for Thanksgiving—I said, 'Whose do you want?' She [sister] said, 'I'll take Leland's.' You were so sweet to think of us—Daddy all worn out so we *were* really glad to see him slide into 'Whatever.' Thank you very much from us all—Affectionately, Kate."

Back on the Coast the next summer, Kate suffered another shock: while on their way to a picnic at Malibu, Spencer collapsed with severe chest pain. Kate immediately called the Zuma Beach fire department, and they arrived with oxygen in a matter of minutes. Spencer was rushed to St. Vincent's Hospital, and the Kanins and the Chester Erskines were given the alarm. Kate, acting with her customary sweetness of character, also called Mrs. Tracy immediately. The two women kept alternate vigils by Tracy's bedside until, his sickness diagnosed as a temporary congestion of the respiratory tract, he was released, with Louise Tracy's approval, to Kate's care. She remembers that on the way to St. Vincent's, Spencer's old spirit flared up. "Kate," he said, "isn't this a hell of a way to go to a picnic?"

It was the severe blow of Spencer's collapse, following so closely on her father's death, that made Kate decide to retire from the screen in 1963. Spencer toyed with several scripts he received from his agents, almost coming to terms with *The Cincinnati Kid*, a story about gambling in the South, which amused him. Stanley Kramer wanted him to appear as the ship's doctor in a version of Katherine Anne Porter's famous novel *Ship of Fools*, and though Spencer turned the part down, he frequently dropped by the set to watch the shooting. In September, 1965, Spencer became ill again, his sickness diagnosed as an inflamed prostate gland. The prostatectomy was difficult, and once again Kate and Mrs. Tracy kept vigil in alternating day and night shifts. For six weeks, Spencer lay in severe pain; when he was finally released, he went home to his place on St. Ives Drive, to a life of almost total seclusion. He was virtually inactive for almost two years, breaking the silence of his absence with a brief job of narrating a documentary, *The Ripon College Story*. Often he went walking with Kate in the Hollywood hills. Occasionally, passersby saw them: Kate, her coppery hair blowing free in the wind, in slacks, and Spencer, worn and leathery, flying brilliantly colored kites, watching them soar into the sky with the joyful wonder of children.

The general view seems to be that those years of isolation from picture-making were painful for Kate and Spencer. Yet one may speculate that they in fact were filled with happiness. Free of the demands of movies, they were no longer burdened by distractions from their loving companionship. The give-and-take of their personalities, the interests shared, the arguments, had so often been played out through their screen roles in front of the world. Now they could enjoy them unwatched. No one other than Kate will ever know what happened between them in those days they spent together away from even their closest friends. Yet one likes to believe that for these two great actors fall was indeed a golden season.

As so often in the past, events toward a filming occurred without Kate's knowing about them. Stanley Kramer, electric and obsessive, had become consumed with the idea of teaming Kate and Spencer in a film again; fired, too, with the idea that the return of Spencer to the screen would be of great therapeutic value to him. Above all, Kramer felt that the world should no longer be deprived of the most beloved of stars.

In the late fall of 1966, he dined with the British writer William Rose, who had written for him the slapstick comedy *It's a Mad, Mad, Mad, Mad World*, in which Spencer had appeared. Rose began talking about an idea he had for a story —originally set in England—in which a young white girl,

daughter of socialite parents, falls in love with a handsome
black man. Kramer, who had made other films dealing with
the racial problem, was intrigued. After dinner, the two men
walked through Beverly Hills discussing the theme, and the
plot began to evolve: they would show the reaction of both
black and white parents to the situation, and would make the
treatment highly controversial. In order to make the project
feasible, Kramer went to Sidney Poitier, because he had to
have as his black hero a man good-looking, noble, and very
successful; he had to have someone to whom the only possible objection was his *blackness*. Poitier accepted at once.

Kramer decided to engage Kate and Spencer to play the
white WASP parents whose daughter wants to marry a black.
Kramer went over to see Kate, who was at Spencer's house
that afternoon. When Kramer arrived, Spencer said, "Stanley, you talk to Kate separately about all this." Kramer told
Spencer there was only one person to play the well-meaning
but obstinate head of the white family who opposes the wed-
ing. That person, of course, was Spencer. Kramer told Kate
the part of Tracy's wife would be perfect for her. He went
on, "They call me a discarded liberal, a 'message man' who
failed to deliver the message. Here's a chance to do something. And it's better for Spencer to be working than sitting
at home and vegetating. And of course you must be with him.
Then comes the rough part. You and I are going to have to
put up our salaries in lieu of the insurance money—Columbia
won't make the picture unless we do that." She agreed.
"She's that kind of a remarkable woman," says Kramer.

Kate was attracted by Kramer's theme, but she was very
worried about doing the picture. She felt that Spencer wasn't
strong enough to carry the work load. She agreed only when
Poitier came over and pointed out to her that this would
probably be Tracy's last picture, that she owed it to the world
to appear in this important story urging racial tolerance.

Spencer was often bedridden during the period, and Kate
acted as his nurse, supervising his meals, making sure he had
his medication at the correct hours, and watching for every
symptom. Meanwhile, Kramer flew over to see William Rose
on the storm-swept Channel island of Jersey. They worked
for five weeks on the script.

The screenplay pleased everyone—Kate, Spencer, Sidney Poitier, and the executives at Columbia Pictures, who had agreed to make the picture only if both stars waived their salaries and agreed to a percentage deal, and if Kramer personally guaranteed them against losses if Spencer died during the picture. "My head was on the chopping block," Kramer says. "Spencer was shot to pieces by all those years of drinking. If he died, I'd be ruined."

Making *Guess Who's Coming to Dinner?* became an enormous task of courage for everyone connected with it. Spencer knew he was risking his life to make it. Kate was risking losing him. Kramer was risking his bank balance and his career. Yet everyone felt so passionately that the WASP public needed to be jolted out of its anti-black bias that they went ahead with a total and dedicated commitment to the material.

A serious problem for Kramer was casting the white daughter of Kate and Spencer. Without pushing her excessively, Kate got behind her niece, Katharine Houghton, for the role. Kramer asked Kate, "Does she have talent?" and Kate said, "Yes. Why don't you test her?" Kramer says, "She did a good test and I hired her, but I found her strange. I don't know whether she was under Kate's influence, or whether she was making a declaration of independence away from Hepburn, but nothing in our professional relationship was ever very smooth. There were problems—the publicity guys would want to take stills of her, and she'd say, 'I don't want to do that kind of publicity.' We had a *Vogue* layout all ready to go—it was her first picture—and she nixed it. My publicity man, George Glass, had aggravation all the time. Her Aunt Kate didn't want to do anything, as usual. At the outset, I said, 'It would be nice to launch the picture if you had a press conference at the Waldorf in New York—just one—and after that we won't bother you. Any personal questions you're smart enough to fence and say, "No comment." ' She said, 'Absolutely not.' Finally she said, 'All right,' and when she was booked for half an hour, we couldn't get her off. For two hours she wouldn't shut up!"

Once he got into production, Kramer realized, "I could only direct Spencer from nine to noon each day. He didn't have the stamina for any more work." Kramer had to observe him every second, telling him to raise the level of vitality when it was visibly sinking low. Because of this situation, Kate had to play many of her scenes to blank space, with Spencer cut in later. It was very difficult, and sometimes her patience frayed. At the end of one morning, three days before end of shooting, Kate heard Spencer say to Kramer, "You know, kiddo, I've been looking at this script, and if I died tonight at home it wouldn't make any difference—you could still release the picture."

Kramer says, "In the rehearsals, I drained Kate and Spencer. I made them simply give out every single idea, every concept they could. Once I came to shooting, I'd exhausted all the avenues and that was going to be the best I could do. But Kate still had ideas even *after* rehearsal when we started shooting. There was a scene with Katharine Houghton in the bedroom—Kate wanted to use an ironing board during a conversation. I told her, 'No. It's so cliché. I hate to do it. We could do almost anything else—packing a bag, for instance.' When I went home that night, I thought, 'Am I objecting to the ironing board simply because she's suggesting it, or because the ironing board won't work?' Next morning I said to her, 'You know, I'm willing to go with that ironing board.' And she said, 'You're really a hell of a fellow. I don't really give a damn about the ironing board.' But we did it her way."

Kramer adds, "Once I got into working with Kate, I was amazed at her control. You could take nine, ten takes, and she would make the tears flow at the exact same moment on the screen. Only Vivien Leigh in my experience could do that. It's not so much a talent, it's a weapon she uses. She uses her eyes as a weapon in other ways also. They're fantastic eyes. When she speaks emotionally, the shine in her eyes is tremendously affecting.

"She has learned softness from the privilege of failure. God knows she has 'bitten the bullet'; she has made many failures. That has made her more tender.

"We had some tensions on the picture. I was irritated by her fear over her so-called 'ugly neck'—she wore scarves and high collars, and 'played low.' Many times she would come in a room and kneel, or sit down at once, so people wouldn't

be aware of her neck. During rehearsal, Tracy would be
sitting there; suddenly she's come in and she'd kneel. He'd
say, 'What the hell are you doin', kneeling?' And she'd say,
very grandly, 'Spencer, I just thought it would be appropriate,' and he'd mock her highfalutin accent, saying, 'Spensah!
Christ, you talk like you've got a feather up your ass all the
time! Get out of there, will yah?' And she'd start to say, 'I just
thought that—' and he'd snap out, 'Just do what the director
guy tells you, will yah?' and she'd reply, humbly, 'All right.'
She'd take anything from him. She'd take nothing from anybody else, from him everything. And despite all the bad-
mouthing he gave her, she was a perfect nurse to him.

"She and I had a strange relationship, because I loved
Tracy, and I think he loved me, and, in a way, I felt for a
while Kate and I were rivals. Isn't that a peculiar way to feel?
Of course, we weren't. But he'd keep saying to Kate, 'Don't
bug him, don't bother him. Jeez, he's worked it out, for
Christ's sake.' Tracy was a very simple actor to work with. He
liked to be told by a director exactly what to do: to be told,
'Here is the frame, go in that door, and we'll play the scene at
this table. There are your sidelines.' He'd come in that door
and get to that table, and he'd do exactly what was called for.
With her, no. She'd say, 'I want to stay at the door.' Now, to
do that, and cover both actors, you'd have to shoot them
separately. Or she'd say, 'No, I don't want to go to the table,
I won't sit down this way, that way.' It was rough. She had
to run free, with and around a director. She was always creative, one of the two or three most creative artists I've ever
worked with. I've never known anyone who matched her in
terms of independence vis-à-vis a director. She *thinks* like a
director.

"She's a set decorator also. She'd say, 'What *is* that, a *fake
fireplace?*' I had to stop her from ripping out the set and
putting in a *real* fireplace! Spencer created within the realm
of himself—he was a *reactor*, she was a *protagonist*. With
Spencer, you could give another actor all the pages, he'd
listen—and he'd steal the scene, nobody would look at the
man who read the lines.

"She was a driving worker. Work, work, work. She can
work till everybody drops. The goddamned scarves, switch-

ing around, pulling 'em over! What a performance! We quarreled often.

"My impression of her was that she had a wilderness of personal defense mechanisms, but that she was still extremely vulnerable. I'm deeply fond of her, and I understand her fierce desire for privacy. My daughter is named for her, and is her godchild. It was supposed to be a boy called Spencer!"

Guess Who's Coming to Dinner? proved to be the greatest success of Kate's career. It grossed many millions of dollars and helped Columbia, which at the time was in financial difficulties. Despite the fact that it presented too simplistic an argument for the improvement of racial relations, and that much of the writing was heavily sentimental, there was much praise from the reviewers for the two central performances.

Kate's grief at Spencer's worsening physical condition was painfully apparent throughout, sometimes unsettling the balance of particular scenes. In others, she came through with striking force, fiercely arguing a liberal position, while Spencer powerfully suggested a crusty conservative, gradually melting into an understanding of his daughter's needs. Despite the schmaltzy, opportunistic quality of the movie, the playing of the two together was deeply touching, a portrait of love imminently threatened by death. Even though the picture was weak, the emotional tension created by the public's knowledge of what went on during and after it assured its place in the history of the screen.

In the weeks following the conclusion of *Guess Who's Coming to Dinner?*, Kate made it a practice to sleep in a small room at the end of a corridor by Spencer's bedroom. She would often leave a small light on so that she could get up quickly if he needed anything.

She had not been sleeping well in the early-morning hours of June 10, 1967. She heard a sound and realized that Spencer had risen and was walking down the corridor. He went into the kitchen. Sometimes he did this to fetch a glass of milk. She decided there was no need to get up and help him, as his step sounded sufficiently firm. She heard the refrigerator door open and the scrape of a chair that indicated Spencer was sitting at the kitchen table. She heard an odd sound that disconcerted her, and she decided to get up and have a look. When she reached the kitchen, Spencer was sitting in his chair with the milk in front of him. He was very still. When she touched him, she knew at once that he was dead.

Ten

The end of Kate's life with Spencer was also a beginning. There could be no question of another romantic involvement for her. Spencer was her first and last great love. Faced with the agony of separation by death, she had to take stock, to rest, to shore up the ruins. She was not guilty of self-pity; her discipline asserted itself. She still had her beloved sisters and brothers, and her friends: the Kanins, the Chester Erskines, Lawrence Weingarten, the Jean Negulescos, Bobby Helpmann and Michael Benthall in England, Laura Harding in the East. She moved back East, spending California visits at Spencer's warm, informal cottage on the Cukor estate. She scrubbed floors, sewed, cooked, entertained modestly, rose and retired early, walked with her dogs, baked Thanksgiving pies, and made Christmas wreaths, living the quiet, orderly, decent life of a Connecticut gentlewoman, with Phyllis as her only companion.

Nobody grew older more gracefully. Not for her the face lifts, the skin peelings, the pathetic American quest for a simulacrum of youth. Her hair darkened, losing its reddish sheen; her face became creased, the strong character emerging more beautifully with the onset of time; the blue-grey eyes grew misty, lovelier with pain and loss. Inside her weakened body, the spirit still burned like a flame. She was, in her late middle age, quite unquenched. Her griefs of those years —the deaths of Lawrence Langner and Theresa Helburn and the homosexual murder of her director at Stratford, Jack Landau—were borne with an agonizing fortitude. She did experience a brief joy—winning an Oscar for *Guess Who's Coming to Dinner?*—though she did not accept it in person.

In the late 1960s, Kate cut out smoking completely, realiz-

ing she was being smothered by the habit. She felt more
deeply than ever that pure, unsullied concentration was the
secret of success in any art. She tried to strip every essential
from her life. Since her body no longer served her as well as
it had, it must be more rigorously trained. She swam every
day she could in her neighbor Lawrence Weingarten's pool.
She grew even more fiercely defensive against the world,
determined not to be broken by its inquisitiveness and its
cruelty. She became a nun in an enclosed order created by
herself, obeying her own rules religiously. To her family, she
was adorable, eccentric Aunt Kath; to herself, she was just a
hard-working old actress, waiting for a good part to come
along.

A few weeks after Spencer's death, Kate rested quietly in
Martha's Vineyard with the Kanins and Phyllis Wilbourn,
loving the environment, the water, the yacht sails, cool, re-
freshing walks along green lanes. The telephone seldom
rang; but one day it did, and it was her agent, Abe Lastfogel,
on the line.

Lastfogel asked her, "Can I give a man called Martin Poll
your number? He's a producer. He wants you to do a play
he's gotten hold of, *The Lion in Winter*." Kate said, "All
right, I'll talk to him."

Poll called her from London, and she agreed to read James
Goldman's historical play; it was the story of Eleanor of Aquitaine and Eleanor's relationship with her husband and family
in twelfth-century France. This elaborate drama had been
unsuccessfully produced in New York, with Rosemary Harris
in the leading role. Kate says, "The play arrived, and I read
it in a morning on Martha's Vineyard. I handed it to Phyllis
and said, 'Don't get up, just sit there and read this. See what
you think.' Phyllis read it, and agreed it was perfect for me.
So I called Abe Lastfogel and told him immediately, 'I'll do
it. It's absolutely fascinating.'

"Then Peter O'Toole called me from London. He told me
he had had a sleepless night reading the play, had fallen in
love with it, and longed to play Eleanor's husband, Henry II
of England. I knew Peter: he's a lovely actor! I had gone
backstage when he did a play in London called *The Long and
the Short and the Tall*, and congratulated him on his perfor-

mance. Later, I recommended him to David Lean for the role of T. E. Lawrence in *Lawrence of Arabia*.

"Peter started telling me about a director I had never heard of, Tony Harvey, and I said, 'You'd better talk to me about this personally. I'll be back in Hollywood in two weeks. We can talk then.'

"Back in Hollywood, Phyllis and I picked him up at the Los Angeles airport, brought him over to the house, and fed him a fine dinner. He went very, very slowly on the champagne —which he sometimes over-enjoys—and then he said, 'There's a picture I want you to see playing down here at the Pan Pacific. It's a short picture, *Dutchman,* about two people on a subway. It was shot by a friend of mine, Tony Harvey, in a week. Tony Harvey's the man I want to do *The Lion in Winter.*'

"So he dragged me down to the theatre. I said, 'Oh, no. I've never been to a picture at eleven o'clock at night.' But he *insisted.* I thought I'd die—but when I got there, I liked the film. I thought it was very well done. But I still didn't know if Tony Harvey would be right for this picture. How in the hell're you going to tell—well done, not well done? I never know if a thing's any good. You might get a brilliant person and he'd do a bad piece of work. Well, anyway, I called Peter next morning, and I said, 'If you think he's that good, I can't think of anything against him. It's fine with me.' Peter flew back to London, and that's how we came to do it."

Peter O'Toole said later, "Meeting Kate was the great experience of my life. I had met her first in London, when I was in *The Long and the Short and the Tall,* and I was pissing in the sink, because someone was using the toilet, when she walked into my dressing room. I heard her say, in that unmistakable voice, 'I'm Kate Hepburn.' I pretended I was washing my hands and adjusted my clothing hastily. She was like a press agent, she called me constantly, she was crazy about my work. She even came to Akuba to wish me luck on the filming of *Lawrence of Arabia.* If it had been twenty-five years before, I would have broken Spencer Tracy's fingers to get her. When *The Lion in Winter* was due, I said yes at once!"

With Kate, Peter O'Toole, and Anthony Harvey firmly set,

Martin Poll still had great difficulty in obtaining financing
and a guarantee of distribution for the production. Finally,
after everyone had turned James Goldman's script down,
Poll managed to arrange a deal with the independent producer Joseph Levine. The arrangements dragged on, and in
the meantime Kate agreed to make *The Madwoman of
Chaillot*, from the play by Jean Giraudoux, for her old friend
Ely Landau.

Martin Poll was faced with completing a major production
in a very few weeks, in order for Kate to be released for the
second production. To save time, everybody began working
at once. Kate undertook the research, reading every available book on Eleanor of Aquitaine and adding many touches
to the script. Peter O'Toole began casting, touring England
and calling various friends for suggestions, looking at many
repertory productions, until he finally selected some players.
James Goldman traveled from London to New York to rewrite portions of the script. The art director, Peter Merton,
began preparing handsome designs. The cameraman, Douglas Slocombe, partly French and with a painter's eye, began
working out a rich lighting pattern which would give the
picture the look of illuminated manuscripts. A series of actors
and actresses were tested, with Peter O'Toole present and
often supervising their playing. Many were so terrified of
doing the test that he had to have lunch with them first to
put them in a sufficiently relaxed mood. Kate and Phyllis
traveled to France to see the tombs of Eleanor of Aquitaine
and her husband at Fontevrault. Fascinated, they walked
around the tombs.

Rehearsals took place at the Haymarket Theatre in the
West End of London. Kate returned from France and
checked into the Connaught. There, she had several conversations with Anthony Harvey, a modest, cultured man who
kept calling her "Miss Hepburn." Kate said to Marty Poll,
"Why doesn't he call me Kate?" When Poll challenged Harvey with this, Harvey said, "How can I call the woman I've
worshiped all my life just plain Kate? I have to show my
respect!" But he did call her Kate very soon; they became
close friends.

Kate arrived with great enthusiasm for the first day of

rehearsals at the Haymarket Theatre. Her figure still as slim as a young girl's, she was radiant, glowing with health. She rushed through the heavy iron stage door so fast she closed it on her hand and smashed her thumb. Hearing her scream, Harvey, O'Toole, and Poll ran over. She was in agony, but she refused to be taken to the hospital and insisted on continuing with the rehearsal. Not only had her thumbnail been crushed, but a deep cut ran all the way down to her hand. She was bleeding terribly, and later in the morning Poll begged her to have stitches put in. "No," she said firmly. "If you put stitches in, the wound won't heal in time for the picture." Her stoicism amazed everyone. She proceeded with blood-soaked bandages. Throughout the whole of the rehearsal, she was in severe pain, the thumb throbbing and smarting unbearably. But she did her best not to show it.

The picture started shooting in Ireland. Kate flew to Dublin with Phyllis and began work at Bray Studios, where some of the interiors of the castles to be used in the film had been copied. The location shifted to Wales, and then to France.

Castles were restored, details of walls and turrets spread over hundreds of miles matched up so that they looked as though they belonged to the same castle, and the actors wore their clothes whenever possible before shooting so that they looked rubbed and frayed.

Kate kept adding touches of color to Eleanor: she reminded the costume designer, Margaret Furse, who favored dark clothes, that Eleanor had been on a Crusade to the Middle East and would own many vividly colored clothes.

Kate was as athletic as ever: she bicycled to work in Ireland, Wales, and France; she swam in the biting cold of the Irish Sea; she rose early and took long walks at weekends. She fell in love with the Provençal settings of many scenes; the cool green country around Arles and Avignon was magically beautiful, and Kate and Phyllis adored the little hotel they stayed in outside Arles. Working with Peter O'Toole and Tony Harvey was a great pleasure; and when Tony fell ill with hepatitis and influenza in France, she nursed him loyally.

A number of problems marked the shooting. The weather was distressingly changeable. The actor Anthony Hopkins, playing Richard I of England, fell off his horse and broke several bones, closing the shooting down for several days. Harvey's hepatitis worsened, and he had to have a complete rest, which again stopped production. Affected by the strain of shooting, Kate occasionally lost her temper. She says, "I sent for a makeup man, Bill Lodge, one day when we were shooting in the cellars of the monastery of Montmajour. The makeup man didn't arrive. Someone said, 'He's with Peter O'Toole.' Well, I got mad. I rushed up the stairs to Peter's room and screamed, 'Why won't you let me have my makeup man?' And I biffed Peter hard on the jaw! He was dumfounded! I said, 'Next time I want a makeup man, send him down right away!' He did!"

Almost sixty, Kate was indefatigable on location, never tired, never ill, washing her hair obsessively, showering, observing the same regular habits of her earliest days in Hollywood. Her performance was among the greatest of her career. Her Eleanor was passionate, fierce, cruel, intensely royal, mocking, cajoling, weeping, in a formidable range of emotion, at times stabbingly direct, at times devious and subtle. Goldman described the Queen in his play as "a handsome woman of great temperament, authority, and presence. She has been a queen of international importance for forty-six years and you know it. Finally, she is that most unusual thing: a genuinely feminine woman thoroughly capable of holding her own in a man's world." It was, of course, a description of Kate herself. Kate, weeping before an ornamental mirror, sitting on the floor saying the famous line, "Every family has its ups and downs," skirmishing with her husband, turning from outrageous fits of laughter to even more outrageous outbursts of fury, was in her element. For the second year in a row, she won an Oscar, on this occasion sharing the award with Barbra Streisand.

Many of the scenes of *The Lion in Winter* were shot in the Victorine Studios in Nice; Kate continued work, virtually without a break, on *The Madwoman of Chaillot*. She had agreed to do the film for Ely Landau because he had gambled his resources on *Long Day's Journey into Night*. At first, she entertained the gravest doubts that she could play Aurelia, the madwoman who is appalled that a group of capitalists are planning to turn Paris into an oil field, and enlists the aid of her eccentric companions in thwarting the plan. But she was impressed by Edward Anhalt's script, and gradually warmed to the project. She traveled all over Paris looking for suitable locations. Meanwhile, Landau obtained several major stars to appear with Kate, including Danny Kaye, Charles Boyer, Dame Edith Evans, John Gavin, and Yul Brynner. John Huston was asked to direct. But when Landau and his assistant, Henry Weinstein, went to Ireland to visit Huston at his estate, they found they had basic differences of interpretation. Landau crossed over to England and hired Bryan Forbes as director instead. Kate was upset because of her loyalty to Huston, but gradually came to understand Landau's point of view.

Once the picture started shooting, Kate turned out to be its unifying force. She bicycled to the studio every day from her small rented villa in Nice, briskly working out internal problems on the set. She quarreled violently with Forbes on the interpretation of scenes. One afternoon, she stormed off the set. He had a dinner engagement with her that night. He arrived at her villa expecting Phyllis to say that Kate was out. But Kate was there, exquisitely dressed in an evening gown, the quarrel completely forgotten. Kate adored her co-star Dame Edith Evans, and invited her to share her villa. When Dame Edith arrived, Kate said, "Oh, by the way. We're all *very regular*. We're all in bed by seven-thirty at night." And Dame Edith responded in her haughty, flutelike voice, "Oh, that would *never* do for me. Seven-thirty at night is the time I start to live!"

Toward the end of shooting, there were a number of student riots in Nice. Everyone went home at once, except Kate. Ely Landau says, "She stayed on, the studio supplied food and money, and she remained barricaded indoors. When the franc became valueless, the prop man found some louis d'or, gold pieces which were still valid currency, and delivered them to her in boxes. Finally, she did agree to return to London."

The Madwoman of Chaillot was a fiasco both critically and

commercially, largely because of Bryan Forbes' inept direction and Kate's softening of the central role of the madwoman. She miscalculated by letting her own warmth and
strong sentiment override the acid charm of the personality
Giraudoux had drawn, and Forbes miscalculated by going
along with her in this interpretation. Landau says, "We lost
Madwoman in the production. We lost it because it was too
romantic, too sentimental. A fantasy is difficult for pictures
anyway, and it lacked bite. Eddie Anhalt's script was brilliant, marvelous, but it was thrown away. I blame myself as
much as anyone else."

In those years, Kate's plans often overlapped. *The Madwoman of Chaillot* had been brought to her attention during
preparations for *The Lion in Winter*, and her next major
venture, the musical, *Coco*, had been discussed even before
The Madwoman.

Alan Jay Lerner, the neurotic and talented creator of *Coco*,
a musical life of Gabrielle ("Coco") Chanel, had called Garson Kanin only a week after Spencer's death and asked him if
Kate would be interested. He had been working on the musical for almost a year, and was convinced she would be perfect
to play the temperamental, fiercely committed High Priest-
ess of Fashion. At first, Kanin rejected the idea; then he
promised to help act as a go-between. He talked to Kate
about it. She was at once horrified and intrigued. She had
never even seen a Broadway musical.

A combination of curiosity and competitiveness made her
take the part. The fact that it was a new experience was what
intrigued her most. Alan Jay Lerner fascinated her. She had
known him through George Cukor, who had directed Lerner
and Loewe's *My Fair Lady*. Afflicted with a nervous disease
which made the skin of his hands shred, and forced to take
heavy medication, he constantly wore white gloves. So mani-
cally over-energetic he seemed almost to be insane, he was
a dazzling wit, kept afloat by massive injections of vitamins.
He and Kate became friends. Though he wanted her for the
role of Coco, he was afraid she wouldn't be able to sing. She
settled his doubts by going all the way back to her characteri-
zation of Lady Babbie in *The Little Minister*, croaking "Auld

Lang Syne" while he pounded away at his piano. He accepted her at once. Kate also sang for the producer, Frederick Brisson, the Alan Jay Lerners, Patricia Lawford, and Irene Selznick at Irene's apartment at the Pierre. Roger Edens played the piano while Kate, in slacks and three sweaters, croaked away gamely at Cole Porter's "Miss Otis Regrets," "Mrs. Lowsborough Goodbody," and several other songs. Her amusing, touching *Sprechtsingen* delighted everyone.

To celebrate the partnership, Kate decided she would give Alan Jay Lerner a handsome pre-Columbian carving of a jaguar's head. She invited him to dinner and left the carving on the dinner table. In the middle of dinner, she said to him, "Alan, I can't see you properly. Help me to move this." Without a word, he got hold of it and put it on the floor. She said, "You just lost yourself a damn nice present." And she didn't give it to him.

Kate trained for the musical role with Roger Edens, a slow-speaking, solid man with closely cropped hair, who had once been Ethel Merman's pianist and who had become one of the best musical arrangers in the business. They worked at the home of Lillie Messenger in Beverly Hills six days a week, exercising Kate's voice assiduously. She spent her early mornings playing tennis, and her late mornings and early afternoons with Edens, who taught her to give at least an impression of singing. Amazed by her audacity, she was still more amazed when she agreed to Alan Jay Lerner's suggestion that she should visit Chanel in Paris.

Kate told me, "At first I was petrified by the whole idea of meeting Chanel. Here I was, supposed to be playing this great figure of fashion—and look at me! Alan Jay Lerner insisted on it, and then I thought, 'Oh dear, here I am, I've worn the same coat for forty years—literally—and my shoes —the *works!*' I thought, 'What will she think of me?' And then, 'If I don't like her and I have to play her, it will be an agony.' I said to Alan, 'I'm not going to like her, because she's rather fancy and I've heard she's difficult,' and Alan Lerner replied, 'Don't be silly. When you meet her, you'll like her.' Finally I told him, 'All right,' and we went over to Paris to meet her. She was *fascinating!*

"We went to see her in her apartment over her shop. It was exquisitely furnished—wonderful things! Such a cultivated creature! Stylish—but more than stylish; she had a good smell for the real thing. I had with me a little African brass medallion as a present for her. I had bought it from Ella Winter, Mrs. Donald Ogden Stewart, who had a collection of wonderful African things. I thought, 'I'm not going to give it to her, I'm just going to leave it on the little table near the front door with a note.' Because she spoke only French, and my French is very faltering, I thought, 'If she finds it, all right, and if she doesn't find it while I'm there, that's fine, she'll find it afterward.' We had lunch—after she made a carefully timed great entrance—and she was charming. Lerner and I went to see her fashion show and sat on the stairway. She returned to the apartment meanwhile and found the medallion. She was like a little girl, she was tremendously pleased; and I realized she was wonderfully on the level, amusing in a good sense—great fun—and at the same time very, very touching. She really 'got' to me. She made it easier to play the part. After we left, I found I had left something behind, and I returned to the salon. She was lying on the sofa, in her great big glasses and her big hat and her suit, very neat, having a snooze! Now I *knew* I could play her. She was a human being!"

Kate loved Alan Jay Lerner's work, and spent weeks studying the material. Under Frederick Brisson's production hand, André Previn was engaged to write the music, Cecil Beaton to design the sets and costumes, Robert Emmett Dolan to supervise the musical direction, Michael Benthall to direct, and the tense young Jed Harris of the 1960s, twenty-eight-year-old Michael Bennett, to choreograph. As always, Kate took a major hand in the casting, designs, and clothes. She was present at almost all of the auditions.

The first day of rehearsal at the Mark Hellinger Theatre created a nervous hustle and bustle, with New York *Times* photographers scurrying about, everyone shouting at everyone else, and Kate in passionately intense conference with Michael Benthall. She amazed actors who had never known her with her direct, childlike excitement and furies at everything, her violent alarums and excursions. Pulling her scarf tight about her neck, she strode about barking directions, cracking jokes, bursting into laughter, beaming glittering smiles, eyes brimming with tears, her voice alternately acidly humorous, querulous, and alive with appreciation. She showed no patience for uncertainty or error. She was consumed with worry over final results, unable to tolerate the various trivia of a production. She was put off by the necessary paraphernalia of a Broadway musical, yet, paradoxically, she was concerned with it. Everything, she felt, depended on her. She could not tolerate delays of work. If she found that a rehearsal had to be postponed because the orchestra would have to be paid overtime, she was driven almost mad with impatience, and had the overtime money taken out of her own pocket. No matter what the cost, everything must proceed at her dynamic pace.

Michael Benthall turned out to be a problem. Still the gifted man who had directed her in *The Millionairess* and in Shakespeare, he was not entirely at ease with the musical form. She had wanted him because he had taste, and she could trust his eye for detail; but he proved totally ineffectual in marshaling and controlling the large company, the elaborate sets. Kate stood loyal to him as far as possible, but an old drinking problem recurred, and he began to drop out of the picture.

Finally, Michael Bennett, the lean, fiercely uptight young choreographer, took over virtually everything, and the rehearsals became quite explosive. Kate had more or less controlled Michael Benthall, using him as her man on the job; Michael Bennett proved to be much firmer. They collided violently, but she learned to respect him. She learned to deal with his aggressive, high-strung personality, while astonished by his habit of leaping about the stage, screaming and pulling his hair. He confronted her, and she admired him for that. She even learned to depend on him to choreograph her movements. "No, no, no!" she'd scream. "That's absolutely wrong!" But when he explained, when he articulated his point of view, she calmed down magnificently. If he had yielded at all, she would have despised him.

Kate found it difficult to adjust to the numerous changes Michael Bennett demanded. Alan Jay Lerner also objected to these changes. Bennett, who had spent six weeks watching

Chanel present a collection in Paris, had very strong preconceptions, which he refused, point-blank, to alter. He wanted Kate to become more Chanel, less Katharine Hepburn, and this proved to be a problem. Moreover, he grew more and more openly to despise the show itself, feeling it to be an atrocious, old-fashioned travesty of Chanel's life, and this did not add to anyone's peace of mind. He was irrevocably opposed to Alan Jay Lerner's idea of filming large segments of the show, with girls stepping through mirrored screens—an idea more suitable for Las Vegas—and he finally and decisively rejected the concept.

Bennett often found Kate harsh and rude, and they fought constantly in front of the company. She loved these battles; Bennett did not. Bennett says, "She often burst into floods of tears, saying, 'I can't do it, I'll never do it, I'm making an ass of myself. I can't, I can't, I *can't!*' Everybody would run off the set—Alan Jay Lerner, Michael Benthall, everyone. I was the only one left. I would stand there and say to her, 'Go on the stage at the first preview and give them the Gettysburg Address. They'll *still* love you!' Every day she cried. She would come on every day seventeen days old at 9 A.M., full of life and gaiety, and at the end of the day she'd be a woman of almost sixty. She was maddened by the fact that her mind didn't work as well as she'd like, that her body wouldn't do what she wanted to.

"Kate normally has very abrupt, sharp movements. I made her walk more slowly, while the music director, Bobby Dolan, did heroic things with the orchestra to have them match the flow of her voice. I could never *show* her anything. Normally, when you direct, you sit and talk until the actor does it for you. Or you can get on your feet and you can demonstrate. Direction *involves* demonstration. I *became* the character of Chanel. I also studied Kate for a while, and became Kate as well, and caught her movements. But she would never let me show her anything. In a musical, that's an impossible situation. You stand there and you say, 'It would be really nice if you'd make a gesture here. With your right hand, preferably.' It takes forever when you have to do that.

"Yet she would understand so much. I'd tell her *emotionally* what I was going for in routines, and then she would be

wonderful. I eventually learned how to block her in scenes.
I would say, 'Come down the stairs and cross to stage right.'
She would say, 'I can't possibly cross the stage that way.' I
would say, 'Well, where can you go?' And she'd say, 'I could
go left.' So I realized that when I asked her to sit she would
stand, and when I asked her to go right she would go left, and
so on. The thing to do was ask for just what I didn't want so
she would go where I wanted her to go after all. When I told
her to exit left, she'd exit right, and I wanted her to exit right
all along!

"Strictly speaking, Kate would not allow me to direct. I
blocked scenes like painting with numbers. I ran around and
directed the people who *would* take direction. It wasn't the
way to work. The revolving stage was a *nightmare*. All the
numbers were worked out at a certain speed—there were
three speeds on the revolve. A certain girl would get on the
revolve at a certain point, while other girls got on and danced
down. Any variance in the speed threw the numbers hay-
wire. Two days before the first preview, the whole contrap-
tion broke down; they fixed it up, and then the three speeds
were all different. I had to redo all the numbers to the new
speeds.

"Cecil Beaton had promised me a cocoa-brown set and he
gave me a *beige* set. I wanted an effect in which the girls
came out of darkness, out of a dream, as I had later in *Follies*.
It would have worked in brown, but *not* in beige. In beige,
you had one light on that set and it looked like the Washington Monument! I was haunted by that monster set of the
salon, and its hideous *drapes!* I could get no magic. A whole
opening number called "Turn on the Lights"—it went 'Turn
on the lights, bum-bum-bum-bum, turn on the lights, fill up
the spaces, with faces, and faces . . ." It was all based on lights
coming on in the salon, emerging from a dusty cocoon, people walking in. But with beige it wouldn't work; you'd never
see lights coming on *pling, pling!* So we cut it, and we had
to put in a whole new number at the last minute. It drove me
a little crazy: I was racing against the clock, Kate had to learn
the whole thing over. And then there was the nightmare of
the clothes, which were terrible—made in England and refitted
for the girls—and the props . . . *Aaaaah!*"

The show was only just pulled together by dress rehearsal. Michael Bennett miraculously made the various fashion parades seem to be fully danced, by arranging the figures in interesting patterns. The only problem with the dress rehearsal was that Kate had forgotten one important detail: she still rose at dawn, worked all day, and retired at night. Since the show was overlong, it did not end until almost midnight, and she very nearly fell asleep in the last act. She changed her time of rising in the morning to a later hour, but this proved difficult for her to adjust to, and she often went without a full night's sleep.

The first day's take was a record $35,000. Opening night was a triumph, with Laura Harding, Irene Selznick, the Kanins, Leland Hayward, and many other friends present to wish her well, while the unfortunate young Michael Bennett flew to London to have a nervous breakdown. The ovation was tremendous, and Kate, who had felt she was wrong for the part, became somewhat more confident as a result. In slacks and newspaper hair curlers, her sweater done up with a giant safety pin, she was a bustling presence backstage all through the run, stimulating, cajoling, maddening, exciting everyone.

Kate's playing of Coco Chanel was as extravagant a phenomenon as Niagara Falls. She was outrageous, petulant, querulous, overpowering; she stormed, she wept, she screamed, she sighed; she marshaled a fashion show as though she were Wellington and this were Waterloo; she seemed to attack the audience, waving one arm so violently it might have contained a golf club or an oversized umbrella. She was her own barker, in both senses; and what she announced was a one-woman carnival. But always she could convey the stillness of the eye of the hurricane: she could simply sit and carry the entire audience on a feather. Her fights with Michael Bennett and firm handling of Michael Benthall had the desired result: she and she alone was the show, and her unfortunate co-star René Auberjonois, playing a flamboyant homosexual, could only flutter attendance, a giddy moth burning itself to death. Her impatience, her manic drive, were here released in a Coco who made *Future Shock* seem as welcome as Christmas. It was a monstrous portrait of a monster with whom everyone, reluctantly, fell in love.

During the run, the student murders at Kent State University took place. René Auberjonois begged Kate to say something to the audience about it. At first she refused, saying that Spencer had always maintained that actors should have nothing to do with politics. ("The first time an actor got involved with politics, he shot Lincoln," she said.) Auberjonois was furious with her, and slammed into his dressing room. She ran after him, hair flying, and said, "All right, all right. I'll do something. Write me a speech." Auberjonois worked with the stage manager, Jerry Adler, on a brief address. Kate ran by and said, all in a rush, "I'll take the whole audience out on the street and have a moment of silence!" At the end of the evening, when the curtain rang down, she changed her mind about taking the audience out of doors into a bitter New York night. Instead, she had the whole company stand onstage with her while she read the speech, rewritten by herself. It dealt movingly with the reality of life and death, and the preciousness and holiness of all life. Many spectators broke into tears.

René Auberjonois says, "At the end of each show, Kate would roar out of the theatre and try to dart past the autograph hunters, taking so long to explain why she wouldn't give an autograph that she could easily have given it in the same time. I remember one time her chauffeur had her Ford ready, and she jumped into the trunk! She waved at us from the trunk of the car as she took off.

"She often kidded me about how outrageous my playing was. Frankly, my part of a homosexual was so superficial that to play it anywhere near reality would be an insult to gay people. So I simply caricatured it. And then she was so bold, so tremendous, that I had to hold my own with her. At one point, I was standing in the wings at rehearsal, and she was standing on the stage reading the terrible reviews of Coco's spring collection. She read them loud, then she tore them up, screwed them in a ball, and threw them in the wastebasket. She stamped on it. I said to her, 'After seeing that, I don't want to hear any more remarks about *me* being too large for the stage.' She turned on me, and I thought for a second, 'Oh, boy! I've done it now!' She started to chase me all over the theatre, up- and downstairs, in and out of the dressing rooms, until finally she caught me and gave me a good kick in the seat of my pants!

"The set was an incredible hazard. It was a huge revolving drum. If you wanted to come downstairs, onto the stage, you had to follow a certain direction of the turntable and then go across a special foot drawbridge. One day, the bridge had not been lowered, and Kate was determined not to miss her cue. So she simply lifted her skirts and jumped—four feet—in high heels! If she had slipped, she would have fallen thirty feet onto the stage and died!

"Another time, the movable escape stairs had been left out of the scaffolding backstage. Kate simply scaled the scaffolding, sixty feet of it, again in high heels!

"In one scene, she had to give me a cue, and she made a mistake. She was very apologetic, and wrote me a note. A few nights later, she made the same mistake. Phyllis came up with an envelope containing twenty-five dollars. And it contained a note from Kate, reading, 'Every time I do that, you'll get another twenty-five dollars.' She never did it again—unfortunately!"

Kate would not tolerate the sticky heat of the theatre's air-conditioning system, and insisted on flinging open all the doors to the freezing New York winter air. When the cast complained of the cold during rehearsals, she equipped them with mufflers, sweaters, gloves, and fur coats, which made them feel even hotter during the dance numbers. In their stage costumes during the run of the show, they simply froze. In spite of all her precautions and a constant flow of medication, many members of the cast came down with severe colds.

One afternoon, when the noise of building the new Uris Theatre opposite the Mark Hellinger became insufferable, she made her way by workman's external elevator to the top of the Uris' metal framework, stepped out precariously on a girder, and asked the construction crew to lay off during matinees. Astounded by this red-headed, trousered phenomenon, they agreed.

The scenery was too heavy for the revolving stage. Whenever the stage stuck, Kate would stop the show, sit down front, and tell the audience about the mechanical problems the stage caused the theatre's engineers.

One day she broke a six-foot mirror, and, without stopping the scene, took a broom and swept up the broken pieces.

Kate often berated the audience. When a rock group played in a nearby theatre and the loud sound shook the stage, she told the astonished spectators that they were gutless for not going out and demanding that the rock group shut up immediately. She punched a truck driver on the jaw because he was parking with a loud throttle outside the stage door. Police and ambulance sirens infuriated her.

Her co-star George Rose recalls, "Kate used to make her first entrance in floods of tears. She sat on a banquette and said, 'Louis, my mind is made up. I'm not going to open a salon.' One night, she had just delivered the line when a little woman in a bright print dress in the front row of the orchestra took a photograph with a blinding flashbulb. Kate jumped up as if she'd been stung, and said, 'Who the hell did that?' She tore a strip off the woman, yelling at her that she should know better than to take photographs in a theatre. 'We prepare a show!' she shouted, to the audience's astonishment. 'We want to give you our best, and you have to do that! You do a stupid, ill-mannered, ridiculous thing like that, you ruin the show for everybody! Ring down the curtain. We'll start again!' "

Coco was a hit, and Kate, who at last felt the audience was on her side, enjoyed an immense standing ovation on her last night on Broadway, August 1, 1970. In her curtain speech, she praised the late Roger Edens, who had died before the show opened, and her subsequent voice coach, Sue Seton. Her last words to the audience were, "Well—I love you and you love me, and that's that." Danielle Darrieux expertly took over the role, but without Kate, the show soon closed.

Before Kate went on a long cross-country tour with *Coco,* she had to travel to Spain to fulfill an obligation to play Hecuba in a film version of *The Trojan Women,* directed by Michael Cacoyannis, with Vanessa Redgrave and Genevieve Bujold as co-stars. First, though, she made a recording of

Coco for the musical director and composer, André Previn. It was a disagreeable experience. Previn and the chief recording engineer clashed, and there was so much music on the record that it was squeezed down too tight and played a trifle too fast. The result was that Kate sounded rather like Donald Duck, and she had to do the entire record over. When she finally took it home to play it, she suddenly realized she had nothing to play it on, because she didn't own a record player. She called George Rose and said, "I can't find a Victrola! Father never believed in them, you know!"

In November, Kate was in Atienza, ninety miles north of Madrid in Spain, making *The Trojan Women*, which she had taken on chiefly because she felt Greek drama should be correctly filmed. The shooting was not inspiriting, and though she played a bold and striking Hecuba, she wasn't too comfortable with the general concept and execution of the material. She compensated for the mistake she had made in going to Spain by learning the local dialect, visiting the holy sites of St. Teresa of Ávila, and climbing up mountainsides for fossils and unusual rocks. These expeditions took her mind off the endless windswept, dusty, and stifling heat of Atienza, and she spent much of the time getting rid of all the furniture in her rented house and replacing it with movie props.

Predictably, the movie turned out to be a flop. Back in America, Kate embarked on a long cross-country tour with *Coco*. She opened the tour in her home town of Hartford. It was there that a ghastly episode took place. Kate says, "There was a woman who had been my chauffeur. By trade, she was a trained nurse. She hid in my father's house one night when I was out. We came home, very late, after the show, and I noticed a window open. I went in and explored. She jumped at me from a closet with a hammer. We struggled, and went over and over, down the stairs. I never knew what her problem was.

"In the struggle, she bit the end of one finger off. Then she ran away. The finger hung by a *thread*. Phyllis got me to a doctor—I was in agony. Next day, I had to go on for a matinee in a splint. My brother Robert, who's a doctor, found a Dr. Watson, a wonderful man, who grafted it back on. The human bite is very, very dangerous. It can poison you. But because of the wonderful care I had, I never had the slightest infection. I went from one hand specialist to another when I did the long tour. I never lost the finger. I simply refused to sink the road tour, or even to interrupt it. Of course, having a finger bitten off wasn't compared to having my head bitten off by the home-town reviews! They said I was quite talentless, and should have stayed at home."

The tour successfully concluded, Kate spent much of 1972 planning to appear in a film version of Graham Greene's *Travels with My Aunt*, as a raffish old woman. She began preliminary discussions on the script, conferred with Cukor, and became more and more fascinated by the part. Speculations on her subsequent dismissal from the role were legion. She says she does not know why she was fired. The fact is that she continually rewrote the first draft screenplay by Hugh Wheeler, adding much dialogue of her own, until she exasperated James Aubrey, then head of MGM. Finally, Aubrey refused to put up with her, and had an entirely new script written by Jay Presson Allen, and a new star chosen: Maggie Smith. With characteristic loyalty, she would not allow Cukor or her admirable co-star, Alec McCowan, to leave the picture in protest at her dismissal: "We all need work too much to give any of it away," she very decently told them.

Early in 1973, Ely Landau called Kate and began talking about his scheme for an American Film Theatre, a series of productions in which well-known plays would be brought to the screen intact and shown on subscription programs in theatres. He had decided to star her as the mother in *A Delicate Balance*, Edward Albee's savage play about a Connecticut family which fights against the intrusion of two unwanted people.

At first, her reaction was decidedly negative. Kate observes, "If you've any brains at all, as you get older you're harder to interest. Repetition is always the way to go downhill. You become limited in what is appropriate for you to do. For years, I had been terribly lucky in having been sent material that was comparatively appropriate.

"Now, in the 1970s, I was casting around for something that

was right. Ely Landau offered me *A Delicate Balance*. My God, that's a depressing play! I acted it in order to understand what it was all about. Finally, I *did* understand it. It's about self-protection. We all are *enormously* self-protective. It was fascinating to do—Albee uses the English language brilliantly. The family had their own lives—miserable though they were or not, their lives were *theirs*. Which is true of all of us; we have our own shell—it's awfully difficult to reach out of it. These two intruders came in, and when they came in and established a position in the house, then they expected to be able to express an opinion. The family didn't want that! Your house is your own little hideaway where you don't want other people to express too violent an opinion. You just want your *own* opinion to be expressed. Then the playwright went even deeper than that, into the total separation of the husband and wife, who had never contacted each other at all. My husband had become a very stuffy fellow, and I had become very bossy. My sister had taken to the bottle. Everyone was leading a totally frustrated life.

"There was a problem in that it was hard to *connect* to the play. There is a fashion now in which it is not necessary for audiences to connect, and I don't think that's a good idea. Life is puzzling enough, people are baffled by it, so why should art be puzzling as well? I feel I made that play as understandable as possible. It's enormously complicated. Now, *Long Day's Journey into Night*—O'Neill wrote it with great simplicity and honesty. It's a tragedy that everyone, the whole human race, understands. As for *A Delicate Balance* —I said to Ely Landau, 'What's it about? I'm a simple, nice person. I like to make Christmas wreaths, sweep floors, cook meals. I don't *understand* all this complicated stuff! I'm like my sister, who says the worst problem she wants is carrying two pails of milk over a fence.' "

Finally, Kate decided to go ahead. She became more interested when she heard that Tony Richardson, whom she had greatly respected, was going to direct, and was thrilled when she heard she would be co-starred with Paul Scofield, one of her idols, in the role of her husband. Above all, she felt that the American Film Theatre itself should be encouraged in an era of violence and of playing down to the lowest levels of public taste.

She had a series of discussions with Tony Richardson in New York and London. Tall, thin, with a tense, chilly manner and withdrawn, pebble-grey eyes, Tony Richardson was a strong admirer as well as a colleague. He had known Kate since his early twenties. He says, "When she appeared in *The Millionairess*, I thought she was sensational, and I wrote to her with enormous enthusiasm and said in the letter, rather boldly—I had just come down from Oxford—'Do drop over and have tea.' To my amazement, she came to my flat at Hammersmith. I didn't have enough money to buy cakes, so we had nothing to eat. She was absolutely sweet and charming. The next time I met her was when I was planning to do a revival of Tennessee Williams' *The Milk Train Doesn't Stop Here Anymore* on Broadway, and I wanted to do it with her. She didn't want to do it—I got Tallulah Bankhead, unfortunately—but Kate was marvelous all over again. She had even remembered my aviary—I had owned a lot of birds when I had lived at Hammersmith—and she remembered the river nearby my flat. These two meetings had impressed me deeply, and I was determined to have her for *A Delicate Balance*.

"She loathed the character of the mother she had to play, which is odd, because there's a lot of that same kind of inflexible, authoritarian quality in her. She suited the part terribly well. The obsession with the home—the New England background—all very 'Kate.' I kept trying to persuade her, and it was no, yes, no, yes, no, yes, all along the line. There was no single moment at which she said, 'Ah! I'll do it.' It was a gradual *erosion*. I think finally she sensed it was going to be interesting—fascinating."

Kate rehearsed for about two weeks at Tony Richardson's Victorian house in London, discussing different interpretations of each scene. Then the entire film was shot in sequence at the house, over a period of four weeks. "We argued a great deal, but that was stimulating," Richardson says. "She's a natural boss, and so am I, and I like that quality in her. We'd have quarrels, scenes, when I'd say, 'You don't know what you're doing, you've been in this business for forty years and you don't know the first thing about it,' and she'd say, 'You

don't know anything either.' It was really a kind of match—
a game—and everyone on the picture took it rather seriously
and looked quite alarmed when we started to quarrel. We
were Punch and Judy, and we enjoyed it hugely. She loved
to be given her head, it was like dealing with a very lively
horse. She wants to be broken in, ridden, and she has to
respect her rider, feel that he's fearless. She's incredibly free,
which I adore, and once she *sees* how to do a scene, once she's
conceded a point, she romps in superbly!"

One serious problem during rehearsal was the casting of
Kim Stanley as Kate's sister. Seriously ill, she proved unable
to keep pace with Kate's invincible professionalism and
meticulous time schedules, and had to be replaced by Kate
Reid. The actual shooting began under considerable strain at
a rented house in Dulwich, London. Ely Landau says, "Tony
was limited by the handicap of the location he chose. Physically, it proved difficult to move the camera fluidly around
the house, to use proper lighting, and to use directly recorded sound. I think this hampered the fluency of the camera. He should have used the studio. He didn't."

A Delicate Balance was not a successful work. Richardson's
direction was stiff, unrelaxed, and awkward; the pretentious
ramifications of Albee's dialogue became an annoyance
when presented in cramped rooms with little camera movement; and the ensemble playing was handicapped by ugly
costumes and sets. Kate was visibly uncomfortable in the
playing, at odds with the monstrous character of the mother
from the outset.

She was not much more at ease that same year in *The Glass
Menagerie,* made for ABC television in England under the
direction of Anthony Harvey. She was more sanguine about
playing the part of Amanda Wingfield, the pathetic former
southern belle trying to hold her family together in St. Louis,
though she was a little nervous because of the memory of
Laurette Taylor in the role. "I loved working with Tony
Harvey again, after *The Lion in Winter*," Kate says. "David
Susskind had mentioned my doing *Menagerie* through the
years. Finally, I agreed. It's a great play. It's a *great* play. It

really shows what lack of money can do to the human race. My father having been a Virginian, I understood Amanda's background in the South. I worked with one or two southern ladies whom I knew, to get the accent right. I wore the wedding dress I had worn for the stage performance of *The Philadelphia Story* in the scene when Amanda remembers the South. Did it fit? *Hah!* It had to be let out a little at the back!"

Exquisitely photographed, and with Kate expertly supported by Michael Moriarty and Sam Waterston as the gentleman caller and Amanda's son, the movie was made with extreme care. Rehearsed for two weeks, it was shot in exact sequence. Harvey's direction emphasized the claustrophobia of the cluttered apartment, the fact that the city noises were muffled, scarcely audible beyond the dark alley outside.

Kate was miscast as Amanda, too intelligent and assured to convey the impression that she was a stupid, well-meaning fallen gentlewoman of the South. The reviews were somewhat mixed, but the Nielsen rating was excellent.

In late 1973, Kate, by now thoroughly aware of the importance of television as a medium of communication, agreed to appear on "The Dick Cavett Show." When she arrived at the studio, she expressed fury at the dirty dressing room given her, and on the set she immediately began criticizing the carpet ("ugly"), the chairs ("plastic"), and the table ("unanchored") on which she wanted to rest her feet.

Dick Cavett responded to her with nervous sophomoric awe, apparently so overcome by her presence that he lost his composure and stammered like an amateur. Right in the middle of a highly embarrassing opening discussion, he evidently decided, with Kate's approval, to proceed, and at a signal the show began to be videotaped.

The interview went on for three hours. In slacks, turtleneck shirt, and casual jacket, she looked as fresh, scrubbed, youthful, and tough as a Navy cadet. Her hair, skin, and teeth shining with health, her eyes alive with humor, she treated her awestruck host with an extraordinary combination of scarcely disguised contempt, amused tolerance, exasperation, and a considerate, tender affection normally reserved for the handicapped. Despite the fact that his questions were so clumsily managed that point after crucial point was lost, it didn't really matter; if she had stood on her head and recited Longfellow's "Hiawatha" in pig Latin, she would still have been mesmerizing.

She discussed her childhood, her attitude toward women's liberation, marriage, and children, her friendships with people in the theatre and movies, her increasing fear of everything, her love of nature and need for privacy, her passionate commitment to the craft of acting, and her grueling personal discipline.

Despite Cavett's frequent and irritating interruptions—at one point, he even had the audacity to try to upstage her by referring to his own brief career as an actor—she survived wonderfully. Her edgy, half-humorous, half-contemptuous approach to her fans was never more clearly in evidence, nor her half-critical, half-comically deprecating attitude to herself. She appeared at once egotistical and modest, aggressive and retiring, ferocious and gentle. The interview may have been a disaster in terms of the way it was conducted, but it cast a vividly illuminating spotlight on the endless paradoxes of her personality.

After "The Dick Cavett Show," Kate had the greatest flood of offers for work in her entire career. She acted in George Cukor's Edwardian drama *Love Among the Ruins* in London, with Sir Laurence Olivier as her co-star. She decided to appear as the fairy, Light, in Cukor's version of Maurice Maeterlinck's play *The Blue Bird,* and worked extensively on the script with Alfred Hayes and Colin Higgins, who wrote the second draft. She prepared several pages which were retained for the film, including a beautiful speech about the need of human beings to try to stop the passage of time. Finally, she yielded the role to Elizabeth Taylor. In the fall of 1974, she made a Western, *Rooster Cogburn,* with John Wayne, shot in Oregon, in which she played a Bible-thumping spinster who learns to use a rifle against marauding bandits.

Kate, after saying she would not do so, made a startling last-minute appearance at the presentation of the 1974 Oscars,* to present the Irving Thalberg Award to her old friend and neighbor, producer Lawrence Weingarten. Dressed in a black Mao pants suit, which looked as though it had been hanging in a closet ever since *Dragon Seed*, she swept into the Los Angeles Music Center Pavilion, rejected once again the dressing room given her because, she said, it was dirty, and used the production room instead, thus infuriating the Oscar show producer, Jack Haley, Jr.

Her appearance was greeted with a standing ovation. Although she had endured a recent operation on her hip, she tossed away her stick before vigorously striding across the stage to make the presentation. Her speech was brief, but touching. This public display of emotion was extremely rare for Kate. She had never looked more beautiful than when she said, "It has taken me forty years to be unselfish."

Kate's recent behavior has been as wild as ever. While making George Cukor's *Love Among the Ruins*, she turned her back on a group of set-visiting aristocrats who asked for her autograph. While making *Rooster Cogburn*, she spent every available minute shooting the Rogue River rapids in an inflatable kayak, terrifying the insurance people and her producer, Hal Wallis. During a visit to New York before going to Oregon, she saw a performance of Leonard Bernstein's *Candide* with Phyllis and Anthony Harvey. Irritated by the bleachers, and troubled by back pain, she ran up onstage and lay on the large, comfortable bed occupied by one of the actors. It was her way of protesting that he should be lying down in luxury, while she squirmed in acute discomfort.

But the funniest recent Kate story had as its setting London's Piccadilly Circus. Dressed up in her Edwardian costume for *Love Among the Ruins*, she suddenly ran across the Circus and confronted an astonished John Wayne.

"Oh, Mr. Wayne," she said. "I'm so pleased to meet you. I'm Katharine Hepburn, and I'm really looking forward to acting with you in Oregon next month!"

Before the astounded Wayne could recover, she had run

*Despite the fact that Kate had won eleven nominations and three Oscars, this was her first appearance at an Academy Awards ceremony.

back to the set and recommenced work with Sir Laurence Oliver.

In the late summer of 1976, Kate, after several visits to England to see the aged playwright Enid Bagnold, author of *National Velvet*, completed preparations to appear in Ms. Bagnold's new play, *A Matter of Gravity*. It was a drama ideally tailored to Kate's talents. Ms. Bagnold created the rewarding central part of Mrs. Basil, a wealthy eccentric who lives in a corner of her thirty-bedroom mansion with a curious assortment of people, including a cook who levitates. Her grandson, Nicky, in an effort to keep Mrs. Basil abreast of the times, invites four trendy friends from Oxford University—a homosexual couple, a left-wing intellectual, and a pretty, very mod young girl. Mrs. Basil is shown as a reactionary oddball with some elements (particularly the failure to understand gays) that suggested Kate herself. Clearly the work of a playwright in her later years, this curiosity would have been nothing without Hepburn. With her, it was only slightly more than nothing.

During rehearsals, Kate, following her usual custom of assisting people down a precarious flight of steps to the street outside her West Hollywood cottage, slipped and fell. She discovered to her dismay she had broken a hip. She was rushed to the hospital, where she instantly took charge of everything, virtually running the entire floor singlehanded as she issued instructions to everyone. Not a doctor or nurse failed to fall in love with her. By sheer will, she managed to pull herself and her hip together. In one of the last conversations with her, just before the book appeared, I asked her what her plans were vis-à-vis the play. I pointed out to her that in a wheelchair scarcely anyone else would be visible on stage and that after all the play was called *A Matter of Gravity* so it was only appropriate she should have fallen. Predictably, she and the wheelchair were the sensations of an otherwise feeble show. She manipulated it like a chariot, whirling around the stage with surprising speed and ingenuity, scattering everyone in her path.

The Los Angeles and New York appearances were a triumph for her, but not for the author. This greatly annoyed

Kate, who sternly reminded everyone in sight that an actress couldn't be good without words to play. Everyone was much too nervous to disagree.

In a very characteristic speech, Mrs. Basil states, "The whales are going," referring to the decline of great figures in a collapsing civilization which the pygmies are taking over. It was quite clear to anyone who watched *A Matter of Gravity* that this particular whale was very much afloat.

Perhaps as a reaction to the book in which these words appear, Kate suddenly emerged in the late 1970s as an author! Giving her biographer more than a run for his money, she wrote with great wit and style as a contributor to *TV Guide*. Her first contribution, for which she received (under considerable pressure) more than the usual rates, was entitled "Hooked on John Wayne," and appeared on September 17, 1977. It could have been written by Mrs. Basil in terms of its attacks on contemporary life; its tone of adoring romanticism came from the softer, more tender side of her nature. She began, discussing the rerun of *Rooster Cogburn* on NBC: "John Wayne is the hero of the Thirties and Forties and most of the Fifties. Before the creeps came creeping in. Before in the Sixties the male hero slid right down into the valley of the weak and the misunderstood. Before the women began dropping any pretense to virginity into the gutter. With a disregard for truth which is indeed pathetic. And unisex was born. The hair grew long and the pride grew short. And we were off to the anti-hero and heroine."

Kate wrote with immense admiration about Wayne's eyes, hair, skin, nose, teeth, shoulders, chest, and hands. She added a stab that must have given a twinge of unease to her countless homosexual admirers: "Good legs. No seat. A man's body. Rare in these gay times." Rather oddly, she added the following complimentary words: "Carrying his huge frame as though it were a feather. Light of tread. Springy. Dancing. Pretty feet." She seemed to be writing about Nureyev instead of Wayne at this moment. But what did it matter? She was as readable as she was watchable.

In 1978, Kate was busy again. George Cukor called her at home, in a state of characteristic excitement. Alan Shayne, of Warners' TV, had called Cukor, to suggest doing a new version of Emlyn Williams' *The Corn Is Green* with her. It had been filmed with Bette Davis in the 1940's and had been successfully staged with Ethel Barrymore, among others.

Kate was less than enthusiastic. She said, "Oh, dear! It's been done a hundred times! And what about all those illegitimate babies? Oh, no. I think no."

She was referring to the fact that the play hinges in part on the problem of Morgan Evans, the young miner who may lose his chance of an Oxford education because a girl he has been dating declares herself pregnant. Cukor and Shayne wanted her to play Miss Moffat, the schoolteacher who saves Morgan's future.

Cukor insisted Kate reread the play before she made a final decision—and no one could insist more than Cukor. It arrived within hours. She read it at a sitting and changed her mind. She laughed, she cried; the part was perfect for her. She loved the idea of a story of a woman who drove a tough and uncompromising course through life without regrets, a woman who saw talent in the young miner and would stop at nothing to see that talent grow and bear fruit.

Once she had decided to play Miss Moffat, Kate could hardly wait to go to Wales, where Cukor and Alan Shayne had unhesitatingly decided to shoot the Movie of the Week. First, Cukor and Kate flew to London. They had to find a decent Morgan Evans who would be capable of suggesting both the working class boy of eighteen and the genius who would become revealed at Oxford. They also needed a strongly attractive man with great warmth to whom audiences could respond. The first actor to read for the part was the moodily handsome Ian Saynor. Cukor and Kate were amazed. He read the test scene—of the reading of his first prose efforts which gives the play its title—with such command that it seemed unnecessary to look at anyone else. Cukor was prepared to hire him at once. But Kate felt she dared not ignore all the other potential contestants. After two months, and many other tests, Kate and Cukor settled on Saynor.

There were several disappointments before shooting began. The costume designer and cameraman both backed out at the last minute, leaving the company stranded. Quick replacements had to be found. The location was bleak and rainy.

But Kate was thrilled—no other word will do—with Wales. She helped Cukor select the perfect village, along with art director Carmen Dillon, who was the first to find it. The hamlet was called Isybyty-Ifan. Nearby was the town of Wrexham, and the old Bersham Colliery. It goes without saying that Kate had to go down into the mine in total darkness for thirteen hundred feet through a narrow tunnel with a rough floor, carrying a lamp and a gas detector, with a gas mask on her face. She tramped around the countryside, invaded a farm for the duration of the shooting, parked her trailer in a field, and heaped up blouses, hats, ribbons, scarves, veils, and gloves on the bed in the guest room. She rose at five every morning and devoured a gigantic breakfast of fruit, eggs, bacon, chicken livers, toast, marmalade, and coffee. She was often seen bicycling in the rain. She was given a slate cottage which became her passion. She wrote about the experiences with tremendous vividness in *TV Guide,* on January 27, 1979.

Benedict Nightingale, a name she loved, visited her on location for an interview with herself, Cukor, and the rest of the cast that appeared in the New York *Times* on January 28 of the same year. He described Kate and Cukor arguing over some stage business involving a Cockney cook. At first, Cukor objected to Kate giving the actress Patricia Hayes instructions, then suddenly he gave in and found the business amusing. Throughout the shooting, director and star provoked, nagged, and infuriated each other, only to collapse into laughter, their life-long friendship more firmly cemented than ever.

The Corn Is Green was a skillful and sweet-natured version of the play. Kate acted more warmly and tenderly than Bette Davis had in the earlier version, perhaps reflecting some of the qualities Cukor's great friend Ethel Barrymore had brought to the part. Yet in the scene in which she made mincemeat of the young girl who claimed pregnancy, Kate struck home with a formidable display of anger. It was a memorably shaded, subtle performance, with a core of innocence Kate has never lost.

Never wanting in enthusiasm, Kate discovered a new idol in 1978. This was the young and talented playwright Ernest

Thompson, who at a remarkably early age became successful overnight with his play *On Golden Pond*, paradoxically dealing with the pleasures and agonies of the very old. She saw the play and became captivated by the part of the woman in it, acted in New York by Frances Sternhagen. She correctly saw a tremendous chance in the part and soon decided to appear in it on screen.

Nineteen-eighty was the beginning of an intellectual love affair between Kate and Thompson. Not only did she appear in *On Golden Pond* for Marble Arch Productions in New England, but she also appeared in Thompson's new play, *The West Side Waltz* in Los Angeles, starting in January, 1981. At time of writing, a few scenes from *On Golden Pond* have appeared on screen: in a finely-honed, expertly assembled two-hour tribute to Hepburn on public television. Directed by Mark Rydell, the picture shows Hepburn at the peak of her powers.

On Golden Pond united her for the first time with Henry and Jane Fonda. Incredibly, she had never met Henry Fonda before they started work. Long admiring him as an actor, she offered him the ultimate compliment. Just before shooting began, she gave him Spencer Tracy's beaten up old hat. He started to cry.

The actor's health was poor during the shooting, and Kate and Jane Fonda, with great tenderness, proved supportive, "covering" wherever this was necessary. The exquisite location and the richly rewarding experience of working with the Fondas were great joys to Kate.

During this period, she finally gave up the house she had shared with Spencer Tracy in West Hollywood, and George Cukor sold it. After struggling with herself for some time, she finally knew that she could only be happy living in the East. She spent much time at the Turtle Bay house. Oddly, the Kanins remained her neighbors, even though she resolutely refused to speak to them. She never forgave them for "Tracy and Hepburn."

In December, 1980, Kate was in Los Angeles for rehearsals of *The West Side Waltz*. She played Margaret Mary, a lonely old woman living in a big, rambling apartment house on New York's West Side. Margaret Mary has once been a pianist; she matches up with a neighbor, a violinist, in an odd, rather awkward duet of talent and spirit. Kate triumphed over the writing to give an unsentimental, clear-cut performance. Only the impossibility of playing at concert standard marred her acting; the pianism had to be matched on tape, with weirdly jarring results. One spent most of the play in silent prayer that the tape wouldn't be turned on too early or too late. It was an unsettling experience in the theater.

Today, despite some ill health, Kate is busier than she has ever been, seemingly the last bastion of discipline, order, and decency in a world gone mad. Her angular figure, her wonderful face with its stark planes and hollows, suggest a great abstract sculpture. Though she has set herself against modernity, she is utterly modern and probably always will be.

Katharine Hepburn has years of work ahead of her. It is an impertinence to try to sum up her life's achievement now. But biographers tend to be impertinent by nature. So I shall try.

She is the greatest actress of our time because she has let us see her life unfold in her playing, and because her technique is so finished it is invisible. Nothing stands between her and the women she plays—she instinctively and compassionately reaches to the spirit of a character and becomes one with it. She holds back nothing, because her honesty demands she must suffer nakedly in front of our eyes. What she avoids in life—a direct confrontation with her audience—she emphatically rises to on the screen. She challenges the audience because she at once removes her own disguises and demands that we do the same. Her purity and cleanliness of spirit can be terrifying. She goes for the jugular vein. In more hypocritical times, she disconcerted her spectators even as they responded to her. Now she does not disconcert us; she tells us that she was ahead of us, and that now, in our modern attempt to reject all pretenses, she is at our forefront. When women were wearing what fashion dictated, she wore what she wanted to wear; when women were supposed to be chiefly good for marriage and children, she rejected both;

when women were not allowed to have an intellect, speak their own minds, or take on men as equals, she did all three.

She is our lifeline. She is a more exciting actress now than she was in the days of her youth and early middle age. Time and pain have stripped her to the essence. She has never looked more powerful than she does today. In recent years, she has experienced physical suffering, and this agony has given a harsh strength to her face. Her hair, still coiled in its defiant bun, has a look of steel. Her face, blue-grey eyes smarting on the brink of tears, boldly confronts illness, old age, and the prospect of death. Her cheekbones are still unflawed masterpieces of God or nature—the bones of a natural aristocrat. The chin is aggressively firm, the body spare and fluid in its movements, with small, compact breasts, slim hips, and a back straight as a Marine's. But her supreme feature is her mouth. Often set in a wide line of resistant anger, it more often curls into happy laughter. It suggests terror conquered by determination, sensuality tempered by discipline, militancy restricted by kindness.

As I conclude, I recall the scene with which I opened this book. She is sitting on the floor of her room, firelight playing over her weathered features, showing me the intricately woven leaves of the Christmas wreath she had made, offering me instantaneous friendship on a chilly, foggy afternoon. And yet, along with the friendship, offering me also a champion's threat of struggle, a bracing test of discipline as I start to talk to her. It is that rest that everyone who watches her feels along with those who are lucky enough to know her. Yet beyond giving us the discipline of great acting and expecting us to have the rigor to understand her, she wants no theorizing about her work. So I have not theorized, and shall not. I have tried only to record—and describe. And now I let her have the last word: "Today, there's too much pretension in everything. Let's throw in the playwrights, the painters. Oh God, the *actors!* A lot of hogwash is written about the business. It isn't all that fancy! I can remember when Nijinsky came in on the set and watched Charlie Chaplin. Charlie was about to receive a pie in the face, and Nijinsky said, 'The *nuance!*' It's a bunch of bunk! BUNK, BUNK, BUNK, BUNK! You learn your craft, you pick up a little bit, you're either funny or you're not—hopefully, you are. It's a *craft!* You're asked to explain the mystique when you're just desperately trying to make something that people would come and see, that would make them laugh or cry, and would have a proper tempo. I think we're all burdened with the effort of the director to get the credit that the actors have always run away with. He was the unknown force. Now, in trying to become the known force so that his ego is satisfied, he has talked a great deal—and everyone is talking more than they should—talk, talk, talk, *talk!* Actors talk too much! I'm not aware of what I'm doing—unless I forget the lines and muck up the scene. Spencer always said, 'Learn the lines and get on with it,' and so does Larry Olivier, and so does John Gielgud. Of all talents, acting is the least. Life's what's important. Birth and love and pain. And then death.

"ACTING'S JUST WAITING FOR A CUSTARD PIE. THAT'S ALL."

Index

ABOUT THE AUTHOR

Charles Higham is the son of Sir Charles Higham, British Member of Parliament and Cabinet member as Minister of Labor. He was born in London and now lives in Los Angeles. He was for many years *The New York Times* Hollywood correspondent.

He is the author of the bestselling biography ERROL FLYNN: THE UNTOLD STORY, and his many books include CECIL B. DeMILLE, ZIEGFELD, THE FILMS OF ORSON WELLES, THE CELLULOID MUSE, AVA, THE WARNER BROTHERS, THE ART OF THE AMERICAN FILM, CHARLES LAUGHTON, DIETRICH, and an upcoming biography of Bette Davis, as well as THE ADVENTURES OF CONAN DOYLE. He has also published five collections of poetry. His verse has been anthologized and published in the *Hudson Review*, the *Yale Review*, and the *Times Literary Supplement*.